About the Bo

"This book peels back the curtain. If you're seeking more than just clichés, if you're looking for a tale that transcends the ordinary and touches the core of human potential, then 'Gotta Keep It Movin'' can become your north star".

Owen Roddy, MMA Coach

"From Ballymun to the heart of Ireland, this book is a manifesto for anyone in pursuit of inspiration. Read it and let your own passions ignite."

Philly McMahon, Dublin GAA Footballer

"A great insight into the life of a remarkable individual and his extraordinary adventures"

Michelle Finn, Two Time Olympian

"Ger's journey is a testament to the power of the human mind. The psychological work that has led him to unparalleled resilience is something I find deeply impressive. The ability to turn personal setbacks and challenges into stepping stones towards greatness is showing the potential that resides within each of us."

Niall Breslin, Mental Health Advocate

"Ger Prendergast is an extraordinary ultra-endurance athlete, and this book chronicles his awe-inspiring journey, a deep exploration of resilience, unwavering determination, and relentless dedication in the face of formidable challenges. Immerse yourself in this remarkable and profoundly human story."

Katie Taylor, Professional Boxer

"Ger Prendergast, the extraordinary ultra endurance athlete has achieved nothing short of staggering feats. Not only did Ger triumphantly conquer ten iron distance triathlons in as many days, but he astoundingly emerged as the victor. Just when you thought his accomplishments couldn't get any more mind-boggling, Ger proceeded to secure yet another glorious triumph at the unrelenting Continuous Deca Challenge. The sheer determination and unwavering perseverance required to complete just one of these gruelling events are truly remarkable, but Ger's ability to conquer them repeatedly is nothing short of spectacular."

Gerry Duffy, Deca Champion, Motivational Speaker

"Having known Ger as a fellow athlete and friend, I can attest that his story inspires a generation. This book is a profound and human narrative that will stay with you long after you've turned the last page."

Keith Russell, Ultra Endurance Runner, Irish and European Record Holder

"Ger Prendergast's journey is nothing short of extraordinary. I've had the privilege of knowing him both as a fellow athlete and a friend and witnessing his transformation has left me with a lasting impression. Coming from a disadvantaged area to conquer Ironman and ultimately achieving the incredible feat of the Continuous Deca, Ger's resilience and dedication are unmatched. What sets him apart is not just his athletic talent but also his commitment to community and mental health advocacy. Ger doesn't just break records; he shatters expectations and inspires those around him to dream bigger. His journey is a testament to the power of perseverance and I'm proud to call him a friend and a source of inspiration in our shared pursuit of overcoming adversity in the world of triathlon."

Ger Redmond, Professional Triathlete

"More often than not, it's the people out of the spotlight who make the biggest difference and provide the biggest inspiration. Look beyond the floodlit pitches and the professional stages and you will find men and women like Ger not only pushing the boundaries of human resilience but lifting others up as they do so."

Emma Bilham, Professional Triathlete

"An experience that showed me the true meaning of what the body can achieve once the mind is willing. Being asked to be part of the crew that supported Ger through this trailblazing journey was such an honour and gave me tremendous pride. He is inspiring a generation and trying to help the lives of so many who suffer, 1 kilometre at a time."

Chris Fitzpatrick, Crew Member

Ger Prendergast achievements:

Ironman Wales 2014

The Race 250k endurance race 2016

DecaUK 2017 winner 🏅

52 iron distance triathlons in 52 weeks 2018 🏅

World's first indoor Deca 10 iron distance triathlons in 10 days 2018

100 mile run on 500m tarmac loop (20 hours) 2018

DecaUK 2022 winner 🏅

Malin to Mizen cycle sub 24 hours 2022

4 peaks challenge record holder 2022

Ironman Barcelona 2023

Ironman Cork 2022 & 2023

200k run at Kerry Way Ultra 2023

Lord Mayor's Award 2023 🏅

GER PRENDERGAST

GOTTA KEEP IT MOVIN'

From Parkrunner to Endurance Champion:
Healing Through Sport

To Rachael,

Keep It Movin'

Ger.

MIND AND BODY FITNESS

ISBN Paperback (Black & White): 978-1-9161298-0-1
ISBN Paperback (Colour): 978-1-9161298-1-8
ISBN Hardback (Colour): 978-1-9161298-2-5
ISBN eBook : 978-1-9161298-3-2

Author: Gerard Prendergast
Title: Gotta Keep It Movin'
Subtitle: From Parkrunner to Endurance Champion: Healing Through Sport

About editorial contributions:
As the author, I extend my sincere gratitude to Gianni Tapinassi from Writers' Garage for his invaluable editorial expertise throughout the development of this book. His keen insights, meticulous developmental editing and thoughtful consultations played a pivotal role in shaping the narrative and ensuring a polished final book. His professional guidance significantly contributed to the clarity, coherence and overall quality of this work.
For editorial inquiries or services you can contact Gianni via email at gianni@writersgarage.net

Book cover design, interior layout and formatting by Francesca Giannotta for

Writers' Garage

Ordering information for quantity sales and orders by bookstores/wholesalers:
Special discounts are available on quantity purchases by corporations, associations and others. For details, get directly in touch with Gerard at the email or phone below.

Contacts:
Email: gerard.prendergast@gmail.com
Phone: (+353) 085 2721770
Website: gpmindbodyfitness.com

Social

Instagram
https://bit.ly/insger

Facebook
https://bit.ly/fbger

Join Our Newsletter To receive updates and exclusive content, send an email to gerard.prendergast@gmail.com with the subject "Subscribe to Newsletter".

For Miriam, Jake, Reece & Ben

SWIM
BIKE
RUN

Dedication to My Father

To the man who ignited my passion for all sports and adventures.

This dedication is not just a simple tribute, but a heartfelt thank you for making me the person I am today.

You taught me the joy of movement and the beauty in nature. You also taught me the power of perseverance and resilience. You always encouraged and nurtured my love for sports and always believed in my potential, even when I couldn't see it in myself.

Our adventures in the Dublin and Wicklow mountains as kids were what dreams were made of. The memories of those seemingly endless hikes, which we enjoyed so much, will forever be etched in my heart. You taught me that the greatest rewards come not from the easy path but from the path less travelled, a lesson that might just be the greatest lesson I could have ever learned.

This memoir is my way of honouring your memory and expressing my eternal gratitude for the love and inspiration you gave me. Without you, I would not have discovered my true passions or developed the strength and resilience that have propelled me forward.

Thank you for teaching me to embrace life's challenges, to seek joy in the unknown and to chase my dreams with unfaltering determination. Your spirit lives on within me as I continue to push the boundaries of what is possible in the world of sport and adventure.

Ger

Summary

Part 6 - Resources

Part 7 - Appendices

Foreword

With great pleasure and deep admiration, I am honoured to introduce you to the extraordinary journey of Ger Prendergast.

Ger came of age in Ballymun, North Dublin, during the 1980s and 1990s. As anyone familiar with the challenges of growing up in disadvantaged areas near Dublin can attest, the allure of drugs and alcohol, the scarcity of resources, and the constant struggle can make it seem like an uphill battle. But it is precisely in these conditions that individuals like Ger demonstrate how we can find our resolve to break free.

Ger's journey is a testament to the power of the human mind. The psychological work that has led him to unparalleled resilience is something I find deeply impressive. The ability to turn personal setbacks and challenges into stepping stones towards greatness shows the potential that resides within each of us.

What inspires me even more is the growing community of athletes like Ger, who are returning, or, as Ger, staying rooted to their hometowns and investing where they come from. This is not just about individual achievement but about creating a ripple effect, inspiring the local community, and igniting a spark of hope. It's about showing that, no matter where you start, with dedication and resilience, you can rewrite your story.

As you delve into the pages of this book, you'll discover the inspiring journey of someone who harnessed the power of sport, health, and fitness to heal deep wounds and achieve what some might call "superhuman achievements." It's educational, shedding light on the transformative potential of resilience. It's informative, not only for athletes but for anyone facing their own trials and tribulations.

Moreover, I share this admiration, having faced my own challenges in the realm of endurance sports. Having completed an Ironman in Copenhagen, I can attest to the mental and physical demands of such endeavours, though the thought of doing ten in ten days is a feat that gives me nightmares.

So, my friends, join me in celebrating Ger's path to greatness. I couldn't be prouder to see someone from Ballymun making such a significant impact. As you read his story, I hope you'll find inspiration, hope, and a reminder that no matter where you come from, you have the power to keep it movin'.

With admiration and respect,

Niall Breslin - Bressie

Note by the Author

During the development of the book, in collaboration with the editor, we decided to keep my tone familiar throughout the entire book. I wouldn't have felt comfortable releasing a book with formal expressions that wouldn't match my personality and my will to communicate sincerely with you, the reader of my book (I still can't believe it!).
I also wish to say that this memoir is an attempt to explore the physical and mental facets of sport. As you explore this memoir you'll find a blend of personal anecdotes, narratives, biographical insights, and technical details woven together to provide a comprehensive understanding of the intricacies and motivations driving my journey. In these pages, I aimed to reflect on my inner experiences to capture the essence of the countless moments that occurred along the way.
As you embark on this journey through these pages, I hope you recognise that you're not merely entering my world but you're stepping into the shared space of love for sport that unites us. So, whether you're drawn to the narrative or the technicalities, let the adventure unfold.

Ger Prendergast

Part 1

Starting Block

Chapter 1: The Urban Farm

Born and Raised in Ballymun

Our home in Ballymun resembled a farm, bustling with life. Nestled right in the heart of Ballymun, it housed a large family of fifteen, with two dogs, two geese, thirty hens and one particularly boisterous cockerel. This crazy bird possessed an impressive vocal range, starting his loud crowing in the middle of the night and persisting until the break of day. His enthusiastic calls would set off a symphony of barking from the neighbouring dogs, creating a lively chorus of sound. While our neighbours never voiced their frustrations, I couldn't avoid feeling their possible discontent with the noise. I had entered the world not in this house but at 65 Sillogue Gardens in Ballymun, Northside Dublin. Unlike my siblings, whose births took place at well-known hospitals, such as the Rotunda Hospital or the Coombe, I arrived unexpectedly on the staircase of this house. This extraordinary event earned me the title of 'The upstairs-downstairs baby' on the front page of the *Evening Herald*, a popular Dublin newspaper.

We spent the first year of my life at that address before eventually relocating to Coultry, just a short ten-minute walk away, where the urban farm began.

Our family home stood out from the surrounding residential area like a farm in the middle of a city. With its front, side and back gardens, it occupied a sizable space that would now be hard to come by in Dublin. To find a property with comparable roominess, one would need to venture out to the countryside. While not as large as a rural farm, there was enough space for growing crops and my father used every available inch to create the best possible yields.

In a scenario that is hard to fathom now, our large family of 15, consisting of our parents, six girls and seven boys, once lived under the same roof in our four-bedroom house. Countless memories were made in that crowded house. The six boys shared a single room with David, the eldest, followed by John, Robert, Matthew, myself, Kevin and Philip. The two oldest boys occupied the top bunks, while the remaining four squeezed into the two bottom bunks. Our youngest brother, Phil, slept in a cot placed in our parents' room, since he was just a baby at the time. My sisters were fortunate enough to have more space, as they shared the other two bedrooms. Sandra, the eldest, was the first to marry and move out, followed in age by Sharon, Rebecca, Jude, Paula and Elaine, the second youngest in our family. I fall in as the fourth-youngest. As we grew older, siblings began

to fly the nest, which freed up beds for us younger ones. This was particularly fortunate because we boys all measure between six feet and six feet five inches in height.

With the passage of time and the departure of our older brothers, John and David, we eventually had the privilege of having our own bunk beds. Being the older brother on my side of the room, I was assigned the top bunk, while my younger brother Kevin would have inherited it if it were based on height alone. Interestingly, we were often mistaken for twins, as I was slightly smaller but heavier in build than Kevin.

While my dad's devotion to gardening stemmed primarily from the need to provide for our family rather than a genuine passion, he always put in a tremendous amount of effort overseeing our side and back gardens. He cultivated a wide variety of vegetables, including cabbage, potatoes, cauliflower, kale, onions, turnips, Brussels sprouts, green beans, runner beans, peas, carrots, beetroot, tomatoes, leeks, scallions, lettuce and even rhubarb. Personally, rhubarb was not my cup of tea.

It wasn't until my father helped me grow potatoes on my own plot of land that I truly gained an appreciation for the skill, hard work and time required to cultivate all those splendid vegetables. Even then, my dad took on the lion's share of the labour.

When my wife Miriam and I started growing on our own allotment just around the corner from our home, my dad came to help. 'The soil is quite poor', he explained. With that in mind, we decided to keep things simple and focused on growing potatoes during our first year, which turned out to be a success. Even now, I continue to grow potatoes only, but my responsibilities have expanded significantly as I've taken on the task of raising chickens and keeping bees. Given the time and effort required to care for the chickens and bees, I am content to keep my gardening tasks uncomplicated.

As children, we dreaded being summoned to assist my dad in the garden. Gardening held no appeal to us at the time and like any typical kid, we simply wanted to play football in the adjacent field instead of tending to the vegetable garden.

Our football matches often led to the ball getting lost amidst the towering kale plants, which had grown to almost tree-like proportions. Retrieving the wayward ball meant crawling beneath the dense layers of kale leaves and navigating through the carefully planted trenches. The kale had grown so tall that it felt as if we were venturing into a mini rainforest of kale. And if we were caught in the act, we would receive a tongue-lashing.

Near our house, there was an area that had become a dumping ground over the years. Lazy residents who couldn't be bothered to bring their old furniture and other unwanted items to the landfill would discard them here. Fondly referred to as the 'back hills,' this stretch of land lay at the back of our houses, consisting of

mounds of muck that gradually became covered with grass and weeds over time. However, as part of the Ballymun Regeneration plan, this area was eventually transformed. Today, it stands as evidence of progress, with new homes replacing the old flats and tower blocks, offering residents a fresh start and a revitalised community.

We would frequently find discarded items in the 'back hills' dumpsite and use them to play with. One particular object, discovered during the summer of 1987, would have a lasting impact on my life.

A childhood friend and I stumbled upon an abandoned child's cot or crib. We decided to drag it to the grassy area beside my house, which we referred to as our 'football pitch.' This rectangular field served as the backdrop for all our childhood sporting activities, including football and various other games.

We took apart the crib to retrieve the pieces that make up the sides, which prevent the baby from rolling out while sleeping. First, we would pretend we were pirates and other sword-wielding characters. When that got boring, we started to long-throw the sticks like a javelin so that when they landed, they would stick in the ground. We would then retrieve the sticks and start again.

Once we finished our rounds of javelin, I joined my friend in retrieving our sticks that were lodged into the ground. He began kicking the sticks to dislodge them, but in an unfortunate turn, one of the sticks veered towards me and struck my eye.

Interestingly, I have no memory whatsoever of that incident. I cannot recall the sensation it caused or even my reaction at the time.

Rather than experiencing immediate blindness, the eye that was struck by the stick became infected. Over a brief period, the infection worsened to the point where I ultimately lost my sight in that eye.

At the age of seven, this loss of vision significantly affected me. As a teenager, I particularly struggled with my visual impairment. In the early years of secondary school, specifically from first to third year, I was a student at the nearby post-primary school, Ballymun Comprehensive.

The school, formerly known as Ballymun Comprehensive, now recognised as Trinity Comprehensive School, holds a significant place in my life, as I currently work there and my gym is located in the sports hall of the school. I have strong ties to the school and a deep fondness for it.

During my first three years of secondary school, Ballymun Comprehensive was an all-boys' school. When I progressed into 5th and 6th years, the classes became mixed, with both boys and girls. I faced challenges in the all-boys environment due to being a year younger, smaller in stature and carrying some extra weight. While I excelled at playing football at home with my brothers and friends, the pressures and anxieties of physical education classes at school crippled me. I struggled to express myself, even through the sport I loved.

It had been a similar story during my time in primary school, where I was noticeably smaller than my classmates. This gave rise to feelings of inferiority and a sense of being different from my peers. In hopes of altering their perception and improving my self-esteem, I became determined to train as a boxer and to work on becoming fitter and stronger. I believed that by transforming my physical condition, I could change how my classmates viewed me and also boost my confidence when interacting with them.

At the age of eight, my dad took a significant step by opening the first gym in Ballymun. Initially intended as a boxing club, my older brothers, John and David, soon transformed it to cater more to bodybuilding and powerlifting. The gym quickly became popular and a valued addition to the local community.

My brothers were skilled boxers, with both John and David achieving All-Ireland Championship wins. My younger brother, Kevin, also displayed remarkable talent in the sport. Prior to the establishment of our gym, we had before trained together at Poppintree Boxing Club. Even after our gym opened, I continued my boxing training, making the most of the resources and opportunities available to me.

I absolutely loved it. The toughness, the bag work, the road runs, the unforgettable scent of the place—I was in love with it all. It was here that I discovered my talent for sport.

Unfortunately, my dreams of competing in boxing events were shattered due to my limited vision and blindness in one eye. Although I sparred during training, it wasn't deemed safe for me to step into the ring. Fighting without the ability to see punches coming from one side would have exposed me to too much risk. A fighter with a formidable right hand would have had an easy time landing punches on the left side of my head. So I had to watch from the sidelines when my younger brother competed in events.

The fire of competition within me grew stronger and I yearned for a way to satisfy it. The frustration of not being able to box competitively, coupled with my dad's instructions to my brothers to protect and watch over me as if I were incapable, sparked a newfound drive within me. When we played football, it was undeniable that I possessed more talent and coordination than my brothers. This only intensified my frustration when I heard our father telling them to take care of me.

Chapter 2: The Shadow of Alcohol

Choosing a Different Path in Life

During the 1980s, disadvantaged communities like Ballymun were devastated by the effects of drug addiction and alcoholism. Fortunately, as children, we were largely shielded from the full extent of the havoc wreaked upon our town and its neighbouring regions. However, as I got older, I witnessed the growing prominence of alcohol first hand.

Like countless others, my father enjoyed indulging in a few pints. In Ireland, alcohol has always held a significant place in our cultural fabric. In places such as Ballymun, alcohol provided an escape from the unrelenting pain and struggles of everyday life.

As I grew older, I developed a habit of avoiding my father whenever he came home from the pub. Perhaps it's a typical teenage inclination to steer clear of parents whenever possible. I didn't like seeing him in a drunken state and would retreat to my room or pretend to be asleep.

In his fifties, my dad found himself in need of a kidney transplant. For a long time before his transplant, he had to undergo dialysis. Dialysis helps maintain the body's balance by removing waste, salt and excess water to prevent a dangerous build-up in the kidneys. Dad spent three evenings and nights at the hospital every week for five years before his transplant. This proved challenging for him, since he has always been an active individual, passionate about walking, hiking and gardening. The toll on my mother was even greater, as she constantly worried about his well-being. Regrettably, as a self-absorbed teenager, I failed to grasp the magnitude of the situation. I was too engrossed in my own life, unaware of the tremendous struggle my dad and mother were enduring. Reflecting on this now fills me with deep shame.

At the age of sixteen, in 1997, I had my first encounter with alcohol. It happened one night when I decided to join my friends for a casual hangout. I purchased six cans of cider for the occasion and within the span of an hour, I managed to consume five of them. From that point on, my memory becomes hazy, but I do recall being helped by two of my friends as they guided me home.

Ironically, my dad was undergoing dialysis treatment at the hospital that night. If he had been home, I would have found myself in significant trouble. In fact, had he been present, I likely would not have engaged in the drinking session in the first place. It's important to note that while I didn't enjoy the experience–disliking the taste, the loss of control, and the inevitable hangover–it didn't stop me from drinking later on. This night, however, taught me the immediate downsides of alcohol consumption.

Once I reached the age of eighteen in 1999, I began to partake in social drinking at pubs. In Ireland, turning eighteen grants you legal permission to consume alcohol. While I was still in school, it became somewhat of a norm among my classmates. This shared experience helped foster friendships and made it easier to socialise with members of the opposite sex.

Engaging in conversations with girls was always a challenge for me due to my eye condition. The appearance of my eye made it difficult to establish direct eye contact and as a result, my confidence suffered. However, when I consumed alcohol during nights out, my inhibitions began to fade. The concerns about my eye's appearance would disappear, allowing me to relax and be myself without constantly worrying about judgement from others. This newfound liberation led to more nights out and, unfortunately, it also resulted in showing up to football matches still under the influence. The anxiety I felt about playing was so overwhelming that I often chose to avoid attending matches altogether. On occasions when I did show up, I would pray to be left on the bench, hoping to avoid being asked to play.

In 1999, at the age of eighteen, I had the incredible good fortune to meet Miriam, who is now my wife, in Ms. English's biology class at Ballymun Senior School. During that class on my first day Ms. English asked Miriam to share her book with me, as I hadn't got one yet. From that moment on, I made a firm decision never to purchase that biology book. I was instantly smitten with Miriam. Our connection grew rapidly and we became inseparable. Just three months after we started dating, we discovered that we were expecting our first child. Our son Jake was born on June 20th, 2000. At the time, Miriam was in the middle of her Leaving Certificate Art exam when she unexpectedly went into labour, preventing her from completing the test. To support our new family, I had left school and taken a job at Lifestyle Sports, a sports clothing store. Just weeks after Jake's birth, I moved in with Miriam to be with her and our son as much as possible and to help out.

Miriam was living with her sister Trisha, her husband Eddie, and their daughter Megan in a three-bedroom flat on Sillogue Road in Ballymun. It was in one of the four-story apartment blocks known locally as the 'Four Stories.' Our household was harmonious, with no significant conflicts, making our cohabitation enjoyable. Eddie and I would often spend hours playing Pro Evolution Soccer on the PlayStation, engaging in playful taunts and celebratory dances whenever one of us scored. It was great fun.

In 2003, as part of the Ballymun Regeneration project, we were offered a new house to share as one family. Knowing this would mean we couldn't have our own separate homes, we requested individual accommodations. Fortunately, our request was granted. Trisha and Eddie received the house, while Miriam and I were given a flat in the 'Eight Stories' apartment blocks on Sillogue Road. We were thrilled to have a place to call our own.

I left Lifestyle Sports for a more stable position in 2000 and from then until 2006, I worked full time as a general operator at a laptop manufacturing company. Over the course of these six years, I took on various roles within the company, but it was primarily a means for me to pay my bills rather than pursuing something I was truly passionate about. My routine consisted of working hard throughout the week and indulging in alcohol and fast food with my friends on the weekends.

There was a stark difference between me and my friends when it came to knowing our limits. I had a propensity to drink excessively, to the point of blacking out at times. It's hard to say why exactly I behaved this way; perhaps I fell into the cliché of having an addictive personality. I would admit that I fit that description. After a night of heavy drinking, I would be incapacitated the following day and often found myself repeating the cycle. As I wrote earlier, drinking is deeply ingrained in our culture. We don't approach it with much logic; it's simply something we do because our parents did it, our friends do it and it's perceived as the norm.

During this time, Jake was growing up, and I have memories of taking him to the park while still feeling the lingering effects of the previous night's indulgence. It is a source of great regret for me, even today. I was physically present, spending time with him and Miriam, but unfortunately, I was often battling a hangover during those moments.

Our family grew in 2006 with the arrival of our second son, Reece, followed by our third son, Ben, in 2007. During this period, Miriam was studying for a degree in Microbiology at Trinity College Dublin, from which she graduated and subsequently secured a position at a leading pharmaceutical company. I had left my full time role in the manufacturing company that year.

In 2004, I opened a small gym with my brother at Trinity Comprehensive School. Operating in the evenings, the gym served the local community with personal training sessions and fitness classes. During the day, I took care of the boys, handling school runs, meals, and daily trips to the park. While I cherished the time with them, it wasn't always easy.

Living on the fifth floor of the Eight Stories presented its challenges. The elevator frequently malfunctioned, forcing us to use the stairs. This was especially difficult when Reece and Ben were toddlers. With Jake in school and Miriam at work, I often had to carry both children, groceries, and a stroller up multiple flights. On one particularly stressful occasion, I left the boys on the fifth floor while I retrieved our shopping, fearing they might climb over the balcony. The experience left me in tears and resolved never to repeat it.

Determined to find a better living situation, I frequently visited the local civic offices, pleading for assistance. The conditions in the flats were deteriorating, with common areas becoming increasingly dirty and unsafe due to drug activity. In 2009, we were offered a house and moved out of our flat. We have happily resided in our new home ever since.

Throughout my twenties, going out for nights with my football team, Sandyhill Celtic, became a regular part of my routine. It was often followed by a match the next morning and win or lose, we would continue the celebration with another night out afterwards. This pattern had become ingrained in my life, forming a habitual cycle that was difficult to break. Unfortunately, this also meant playing soccer matches while still under the influence or dealing with the aftermath of a hangover. Looking back, I can't recall a single match where I felt fully present or played to my true potential. I was consistently disappointed with my performance on the field, feeling like I never lived up to my own expectations.

Alongside the alcohol, another indulgence that accompanied my nights out was fast food consumption. Walking back home from the pub, I would find myself ordering an excessive amount of food, typically meant for two to three individuals and effortlessly devouring it all before even reaching home. One particular night, after enjoying drinks at a local pub, I left with my friends, twin brothers Jonner and Ciaran. We decided to make a pit stop at the nearby chipper across the street. The twins both ordered a half-pounder burger and a curry chips tray, which I also decided to order. However, when the server brought us our orders, there appeared to be a mix-up. Jonner received his burger and curry chips tray, as did Ciaran, but I ended up with double the amount. It seemed that the server misunderstood and thought I wanted what the twins had ordered together. Consequently, I found myself with two half-pounder burgers and two curry chips trays, all for myself.

I paid for my meal and immediately began devouring it as I walked home. I had finished both burgers before we even reached the first street corner and by the time I arrived home, I had polished off both curry chip trays.

This kind of excessive eating was not an uncommon occurrence. I was aware of the harm I was causing to my body, but being young and seemingly unaffected by the consequences, except for my declining performance in sports, I continued on without much concern.

Discussing this topic is challenging for me, but I hope it helps explain why I broke away from the prevailing lifestyle of many around me and why I continue to abstain from drinking alcohol. I possessed a profound understanding of the detrimental effects of this toxin on us and I rejected the notion that I needed it in my life. Moreover, I was determined to set a positive example for others, particularly my children, and to prove that we can thrive without the presence of alcohol.

Growing Through Sport

My father's boxing club was situated in the basement rooms of the flats in Coultry, Ballymun. These seven-story high-rise flats were initially constructed in the 1970s as a temporary solution to meet the housing demands in the area.

For my family, boxing quickly became more than just a sport. It served as a means of keeping us engaged in a positive activity away from the growing drug problem that plagued our neighbourhood. Additionally, learning how to defend ourselves through boxing became crucial when Ballymun started gaining a reputation as a rough area. Many kids from our community eagerly joined the club, leading to its rising popularity.

In the early 1990s, my older brothers had taken charge of the gym's day-to-day operations and transformed it into a weightlifting gym.

Since I couldn't enter in boxing competitions, I naturally gravitated towards a different sport. It wasn't until I turned sixteen that I joined my first football team. However, even before that, I spent every spare moment I had kicking a ball of some kind in the field close to my house.

Typically, individuals who have lost sight in one eye face challenges with depth perception. Surprisingly, I cannot recall this ever being a problem for me, even in the realm of sports. Although I sometimes struggle to press an elevator button accurately on the first try, when it came to sports, depth perception was never an issue.

I dedicated countless hours to playing football in the field next to my house, whether it was on my own, with a friend, or with a small group of friends who happened to be around at the time. My brothers and I would often have matches against the local kids from the neighbouring streets. The lads from Coultry Lawn had their own team called 'The Lawn,' while those from Coultry Drive were known as 'The Drive.' The lads on our street formed their own team called 'The Crescent,' but we had our own team; we were recognised as 'The Prendergasts.' Teams from other areas would even come to play against us, drawn by our formidable reputation.

Spending countless hours in the field, often by myself, honed my football skills and gave me a keen sense of ball control, but those were the ways of street football. My father had always advised us never to venture beyond the field next to our house, which is why we never joined any of the local football clubs. At first glance, one might perceive my father as overly protective and to some extent, he was. However, when I consider what transpired at one of those clubs, involving kids in my own class at school, it becomes clear that his caution was justified. I won't delve into the grim details, but it is heart-wrenching to acknowledge that some of my classmates who played for that club in Ballymun from the late '80s to early '90s endured sexual abuse from one of the head coaches. When viewed

from this perspective, my father's protective nature seems entirely reasonable, especially considering my quiet and shy demeanour, which could have made me an easy target.

Having never been a part of an 11-a-side football team, my exposure to the sport was limited to the streets. Therefore, when I joined my first team at the age of sixteen, I felt completely out of my comfort zone. I didn't even grasp the concept of the offside rule until after I started playing. The team I joined was Sandyhill Celtic, primarily because my good friend Jonner was already a member. Moreover, Jonner's brothers managed the team and I knew they would take care of us. During training sessions, I managed to give the impression that I would be a valuable addition to the team. I can still recall my first official match, where I scored two goals against a local pub team. Despite being clueless about my position or what I was supposed to do on the field, my instincts from street football kicked in. In my own penalty area, I got the ball and started on a mesmerising run, evading several opponents before unleashing a powerful shot from around 25 yards out that soared into the top corner of the net. After that, my involvement in the game was minimal until I scored my second goal, a scrappy effort. The ball found its way to me in the opposition's penalty area and without hesitation, I struck it, watching as it trickled into the far corner of the goal.

The beginning of my football journey was a mixture of promise and disarray, but I could never find true comfort on the soccer pitch. I often felt clueless about where I should position myself or which runs to make. As a result, I never fully committed to the sport, which led to my inconsistent presence in starting line-ups. Although I appeared to excel during training sessions, I struggled to replicate my performance during matches. Over time, this issue worsened as the pressure to perform well mounted. If I failed to meet expectations, which happened frequently, my already fragile confidence plummeted even further. Despite staying with the team for twelve years, I never truly felt comfortable, like one of the team. While I diligently attended training sessions, I would often avoid participating in weekend matches due to my lack of confidence. I simply never grasped the fundamentals of the game and, as a result, never developed the confidence I needed to use my natural abilities.

At the age of 26, I realised that alcohol was exerting a negative influence on every aspect of my life. Physically, I carried more weight than I should have, which I recognised as a consequence of excessive drinking. Emotionally, I found myself trapped in a sport, specifically 11-a-side soccer, that I didn't enjoy. Moreover, my family life suffered greatly due to my drinking habits. The time spent indulging in alcohol meant time taken away from my loved ones and the aftermath of nights out left me mentally absent and disconnected in the days that followed. It was evident that I needed to alter my relationship with alcohol, not only for my own well-being but also for the sake of my family.

Finding Confidence

In 2007, I began searching the Internet for information on sporting activities I could participate in despite my visual impairment. Recognising an opportunity to turn my disadvantage into an advantage, I was determined to find something that would align with my decision to quit drinking and prioritise my overall health and wellness. That's when I discovered futsal.

As fate would have it, I came across the contact email for the manager of the Republic Of Ireland VI (Visually Impaired) Futsal Team. After I reached out, the manager invited me to join the training sessions with the team at Blanchardstown Institute of Technology. I had concerns about my endurance, fearing that I might not be able to keep up with the other players if they were accustomed to longer training sessions that lasted for three hours.

At the training sessions, it became apparent rather quickly that I was already in better physical condition than most of the team. After I had trained with the guys a few times, the opportunity arose for me to play in a friendly match at DCU. Despite my relative fitness, I knew there was still room for improvement and that I needed to maintain my rigorous training schedule while also eliminating alcohol from the equation.

Joining the Visually Impaired International Futsal Team strengthened my commitment to the decision I had made months earlier. If I truly aimed to compete at an international level in any discipline, I had to be at my absolute best. Consuming alcohol and the associated behaviours would only hinder my progress.

This became my driving force; the answer to my 'why?' It became effortless for me to turn down any offer of an alcoholic drink and with each refusal my self-discipline rocketed.

After training with the team for several weeks I was given the opportunity to attend my first match. Despite not having played even a practice match, I found myself selected as a substitute player. In futsal, however, it is common to have more substitutes than active players on the court at any given time, similar to the setup in basketball. Unlike outdoor football, where two teams of eleven players face off against each other, futsal is played indoors with five players on each side. Swapping players every few minutes to optimise their performance was an essential part of futsal strategy.

Shortly after joining the international team, the FIA launched a new futsal league sponsored by Eircom, aptly named the Eircom Futsal League. Top clubs from Dublin entered teams into the league. We decided to enter all the players from the VI International team as a club team. The goal was to enhance our game by competing against top-tier opponents on a weekly basis. We based ourselves in Ballymun, training in the PE hall at Trinity Comprehensive School. This arrangement was ideal for me, as I worked there, eliminating any extra travel or disruption to my schedule. Additionally, the new national futsal arena was constructed on the school grounds. We had the honour of being the first team to play an official match there, facing the English VI international team. Unfortunately, we lost 2-1.

When I first joined the international team Paddy Coates, a prominent figure in the team, served as our anchor player. He consistently started and finished every game without being substituted. Playing in the anchor position meant he was positioned in front of the goalkeeper, forming the base of a diamond shape, with wingers on each side and a forward positioned at the top of the diamond. I was instructed to position myself on the right side of the diamond and get the ball from Paddy. The moment arrived for me to enter the game and I hurriedly sprinted from the bench across the pitch to take my place on the far right side of the court. Just as I reached my position, Paddy charged towards me with the ball, leaving me with no time to react or evade him. Our collision resulted in losing possession and the opposition capitalised on the opportunity by scoring. Rob Moore, the team manager, summoned me back to the bench. At that moment, it seemed like he was questioning my ability. Being subbed on and off within a few seconds was very embarrassing. To be fair, the mishap wasn't solely my fault; Paddy should have passed the ball and anticipated my return. However, Paddy's limited peripheral vision may have hindered him from noticing my presence.

That was my initiation into the world of futsal and despite feeling like an outsider, I was determined to prove myself. When I arrived for the next match, the atmosphere in the dressing room felt cold and unwelcoming. No one greeted

me or acknowledged my presence; it was clear that I had not yet been accepted, likely due to my less-than-ideal debut in the previous match. I doubted they even knew my name.

As we were playing in a tournament, there were multiple games scheduled. Unfortunately, I could only participate in the first game because of a prior family commitment. Rob, aware of my limited availability, chose to start me in the opening game. This was the chance I had been waiting for and I was determined to make the most of it. I was positioned at the top of the diamond as the front man, ready to seize the opportunity.

Each game in the tournament had a shortened duration of only ten minutes per half. In the first ten minutes alone, I managed to score three goals and completely destroy the opposing team. The expressions on my teammates' faces were priceless; they were in awe of my performance. The second half brought more of the same, although I only managed to score one more goal, bringing my total to four for the game. It was a beautiful goal. I started from my own penalty area, fending off an opponent for the entire length of the court. Having noticed the goalkeeper's tendency to slide on his knees towards us to make saves in the first half, I anticipated that he would dive in an attempt to stop me. I chipped the ball over him as he rushed towards me, effortlessly guiding it into the empty net. After that game, we returned to the changing rooms. I was preparing to leave, but my teammates were staying on for the next match. As I made my way out, I bid them farewell, saying, 'Bye, lads.' To my surprise, every player responded with, 'Bye, Ger.' If they didn't know my name before, they certainly knew it now. Following that game, my confidence began to soar as I consistently found the back of the net in every match I played. However, it wasn't until a friendly game during a training session that I discovered my true position. This particular match was officiated by league officials and arranged by Rob, our Visually Impaired team manager. It was a serious game and each player was determined to showcase their skills and worth. With the world championship in Argentina just a few months away, we were all eager to secure a spot on the team representing our country.

I started the game as the frontman in the diamond, with Paddy as the anchor. However, due to a minor injury, Paddy had to leave the game. As a result, I was asked to fill his position as the anchor. Stepping into this role, I took control of the game, both offensively and defensively. I orchestrated plays, created scoring opportunities and prevented the opposition from having any chances at our goal. From that pivotal moment on, I became exclusively known as the team's anchor. This position proved to be a perfect fit for me. It allowed me to have a clear view of all the players in front of me, enabling me to make strategic passes, determine when to attack or defend and communicate effectively with my teammates. Surprisingly, I discovered that I became more vocal in this position, a trait that I had never possessed while playing 11-a-side football. Filled with newfound confidence, I continued to excel as the team's anchor from that day until my last game.

One would assume that, as a Visually Impaired team, our level of play would be inferior to that of the senior futsal International squad. However, the reality was quite the opposite. We proved our quality by defeating them in a friendly match. Our team, having competed together in international competitions for a couple of years prior to their establishment, had developed a strong chemistry and cohesive playing style.

I had the privilege of participating in numerous matches for the Visually Impaired Futsal international team, and it bestowed immense pride upon me to represent Ireland in major tournaments held in countries such as England, France, Turkey and Argentina. However, in 2011, we received the disheartening news that we would no longer receive any funding from official sources for future tournaments. As it was, we had received very little support to begin with. As a team, we covered our own travel expenses and organised fundraising efforts. Nonetheless, this announcement came as a severe blow. Faced with the harsh reality of playing without the support of the Football Association of Ireland, we were left with no choice but to stop playing internationally. Regrettably, the dissolution of the national team also led to the disbandment of our club side.

When I was younger, anxiety weighed heavily on me, trapping me within its grip. However, through my involvement in futsal, I discovered an outlet to express myself and release the pent-up frustration. It felt as if I had two distinct personalities: off the field, I was reserved and kept my opinions to myself, but on the field, a different persona emerged—one that didn't hold back and didn't care about pleasing others. I acknowledged that my on-field personality could be perceived as abrasive, but the aggression it brought allowed me to tap into my competitive nature. It felt akin to a state of hypnosis. The referee's whistle signalled the start of a game, my on-field persona awakened and eagerly sought to dominate the opposition, much like the transformation of Dr. David Banner into the Incredible Hulk. Yet, as soon as the final whistle blew, this fierce persona disappeared and my more composed self returned—until the next time the Hulk within me was called upon.

Ditching Alcohol

As I have already written I felt compelled to become a positive role model for my son Jake, and recreate the special activities my dad used to do with us. My dad would take us camping every weekend to wild spots in the Dublin or Wicklow mountains. He instilled in us a great sense of adventure and a love for the outdoors, sports and health and I wanted to do that for my son too. My father's presence in my life was an immensely positive influence. Looking back, I can acknowledge that his struggles with alcohol also played a significant role in shaping my ability to make wise choices and to listen to my inner compass.

I have vivid memories of leaving behind alcohol and joining the V.I. Futsal Team. It was a pivotal moment when I realised something incredibly positive was unfolding in my life. By abstaining from alcohol, I experienced newfound strength in the gym, improved agility during training and overall increased fitness. Not only that, but I underwent a transformation on a personal level. I felt an overall sense of happiness and clarity of thought that I had never experienced before. I was less nervous, less anxious and my relationships with people seemed much better. A combination of a few things all at once made it easy for me not to drink anymore, just like that. I realised I could perform much better. I wanted to be a better father; I wanted to be a much better partner. I didn't like the way my life was turning out and the direction in which I felt it might be going.

The benefits were immediate. The body's ability to recover and adapt is simply amazing. I was training at least once a day between futsal and the gym. I was still into bodybuilding and I felt that my frame at the time had great benefits on the futsal pitch. I was performing really well for club and country, scoring goals every time I played, even though my primary objective was defending.

A life free of alcohol also gave me the ability to think more clearly. I find this hard to really explain fully, but I was more compassionate, had more empathy and was much less selfish. Since then, sixteen years later, I have drunk alcohol twice: once at a friend's wedding in Italy and the second on my wedding night. I did enjoy both occasions and it definitely allowed me to get more involved with the celebrations. But now, I am so aware of my relationship with alcohol that I know I can allow rare occasions to occur. My wedding was in 2015 and since then I have not drunk alcohol, even though I have been to more family and friends' weddings. I have no plans to get married again, so I have no plans to drink again!

Part 2
'Let Food Be Thy Medicine and Medicine Be Thy Food'

Chapter 3: Embracing a Plant-Based Lifestyle

As a child, I had no interest in the vegetables my father grew in the garden. I only cared about avoiding his wrath when our ball landed on his precious kale plants. The whole concept of vegetables, gardening and plant cultivation that my father loved so much meant absolutely nothing to me.

Even at dinner time, I failed to appreciate the incredible freshness and beauty of the food that was served to us every single night. Our meals were structured like a restaurant, with assigned seating and strict timing. The youngest member of the family was fed first and being late meant risking having your plate swiped by one of the elders. We had to be punctual and quick, making way for the next group to eat. Meanwhile, my mother would spend her entire day preparing and cooking the vegetables from the garden. She was always on her feet, working tirelessly. We would hear her calling out our names and when we arrived at the table our plates would be waiting for us.

Stew was a staple in our household, especially on Tuesdays when my Mam would make it without fail. I used to eagerly anticipate it and the flavours would only deepen and intensify as it sat overnight, making it even more delicious on Wednesdays. The main ingredients were fresh carrots, potatoes, parsnips and turnips straight from the garden. As for the meat, oxtail was added to the stew and contributed to its rich flavour. The meat would become so tender that it effortlessly fell off the bone as you picked it up to eat.

On Saturday mornings, we were woken up for a hearty bowl of porridge. There was no escaping the noise of the rooster and his pack of noisy hens, so we would get up and start our gardening duties. Tasks included cleaning the chicken coop, cutting wood and turning the soil in one of the gardens. I absolutely despised cleaning out the chickens; I found myself gagging every few seconds. However, I did enjoy cutting wood because it meant I got to handle the saw and even better, I got to swing the axe to chop the logs into sticks. One of the most undesirable tasks was dealing with the cow manure deliveries. A friend of my dad would reverse his truck up to our front gates and unload tonnes of pungent cow crap right at our doorstep. It was then our responsibility to shovel this smelly mess into wheelbarrows and transport it all the way to the back garden, which was easily a hundred metres away with several twists and turns. It was a truly unpleasant job.

To make it somewhat more bearable, my siblings and I would occasionally play a mischievous game of throwing bits of manure at unsuspecting passers-by, quickly hiding behind the bushes before they realised what had happened. Yes, we were literally playing with shite and yes, it was a bit bold. However, we understood that the manure was an integral part of cultivating and growing our beautiful fresh vegetables, of which we had a plentiful supply.

In my late twenties, I had a profound realisation about the importance of eating well. As a fitness instructor, I had read extensively about nutrition, but something never quite felt right. I consumed copious amounts of chicken, fish, protein powders and all the other things that fitness professionals insisted were essential for optimal health. However, it became clear that their concept of what constitutes a healthy diet and my understanding of physical well-being were different.

The current wisdom surrounding 'healthy' eating simply did not align with my intuition on how to achieve greater fitness, strength and endurance. The gym scene itself became warped – quick results, mystery supplements, and weekend hangovers. This toxic culture wasn't for me.

The rise of gym culture has moved away from genuine training and achieving fitness and well-being towards focusing mainly on superficial goals like appearance, influenced by market trends and fads. As a personal trainer, I had to look the part. And I tried to fit that mould. I ate plenty of meat because it was believed to bulk you up and give you the appearance of greater strength. However, I often wondered if this was due to whatever substances had been pumped into the animals and were now in my system. Did it truly make me healthier? I wasn't quite sure. It did succeed in creating the desired external image of health, but internally, I didn't feel the same.

Although before I engaged in a lot of high-intensity interval training (HIIT) and attained a respectable level of fitness, I always felt fatigued and sluggish. There was a heaviness within me that I couldn't shake off. It wasn't until I made a change to a wholefoods plant-based diet that I realised that merely looking fit, strong and healthy doesn't necessarily equate to being truly fit, strong and healthy.

I never had the desire to flaunt my physique and show off the results of my countless hours spent in the gym. I grew weary of the constant focus on vanity within the fitness community. Don't get me wrong, there's nothing inherently wrong with wanting to look good. After all, it's a major motivation for many of us to engage in training. Looking good can boost confidence, self-esteem and overall happiness. However, an issue arises when individuals become fixated solely on their appearance, losing sight of everything else and their sense of perspective.

It's disheartening to witness people becoming consumed by the pursuit of physical perfection, obsessing over their looks and constantly striving to improve their physical appearance. There is so much more to life and personal fulfilment than simply looking good.

In 2011, when I pushed myself to complete a 5k run in the park, it was an immense struggle. My body and all its systems were sent into shock. I was well aware that distance running and bodybuilding were contradictory pursuits. I knew that running would break down the muscle I was trying to build with weight training. Yet, I also recognised which activity truly made me feel 'healthier' both mentally and physically.

Running became a respite, an escape from the demanding expectations of looking like a stereotypical fitness professional. I felt the constant pressure to have bulging arms, a chiselled chest and, of course, a visible six-pack. At that point, I was mentally exhausted, burdened by the belief that I had to maintain this appearance at all times. Running allowed me to shed the excess muscle and

REVISED AND UPDATED EDITION
FINDING ULTRA
REJECTING MIDDLE AGE, BECOMING ONE OF THE WORLD'S FITTEST MEN, AND DISCOVERING MYSELF
"Finding Ultra is Rich Roll's incredible story of mental, emotional, and physical endurance. An essential, inspiring read."
—MICHAEL GREGER, MD, FACLM, New York Times bestselling author of How Not to Die, founder of NutritionFacts.org
RICH ROLL

liberate myself from the constant obligation to look 'in shape.' It granted me a newfound sense of freedom. Dedicating more time to running, gave me more time to reflect and to think, which had a profound effect on my mental well being. I realised that my mental state was just as important as my physical fitness. Without the need to focus solely on building muscle mass, I found myself questioning what I should be eating. The knowledge passed down by my father about the goodness packed in vegetables came to mind. A common misconception in society is that all vegetarians and vegans are pale, thin, weak and unhealthy-looking individuals and I was certainly concerned that if I was to solely rely on vegetables for my diet, I too would become one of these emaciated figures associated with non-meat eaters. Driven by scepticism, I conducted thorough research on the subject.

My awakening came when I stumbled upon Rich Roll's memoir, '*Finding Ultra*.' Rich Roll is a renowned ultra-endurance athlete and advocate for a plant-based diet. His words resonated deeply with me, when he described his progress as an athlete and the benefits he experienced from adopting a plant-based lifestyle. It was as if a switch had flipped in my mind. Despite eating what was considered a healthy diet by conventional standards, I knew that something wasn't right. Foods like pasta, rice, meat and dairy products left me feeling bloated and sluggish. This was not how I should be feeling, especially considering my commitment to training. I realised that I could achieve a higher level of fitness, become lighter and improve my overall health by embracing a plant-based lifestyle.

During the initial transition from a standard to a more plant-based diet, I faced challenges in adding variety to my meals. It was frustrating to be eating the same things over and over again. Avocado toast became a staple for me and continues to be, but like with training, my approach to nutrition needed to evolve. I dedicated a significant amount of time to researching recipes and discovering new plant-based foods that would suit my taste buds. I immersed myself in articles and videos that provided valuable insights into good nutrition.

In my quest for knowledge, I turned to experts like Rich Roll and Joe Cross. Their wealth of information helped shape my understanding of plant-based eating. Additionally, I found resources that provided me with valuable information. Along the way, I honed my skills in the kitchen, becoming more adept at preparing and cooking plant-based meals.

Not long after, I discovered 'The Happy Pear' twin brothers who have been following a plant-based lifestyle for years. David and Stephen Flynn, the founders of The Happy Pear, not only run their own plant-based shop and café, but are located only a 50-minute drive away from where I live. Their enthusiasm and passion for plant-based living is infectious, and thanks to their recipes and guidance, I was able to train for longer periods and recover quicker.

One dish in particular that stood out was their lasagne recipe, which I found on their YouTube channel. I never thought I would have lasagne again, but their plant-based version blew me away. The flavours were incredible and the noises I made while enjoying it attested to just how delicious it was. Discovering 'The Happy Pear' opened up a whole new world of nutrition for me.[1]

Embarking on a plant-based diet seemed daunting at first, especially since I was a big consumer of different meats. However, it turned out to be much easier than I had anticipated. There were numerous alternatives available. Rather than using meat in traditional stews and coddles, I simply omitted them and found that the flavours were even better.

I experimented with ingredients like chickpeas, butter beans, tofu and tempeh as substitutes for chicken in my curries. It was a revelation and it introduced me to a whole new realm of flavours and recipes. Thanks to the helpful videos by 'The Happy Pear', following plant-based recipes became a breeze. I started cooking from scratch using fresh herbs and spices, creating delicious recipes without relying on jars of prepared sauces, laden with sugar. It was a refreshing change and made me appreciate the vibrant and wholesome nature of plant-based cooking. I took suggestions from recipes I found in books and changed ingredients in recipes suggested by the Happy Pear twins to come up with recipes that suited my own personal tastes, and sometimes what I could afford to buy!

Nowadays, I can create vegan versions of all my favourite dishes, evoking the same feelings of comfort and nostalgia. The exact recipes for classic homemade staples like Irish stew, lasagne, and shepherd's pie, in my vegetarian and vegan versions, can be found in the 'Plant-Based Food Plan' in the 'Resources' section of the book.[2]

Smoothies also became part of my everyday diet providing a quick and efficient way to consume nutrient-rich foods while also being gentle on the gastro-intestinal tract since they require minimal digestion. However, they can be high in sugar. I'd recommend a 3:1 ratio of vegetables to fruit and also using them as part of an active lifestyle.

My Journey to Plant-Based Living

Quitting alcohol sparked a health revolution. Embracing a plant-based lifestyle fueled by smoothies, fruits, and whole grains became my focus. Beans replaced meat, with veggies sneaking into every dish. Energy skyrocketed!

As my cooking skills improved, I developed a rewarding routine - shopping fresh ingredients, prepping, cooking, and relishing the abundance of highly nutritious food.

Listening to my body, I adjusted my diet for optimal results. Leafy greens and

1 Check the "The Secret Recipes from DecaUK" in the recipe section at page 244.

2 Check the "The Secret Recipes from DecaUK" in the recipe section at page 244.

nuts became my energy powerhouses, fueling my triathlon training. Weight loss accompanied a shift to aerobic activity, but more importantly, I felt lighter and stronger.

Chicken gave way to chickpeas, lentils, and kidney beans on my plate. Beef morphed into broccoli, kale, and spinach. Pork swapped for celery, cucumber, and coriander. These ingredients found their way into smoothies, hummus, casseroles, curries, and even enjoyed raw. Raw broccoli, cauliflower, and red pepper with hummus became my quick, nutrient-packed snack.

- My suggestion for a practical, progressive implementation:
- Gradual Transition: Ease into plant-based meals to allow taste buds and digestion to adapt.
- Diverse Ingredients: Explore fruits, vegetables, grains, legumes, nuts, and seeds for a wide nutrient spectrum.
- Educate Yourself: Learn about plant-based protein sources for balanced nutrition.
- Recipe Experimentation: Embrace the joy of cooking and experiment with plant-based recipes to discover new flavours and textures.
- Listen to Your Body: Pay attention to how your body responds to the changes and adjust your diet accordingly.

Deeper into plant power, I realised the magic of leafy greens like kale and spinach. Packed with iron, they boosted my oxygen flow, making me feel like a freaking energizer bunny! Nuts and seeds became my secret weapons - full of good stuff like phytonutrients, protein, and healthy fats that give me sustained energy for those long, slow workouts.

Remember my parents always nagging about veggies? Turns out they were onto something! Eating more plant-based foods totally upped my energy and overall well-being. Triathlon training in 2013 pushed me towards a wholefoods plant-based approach, building on their wisdom. Fruits and veggies became my main fuel for training, racing, and everyday life.

I still remember the first week after eliminating meat and dairy from my diet was a revelation. I could immediately feel the difference in my body. I felt lighter and more agile when running and my endurance significantly improved. It was a tangible shift in my fitness level that I could not ignore.

Although some people made negative comments about my weight loss, I felt incredible. It was as if I had transformed into a new person. Embracing a plant-based diet triggered me with energy and vitality. I found myself gravitating towards an increased intake of vegetables and incorporating more nutrient-packed smoothies into my routine.

Weight loss brought all sorts of comments, especially from my parents who worried I looked unhealthy. They grew up with food scarcity and wanted to make sure their kids were always full. This sometimes meant overfeeding, you know? In Ireland, their generation often equated bigger with healthier. But health isn't just about size! I felt amazing, stronger than ever, and knew my plant-based choices fueled my well-being. It was a constant transformation, pushing my body to new limits!

While changing the mindset of others may be challenging, my intention is to inspire and educate through my own experiences. I aim to show that a plant-based lifestyle can bring significant benefits and serve as a catalyst for positive change. In my case, the transformation in my performance was undeniable. From barely finishing a 5k to crushing ultra endurance challenges (like 10 iron distance triathlons in 10 days!), the transformation was unreal!

Part 3

Challenge after Challenge

Chapter 4: Going Solo

An Unexpected Shift

I was always interested in health and fitness, having been involved with my brother John's gym since I was twelve, so when I finished playing soccer, I put my time into extra gym training. It was something I enjoyed, but it didn't really satisfy my needs. I wanted to be outdoors. I was raised on regular trips to the mountains.

When I was twenty-three, I completed a Diploma in Sports Therapy and two years later, I completed a Diploma in Strength and Conditioning. By that time, our family gym, located in the basement of the eight-story flats in Coultry, Ballymun, had been forced to close due to the regeneration project in the area. However, a glimmer of hope emerged when we were offered a space in the sports hall of Ballymun Comprehensive School. This new location provided a gym for students during their PE classes and also allowed them free entry after school. Additionally, it served as a valuable resource for the wider community during evening hours.

I began working at the gym and eventually established my own fitness classes and business, called GP Mind and Body Fitness that I still operate today. I have completed numerous fitness-related courses since then, on topics including sports science, advanced yoga teacher training and triathlon. These certifications have played a pivotal role in shaping my career and have allowed me to expand my services to include personal training in the gym and, more recently, triathlon coaching through my latest endeavour, GP Triathlon Coaching.

I also run fitness classes in my gym and I enjoy organising and offering this service to my groups. Many of them have been training with me since 2010.

In my fitness classes, I've had the privilege of meeting countless incredible individuals I might not have crossed paths with otherwise. Guiding people towards self-improvement is deeply fulfilling. Witnessing their increased happiness and improved mental well-being is a gratifying ripple effect.

Anna's journey from despair to triumph is truly remarkable. Initially diagnosed with C.O.P.D. and having undergone lung surgery, she found hope and vitality in my classes. Witnessing her fitness and mental well-being soar has been immensely fulfilling. Now, she's training for her first marathon, a testament to her inspiring dedication to health. Feedback like Anna's resonates deeply, reinforcing my purpose in offering these classes.

Similarly, the news of breast cancer diagnoses for two of my clients, deeply affected me. Mary, in her mid-30s, faced gruelling treatments that took a toll on her physically and emotionally. Witnessing her transformation was extraordinary. She bravely ditched alcohol, earned a degree, and completed a half-marathon, with her sights set on a full marathon. Mary's resilience continues to inspire those around her, reminding me of the profound impact of support and determination in the face of adversity.

At the age of thirty-two, I had finished playing soccer and futsal. Finding myself without a sport to focus on, I realised I was accustomed to playing with teammates. Soon I would find myself going solo with nobody to rely on but myself.

We had built a great camaraderie within the fitness class group. One of the group members suggested we run a 5k road race and we all agreed that it would be a great idea to do it together.

Some of the group decided to run the 5k for a charity and I wanted to show my support since they had supported me by regularly attending my classes. The run was the Simon Fun Run and it was held in Phoenix Park, Dublin. It was a beautiful, warm day in June. I showed up in Under Armour Cold Gear, which is worn on cold days to keep you warm, so it was like I was running in a sauna. On top of that, I wore shorts, which were unnecessary as I was already wearing leggings. This would be like wearing two pairs of trousers to work and to make myself overheat even more, I wore a cotton t-shirt over my long-sleeved top, which would trap all the heat in since cotton is not a breathable material for running. I also ran in Nike Air Max shoes, the ones with bubbles. Let's just say I could have run faster in a pair of wellies. I wish I could talk to that guy now and tell him how ridiculous he looked.

Anyway, there I was lining up at the start, looking like I was about to go out for a run in December, surrounded by runners wearing singlets and short shorts. You could pick me out in the crowd from a mile away. I was already sweating. The starting gun went and I slowly kept pace with the thousands of people that were ambling off ahead of me. I was running with a few women from the fitness classes and was feeling pretty good, but a bit too warm. The ladies I was running with were chatting away and having a laugh. I thought that people did this whole running thing because it was exciting and that something great would happen when I did it. Well, I was waiting for something exciting to happen, but it didn't feel like it was coming anytime soon. 'Christ, is this over yet?' I asked myself, but I knew it had only just started.

I think one of the ladies sensed my frustration. 'Why don't you go ahead there, Ger?' she asked. 'We're only slowing you down.' 'Sure, I don't mind; I'm here to run with you guys,' I replied. She then went on to say, 'We'll be grand; you go on there and catch up to the front.' It felt like I was being given permission and felt obliged to run faster, so I did.

Did you ever see a dog in a fast-moving car with its head out the window and its tongue hanging out the side of its mouth? Well, that's how I felt and I'm sure it's how I looked. I was nipping in, out and around people as I whizzed past them, making my way through a sea of runners. It was a similar feeling to running full speed with a futsal ball, beating players and sticking the ball in the net. I couldn't stop smiling, but that changed after I passed the 3k marker.

My poor choice of running gear was starting to take its toll, I was really overheating. The last 2k were horrendously tough. My runners felt like they were made of lead. Every stride felt like I was climbing up a mountain as I slogged my way around the bends and up the hills in Phoenix Park, eventually reaching the finish line.

I sat in the grass and removed my overweight shoes and sprawled in the grass like a starfish. It took my body some time to cool down. After a few minutes, I could start to breathe normally again and I then began to think about what I had just done.

I had finished the 5k in twenty-one minutes which wasn't bad considering my poor wardrobe and footwear choice. Most significantly, the run planted a seed. The weather was glorious and the atmosphere was exciting. When I got home, I started looking into doing more running events.

Shortly after that 5k, I took part in a 6k obstacle course race with the same fitness class group. It was held in Puddenhill and ran by a group called Braveforce. This was another seed planted. It wasn't like road running, but I loved the adventure side of it. Firstly, it started at night, so it was dark. The race was through fields, into ditches, up hills and along muddy trails. Every few hundred metres or so, I was confronted by some kind of obstacle. A lot of the obstacles involved crawling through tight spaces on your hands and knees in the dark. There were also obstacles that involved climbing up cargo ropes to get to a high point and then climbing back down. There was even a hand ladder that you needed good upper-body strength to cross; if you slipped, you would find yourself in a pond of muddy water. It was a lot of fun.

I quickly realised that my gym fitness was benefiting my endurance, but I didn't consider myself a runner. I did want to do more, however. I felt a great sense of achievement from finishing that event and I wanted more. I also loved the freedom I felt when I was out running. I started adding running into my training and it became my favourite type of workout. I could almost drift away and think more clearly about other things in my life while I was out running and some of my better ideas and thoughts have come to me while I've been out running.

I started to let go of my weight training since it felt like it worked against my running training. I was adding body mass with weight training and then burning off the muscle gained from that weight training while out running. What happened next I did not expect. I gradually noticed that my once overpowering desire to appear muscular was gradually fading away. The pressure to train solely for the purpose of impressing others or feeding my own vanity diminished, bringing about a newfound sense of liberation. As a runner, I no longer felt the burden of conforming to society's expectations of what a personal trainer's physique should resemble. I embraced the freedom of not needing to fit into that mould.

The Magnetic Pull of a Multisport Challenge

After a couple of years of running, my curiosity was piqued when I stumbled upon a post on social media about an exhilarating sport that combined three different disciplines into one: triathlon. "These individuals must be out of their minds, but they also exude an extraordinary level of athleticism!" I thought to myself. In that instant, it became clear that I too would become one of them. Having already made the decision to quit drinking a few years earlier in order to enhance my health and fitness, venturing into the world of triathlon felt like a natural progression. The idea of attempting a triathlon journey first came to me in 2012. Prior to that, I had taken part in road running and had even completed a few duathlons. For those unfamiliar, a duathlon is akin to a triathlon but without the swim. Instead, it replaces the swim with an additional run. Similar to triathlon, duathlons take place over various distances and involve a sequence of running, cycling and a second run.

My venture into the world of triathlon began to take shape in 2012 when I signed up for the Dublin City Triathlon. My aspirations started to grow and I eagerly pursued greater challenges and amassing a wealth of valuable experiences through both triumphant ventures and monumental setbacks.

Among the events I entered or tried out were Gaelforce West, bog snorkelling and the Liffey Swim as well as an assortment of adventure races (run, cycle, canoe) and road races at all distances.

Dublin City Marathon (1999)

Race: Dublin City Marathon	Type: Marathon	Length: 42 Km
Date: October, 1999	Where: Dublin City	Notes: Zero training at age 19

My very first marathon came in 1999, when my PE teacher, Paddy O'Reilly, asked me and a few friends from school whether we wanted to run. "Lads, do ye want to run the Dublin City Marathon?" Paddy asked us as we sat on a bench in the PE Hall at school, a week before the event. "Quinner couldn't run for a bus Paddy" I joked back. The truth was that none of us had ever run any kind of event before. The only running we did was when playing football.

Noel Dempsey, Martin Quinn, Keith Keeley and I lined up at the start of the 1999 Dublin City Marathon, not having run one kilometre previously. We were young and fit, but our level of running experience was zero. Noel and Keith took off at the start like it was a 100m sprint. Later that night, I heard Keith went to the hospital with a hernia and Noel pulled out after a few kilometres.

Although I knew nothing about running, I did know it was going to be a long run, so I jogged. I enjoyed it, but the lack of miles in my legs was evident early on. I was struggling after about ten kilometres. I started to walk and jog. By the time I got to the halfway point, I was done. I just wanted to go home. But I was far from home and didn't have a clue how to get there.

I saw a phone box. Back then mobile phones were not a thing, so there were still public phones around. I tried to ring for a taxi, in the middle of a marathon, surrounded by thousands of people and road closures. How naive! I had the phone pressed to my face when I was interrupted by "bang, bang, bang" on the door of the phone box. I turned around to find Martin banging the door down. "What are ya doing?" he asked. It was like finding a needle in a haystack, but he managed to find me. I'm convinced to this day he had the same idea as me, get a taxi and go home, but he would never admit it. "I'm getting a taxi and going home" I replied to him. "Come on, let's finish this together," he pleaded. In that instant, I felt assured that we could reach the finish line together.

We started a jog and walk strategy and as the race went on, I started to get stronger and it was Martin who really began to struggle. He was in such pain that he needed the assistance of the medics that populated the course on several separate occasions. Although he was struggling badly, I knew I had to repay the favour and get him going again. "Come on, we are going to finish this," I told him. We struggled on and after 6 hours and 17 minutes, we made it to the finish line. Paddy O'Reilly met us in McDonald's on O'Connell street, after we had finished. We were due in school the next day, but we were adamant in telling him we wouldn't make it.

Fingal 10k (2012)

Race: Fingal 10k	Type: 10k Road Race	Length: 10 kilometres
Date: July, 2012	Where: Swords, Co. Dublin	Notes: First time running this particular distance as a stand-alone race

FINGAL 10K
START

9654
2560

In July 2012, I entered my first 10km - The Fingal 10km in Swords, which was part of the Dublin Marathon series of road races. I had entered with some friends and we lined up on the start line together. The only road race I had done previous to this was the 5k and 5 miles of the Dublin Marathon series and also the 5k fun run in 2011, so I was very inexperienced.

We arrived early to make sure we got a good place at the start of the run. Since we were among the first people there, we got our warm-up done at the start line area. Such was our excitement that we did not realise that we were surrounded by elite-level runners.

The gun went off for the start of the race and we took off at the elite-level pace for all of about 200 metres. After that, we were being overtaken by dozens of 'proper runners.' We did not realise that we were actually a hindrance to the elite runners, forcing them to dodge past us.

A couple of years later, I found a thread online about the race where a lot of frustration was vented over our disruption of the elite runners' race start. We were described as a pair of bollards, which I found hilarious. It was a mistake I would never make again.

Despite the drama at the start, the run itself went well and I managed a 42-minute finish. The feeling of satisfaction and accomplishment from that day remains vivid in my memory. It resonates with the same sense of fulfilment and triumph that I experience today when I complete an ultra-endurance event.

Frank Duffy 10 Mile (2012)

Race: Frank Duffy 10 Mile	Type: 10 Mile Road Race	Length: 10 Miles
Date: August, 2012	Where: Phoenix Park	Notes: First time at this distance.

When the race finally came around, I had accumulated several months of consistent training and I was hitting my stride. Crossing the finish line with a time of 66 minutes, I vividly remember sprinting my final mile in under six minutes, which I was very happy with. It was incredibly satisfying to finish strong. As the year passed, I could see the progress I had made, consistently outpacing my friends in races. Taking place in the beautiful Phoenix Park, which has always been one of my favourite running and racing spots, the race held a special significance for me.

Takeaway point: Finish strong, give it your all; the difference in a couple of seconds could mean a personal best or a much higher finishing position.

Gaelforce West (2012)

Race: Gaelforce West	Type: Adventure race	Length: 67 kilometres
Date: August, 2012	Where: Connemara	Notes: This was my longest event at the time and my first adventure race.

In August of 2012 I decided that 67 km Gaelforce West would be my first endurance event. It consisted of a combination of running, cycling and kayaking through the mountains, rivers and lakes of Connemara. The terrain was tough, especially considering it would be my first attempt at such an event.

It started with a 5k run on the beach and it started fast. I couldn't believe how fast some of the guys took off. I went with them at the start, but quickly realised I was only going to blow up if I kept going, so I slowed it down. The next section was a long cycle which was then followed by a short kayak section around a lake and then back on to the bike.

It was on this bike section where I experienced bonking for the first time. What happens is that you completely run out of energy and continuing your race feels impossible. I hadn't a clue what was happening to me, but I could hardly get a

full rotation of the pedals without feeling like I was going to fall off the bike. I was exhausted.

I was using gels as my primary source of nutrition at the time, so I managed to take one to get going again but I could only move slowly. I managed to get to the transition where the finish line was only about a kilometre run away. I managed to finish in under five hours, so it was a respectable time. As I was new to all this running and cycling, I followed the conventional advice on nutrition, which was the use of gels. Gels were and still are the go-to source of nutrition for many people taking on events. Although they do work in terms of supplying the runner or cyclist with a burst of energy, you must take them for the duration of the event to keep topping up energy levels lost through constant energy output. Many people suffer from gastro-intestinal problems because of this overload of sugar which the human body is not designed to digest over such a short period.

Although I was using such supplements at the time, we all know now that the high content of sugars cannot be good for the human body.
Connemara is undeniably one of the most breathtaking places in the world and having the opportunity to bring my family along to experience its stunning scenery was truly remarkable. Whenever I travel for an event, I remain acutely aware of how fortunate I am to witness such incredible locations and participate in extraordinary activities amidst these natural wonders. I make a deliberate effort to pause and fully appreciate the privilege of being able to embark on these adventures, especially with my incredible family by my side. It is crucial to acknowledge and cherish these moments.

Bog Snorkelling (2012)

Race: Bog Snorkelling	Type: Fun event	Length: 100 metres
Date: August, 2012	Where: Co. Monaghan	Notes: Fun event with friends, non competitive.

In August 2012, I took part in a bog snorkelling event in Co. Monaghan. It was a festival type event that my friends had attended the year before although they were more interested in the festival side of things as opposed to the snorkelling. To be fair, they all had a good go as the event is just a bit of fun rather than a serious race although there is plenty of competition between the people who attend annually. Although I couldn't swim properly yet, I decided I'd give it a go. Bog snorkelling is not like swimming at all. You kick your legs to propel yourself and you cannot use your arms. You snorkel a measured length of the bog by kicking with flippers and breathing face down in the water with a face mask and breathing snorkel. The water is brown so you can't see anything. The fastest time from one end and back wins. You could do this easily without being a swimmer. When my time came I was pretty nervous, although more about making a fool of myself and coming last than about the 'swim' itself.
I just went for it and ignored the fear. I kicked as hard as I could and before I knew it my head was approaching the end of the length which was about 100m. My lungs were burning and my legs were on fire. My gym and sports fitness kicked in and I was able to push on and go again to get back to the start/finish line. I finished with the fastest time at that stage of the event. I was delighted with my effort. Unfortunately, my time was well beaten by a few more competitors who were seasoned pros at the sport, although I was happy to beat Leo Varadkar who has been Ireland's Taoiseach.

Dublin City Triathlon (2012)

Race: Dublin City Triathlon	Type: Sprint Triathlon	Length: 750m Swim, 20 Km by bike, 5 Km Run
Date: August, 2012	Where: Phoenix Park	Notes: My first triathlon

Participating in the sprint event at the Dublin City Triathlon of 2012 marked my first step into the world of triathlons. While I had previously taken part in running events and duathlons, this seemed like the next logical step. However, there was just one problem—I couldn't swim! If you had asked me to swim a single length using the front crawl technique, I would have been utterly lost. Nevertheless, I registered for the event with the intention of getting some practice or even taking a lesson, though that never quite materialised. Undeterred, I decided to show up and give it a try.

Arriving at the Garda Boat Club bright and early that morning, I parked my car and prepared my gear for the impending challenge at the transition area. The Olympic distance Triathlon was in progress before the sprint distance, giving me the opportunity to witness some seasoned triathletes in action. The first to emerge from the water was Irish Olympian Gavin Noble. Observing these remarkable athletes as they prepared, warmed up and completed the swim section was truly inspiring. I was so nervous and this was compounded by the fact that I had come alone, without any support. Forced to step out of my comfort zone, I mustered up the courage to approach a fellow participant and seek help with my wetsuit. It turned out to be a blessing, as this encounter led to a friendly conversation and even some valuable tips.

Knowing my limitations, I wisely positioned myself at the very back of the pack before the race began. Despite my lack of swimming expertise, I found myself pleasantly surprised at how buoyant my new wetsuit made me feel as I entered the river. This slight boost helped lessen my nerves slightly. The sound of the hooter marked the start of the race, and the chaos of the triathlon swim started to unfold. However, I soon realised that many others had entered the river after me, resulting in a scramble of limbs and bodies swimming over and past me. Panic quickly set in.

Before I knew it, those who had initially been behind me were now surging ahead. My swim strokes were far from graceful or efficient, resembling some hybrid of breaststroke and frantic paddling. I swallowed more than a few mouthfuls of Liffey water along the way. It took me what felt like an eternity, but in reality, it took me a taxing twenty minutes to complete the 750m swim.

As I reached the pontoon, two kind helpers pulled me out of the water. I was grateful for their assistance, as I doubted whether I had the strength to climb out on my own. Making my way through transition, I removed my wetsuit and regained my composure. Without missing a beat, I hopped onto my bike for the 20k and began overtaking a few fellow competitors. No significant issues arose during this leg of the race, which provided me with a well-needed boost. I couldn't help but smile as I passed athlete after athlete which only spurred me on to push harder and go faster. I made up significant time on the field of athletes who had left me behind in the swim.

As I dropped the bike and set off on the 5k run, I continued to pass other athletes, and in greater numbers than I had on the bike. I finished in 1hr 05min which, considering I was last out of the water, made me very excited; excited because I knew I could do better.

I began to imagine a future where I could improve my swim technique with focused training and perform even better in my next triathlon.

Dublin City Marathon (2012)

Race: Dublin City Marathon	Type: Marathon	Length: 42 Km
Date: October, 2012	Where: Dublin City	Notes: I trained well for this event and felt nervous.

Even though I had already completed a marathon back in 1999, the 2012 Dublin Marathon felt like a first true test of my abilities, hence, I felt very nervous. I had been training on my own, diligently completing all the runs in the Dublin Marathon Race series. While I felt good about my progress, I still lacked the experience of a seasoned marathoner. As I started the race that day, I did so without any friends or family, determined to maintain a controlled pace, unlike my previous tendency to start too fast.

Around mile five, I unexpectedly encountered Ken Coakley, a local youth from Ballymun who I knew from my football days at Sandyhill Celtic. Ken was not only a talented footballer but also an exceptional runner. While our acquaintanceship was limited at that time, my interest in running and my background in fitness, helped foster a mutual respect. Little did I know that this encounter would lead to a lasting friendship and many shared projects.

I decided to stick with Ken, knowing that he was a stronger runner than me. The miles seemed to pass effortlessly as we ran side by side. At one point, another runner approached us and inquired about our progress. I didn't have a watch or a Garmin to provide an accurate answer, but I had been keeping an eye on the mile markers along the course. "I think it's mile 14," I replied. Ken glanced at his watch and corrected me, saying, "It's mile 18." I couldn't believe how far we had already come.

As we approached the flyover at UCD, Ken turned to me and said, "Let's go." Before I could respond, he surged forward and I followed suit. We were passing other runners as if they were standing still. Our pace must have been close to a blistering six minutes per mile and although it felt like a sprint, I refused to let go. We reached the last few hundred metres and I caught sight of the green carpet leading to the finish line. Determined to finish strong, I unleashed a final burst of speed. It turned into a sprint finish and I managed to drop Ken in that final stretch. However, as Ken had started behind me at the starting line, he ultimately finished with a slightly better overall time, beating me by a few seconds. Thanks to Ken's support, I crossed the finish line with a time of 3 hours and 12 minutes – a result I am forever grateful for.

Dublin City Marathon (2013)

Race : Dublin City Marathon	Type: Running - Road race	Length: 42 Km
Date: October, 2013	Where: Dublin City	Notes: Knee issues pre-race

Determined to surpass the great experience of the previous year and break the three-hour mark, I returned to the start line of the Dublin Marathon in October 2013. I had trained consistently throughout the year, but as October approached, I started experiencing knee pain. Reflecting on it, I believe I was overtraining. At the time, I was also heavily involved in CrossFit, which I thoroughly enjoyed. However, combining the intensity of CrossFit with the volume of running I was doing proved to be too much for my body. I may not have been allowing myself sufficient time for recovery, or the quality of my recovery may not have been adequate. These are common mistakes often made by newcomers to running. The excitement of engaging in the sport often leads us to push ourselves too hard, too soon. We become enamoured by the mental and physical benefits running provides and consequently, we want more and train more. Sometimes, we go beyond what our bodies can handle. Sometimes, we haven't built a strong enough foundation to support our training, resulting in overuse injuries such as runners' knee, which I ended up experiencing. Runner's knee is a condition commonly

caused by excessive and sudden increases in running, similar to tennis elbow. It can be identified by pain felt on the outside of the knee and is caused by tightness in the tendon that runs along the outside of the leg from the hip to the knee.
Despite dealing with this injury, I made it to the start line of the Dublin Marathon and pushed through. I was still on pace for a sub-three-hour finish at mile eighteen. A sub-three-hour finish time is considered a significant milestone for non-competitive participants. However, my optimism quickly turned to disappointment as I started feeling pain in my left hamstring, followed by my left quadriceps, left hip and an intensified stinging pain in my knee that I had been experiencing for weeks. I had to alternate between jogging, walking and limping just to make it to the finish line, with a final time of 3h 30m. My friends and training partners praised me for persevering until the end, but deep down, I knew that withdrawing from the race would have been the wiser decision.

The Race, Donegal (2014)

Race : The Race	Type: Adventure Race Run, Kayak, Cycle, Hike, Cycle, Run.	Length: 250 Kilometres
Date: February, 2014	Where: Donegal	Notes: Extreme weather conditions

In 2014 I entered The Race, a multi-stage endurance race held in Donegal at the end of February or start of March. It totals 250 kilometres and has a cut off time of twenty-four hours. I was worried that I might be a bit out of my league, but I've always felt that one of my best qualities as an athlete was my willingness to reject the fear of entering big events and to take these on as a personal challenge. I trained for the event but I was nowhere near strong enough to finish the first bike section comfortably, which was 100 km of hills, headwinds, dangerous winding roads and driving rain.
The terrain and guaranteed harsh weather conditions are what makes The Race an extremely tough event. The finish rate is generally 50% each year. I started the first run section fairly comfortably having set off at 6 am in the dark, cold, wet surroundings of Gartan House. From there it was a half marathon to Lough Swilly where I got changed into some rain gear for the 15k kayak from Ramelton out to Rathmullan. Although the kayak was 15k I had felt it didn't need too much training attention, and I was right. But most of the race is done on the bike so more attention should be given to training on the bike. The next section was the first bike section, approximately 100k out to Muckish Mountain. It was

the toughest cycle I have ever done. I had travelled to Donegal that year alone as the rules state there is no crew allowed. Yet, while I was battling headwinds, rain and hills I saw other competitors being shielded or drafting behind vans and being fed on the roadside by family members. I didn't mind as, honestly, the conditions that year were rough! I just wished that I had someone there, even for the support.

I managed to get through the cycle and get changed in the tent provided as a changing area. I don't know how the tent didn't blow away that day. Since then, the organisers have switched to using steel containers. I got up to the top of Muckish and back down in an hour which was pretty decent. I had a few slips due to the wet, windy conditions but nothing major. I got a second wind having completed this section so well and was happy to jump back on the bike.

I took off down the road and had twenty kilometres done when the battery that powered my Di2 gear set came away from the underside of my bike frame. My bike's Di2 gears are battery-powered. The battery got caught in my back spokes and snapped the power cable. This meant I had no use of my gears and I was stuck in a high gear and could not even shift it manually. I carried on for another 10k or so until I was beaten mentally and physically. I was annoyed and angry at the time but it was one of many scenarios that forge my mental strength into what it is today. If this happened to me again today, I know I would finish that race regardless. When I made the decision to pull out, it was an impulse decision. Sure I was physically and mentally depleted but it was a decision I would come to regret. After I told one of the race marshals that I had decided to pull out, he got on to the race director to inform him of my decision. I was told I'd have to

wait for the van to come and pick me up to bring me back to race HQ. I sat in the race marshal's car to take shelter from the cold winds. I was waiting for nearly three hours for the van as it was following the last placed competitor. I could have finished the bike leg by this time, even if I had walked up the hills with the bike. When the van picked me up I was happy to be making my way back to HQ. The van followed the last placed competitor all the way back to where the marathon, the last section of the race was to start. By the time we got there, I could have nearly finished myself if I had just kept moving forward. Keep moving forward is now what I tell myself when faced with similar adversity.

To this day, the decision to pull out of the race annoys me greatly, but it helped me become stronger mentally. It's because of this single scenario that I would never again make a similar decision so impulsively. Sure I might pull out from a race or event in the future, but I will ensure I do everything I can to try to continue and take enough time before I make that decision. While I was waiting on the side of the road for the van to pick me up, I came across a guy named Keith Horgan from Dublin. I met Keith a couple of weeks before at the launch of a book called *Tick Tock Ten*, written by Gerry Duffy who coincidentally was the first Irishman to have completed ten iron distance triathlons in ten days. At the event we got chatting and discovered that we were both heading up to Donegal to take on The Race later in the month. When I saw Keith pull up on his bike on the side of the road, he looked shattered. His bike lights had failed and he needed another light to continue. I offered Keith mine, since I didn't need them now. He took the lights and continued on. Later that night, back at HQ, I got to greet some of the competitors who finished The Race 2014. Among them was Keith. He looked tired but on his face was a huge smile and a look of accomplishment that made me so envious. I knew I needed to re-enter The Race again the following year.

I had told all my family, friends and clients I was taking on this massive challenge. So when I failed to finish I felt a little embarrassed. I knew I would have finished The Race that year if not for the bike mechanical issue. When I got home the following day, I got online to check The Race dates for 2015. Again it was being held in late February so I knew the weather would be a big factor. I signed up for 2015. I could not have predicted just how much of a factor the weather in 2015 would prove to be...

Coast to Coast (2014)

Race : Coast to Coast	Type: Adventure Race Run, Cycle, Kayak, Cycle, Run.	Length: 312 kilometres
Date: May, 2014	Where: Sligo to Down	Notes: 10 weeks after The Race, Donegal

As soon as I returned home from Donegal, I wasted no time searching for a similar adventure. Despite not finishing the event, I still felt confident in my performance and believed I would have completed it if not for the unfortunate incident with the snapped power cable. That's when I stumbled upon the Coast to Coast, a 312 km race from Sligo to Down, scheduled for May. Although it was another 24-hour race, I assumed it would be a slightly easier challenge due to the milder weather and flatter terrain in the Midlands.

My optimism soon proved to be wishful thinking. The Coast to Coast race presented us with horrendous downpours and extraordinarily rugged terrain in the Mourne Mountains. The event kicked off with a challenging 5k beach run in pouring rain and with strong winds. The organisers assured us that the wind was only a factor on the beach and that calmer weather awaited us ten miles inland. To my relief, this proved to be true.

After completing the beach run, I hopped onto my road bike to begin the first bike section, covering a distance of 108k. The roads had good surface quality and the weather began to improve. My wife Miriam and her brother Tom graciously volunteered to be my support crew for the race.

Upon borrowing my brother's old van, Tom took on the role of the driver. Their plan was to drive ahead for about an hour; I would follow behind, meeting them at a planned spot. If I needed to refuel or change clothes, I would make a stop. If I felt strong enough to continue without a break, I would push forward.

Unfortunately, at just 60 kilometres into the bike section, my energy levels dropped sharply and it felt as though I had slammed into a wall. I had made the decision to skip breakfast before the event, as I was never keen on consuming a large meal before any run. But this proved to be a mistake for a race as long and demanding as this. I realised the importance of properly fuelling my body, especially in such endurance races.

I fed myself with some pitta bread, potatoes and hummus, taking a few minutes to replenish my energy levels. My primary goal for this race was simply to cross the finish line. However, I found myself wrestling with thoughts of giving up and heading home. It was still early in the event and I couldn't see how I would make it to the end or if I had the willpower to persevere through the challenges ahead. Miriam, sensing my doubts, encouraged me to keep going, assuring me that I could finish if I just kept moving forward. The weight of potentially disappointing Miriam and Tom, who had put in so much effort to support me, weighed heavily on my mind.

In my experience, the cycling portions of endurance races have always been tougher for me than the running sections. I know that running is more physically demanding on the body, but there's a sense of confidence and determination in me when I'm running that allows me to believe I will reach the finish line of any run. So, when I reach the marathon stage of an Ironman, I'm not thinking about the daunting distance ahead; instead, I focus on the fact that

I'm nearing the end. Even if I experience discomfort during or after running, I maintain the certainty that I will ultimately reach my goal. I suppose that comes from experience and I had very little of that when it came to cycling.
The first 108K of cycling proved to be a tough challenge. It led to the start of the kayak stage, spanning 27k of paddling through canals and loughs3 to complete it. It took me four hours to finish this kayak section. The first three hours, particularly on the canal sections, were enjoyable as there was no resistance from the current. However, once I ventured out onto the loughs, battling against the waves and winds became a different story. The last hour of the kayak stage was especially difficult. The initial excitement and appreciation for the scenery had faded away and all I wanted was for the stage to be over. It was an hour filled with persistent effort, but I reminded myself that time always passes and it was up to me whether to keep pressing forward or waste time by staying stagnant and thinking about what lay ahead. With determination, I chose to keep moving forward.
The sight of Miriam waiting at the finish area of the kayak section was incredibly uplifting as I rounded the last bend. I was so happy to see her there but I quickly refuelled with food and changed into my cycling gear for the next section which was a 140k cycle.
While getting changed, I struck up a conversation with another competitor who had been working together with a partner since the start of the race. He mentioned that many other participants were doing the same, teaming up. Considering my relative weakness on the bike, I expressed concern about slowing them down. However, he reassured me, saying, "Not at all, you can just sit behind us." Given the opportunity, I couldn't say no. With that, I set off alongside my new companions, embarking on a challenging 140k ride that would mostly be in the darkness of the cold, wet night ahead.
To this day, it remains one of the toughest cycles I've ever encountered. The roads were in good condition and the terrain wasn't particularly hilly. However, what made it exceptionally challenging was the darkness, the bone-chilling cold and the relentless rain, unlike anything I had encountered during previous cycling events. The heavy rainfall made it extremely difficult to see, resulting in a much slower pace. Yet this wasn't an issue when it came to keeping up with the two guys, as they were facing the same visibility challenges. The downpour was so intense that it caused streams to form on the main roads, further adding to the difficulty of the ride through the night.
After the heaviest rainfall had passed, the weather remained cold and intermittent showers continued to surprise us. Despite cycling through the night, we found ourselves nearing the Mourne Mountains, the location of the upcoming run, as the sky began to brighten and the night began to fade.

---

3 "Loghs" is the Irish/Scottish for "Lake".

Arriving at the transition point, situated in a car park, one of the men had a camper van and a crew prepared to accompany him during his run. His plan involved indulging in sausage sandwiches and having a rest before embarking on his 30k journey. Since I was drenched and shivering, my main focus was on drying off and getting started. As I wasn't keen on eating before running, I decided to forgo food and set off on my own.

The 30k run took me through the mountains, which was something that I was not used to. It started with a difficult climb that required me to hike rather

than run. Once I got past that challenge, I found myself on an asphalt road and the thought of finally getting into a steady pace made me happy. However, my happiness was quickly erased as the course veered off-road once again. From that point until the finish line, the run would consist of trails and mountainous terrain only.

As I overtook a group of guys who were clearly working together, a moment of regret washed over me. If I had known what lay ahead, I would have surely joined them, but my ego got the better of me and I zoomed past them. Determined to keep going, I pushed forward until they were out of sight.

After a while, I realised that I couldn't see anyone around me. A sinking feeling settled in my gut, telling me that I had made a wrong turn or missed a crucial junction. At that moment, I faced a difficult decision: should I backtrack and retrace my steps to find the group I had passed? Or should I just keep pushing on?

Making up my mind, I sprinted back in the direction I had come from, hoping to cross paths with the guys again. It wasn't long before I caught a glimpse of them in the mountains, following a different trail. They were approximately two kilometres away from me across a valley and seemed to be veering off in a different direction. A wave of frustration crashed over me as I cursed my earlier decision.

With determination fuelling my every step, I focused on catching up to them. Although they had picked up their pace, I managed to close the gap, ensuring that I could follow behind them and find my way back on track.

Just as I caught up to them, I began to struggle. My grip on the group slipped away and I could feel myself bonking as I had at Gaelforce West. To my dismay, I had no food on me to replenish my energy. I slowed down drastically and, soon enough, I lost sight of the group. I was on my own once more.

Given my previous wrong turn, anxiety crept in as I was determined not to repeat that mistake. I resorted to walking and occasionally retracing my steps to confirm I was heading in the right direction.

After some time, I regained enough strength to resume running. Although I moved more smoothly, I realised that I hadn't encountered anyone in a considerable amount of time. I had done it again–missed a turn and continued on a trail that led nowhere. This time, I had strayed even farther from the correct path and I was now miles off course. I had no choice but to retrace my steps once again.

To this day, it remains a mystery how I managed to find my way back. As I trudged up the side of a mountain that was a popular spot for visitors, relief washed over me when I reached the summit and encountered a race volunteer. He kindly directed me back down the mountain, pointing me in the direction of the finish line. Years later, after returning here, I realised that this mountain was Mount Donard.

I had reached a point of desperation where I found myself approaching random strangers, desperately asking for something to eat. Unfortunately, no one I encountered had any food to offer. Overwhelmed with distress, I sank down and sat, feeling utterly defeated.

My appearance must have been truly alarming, for I distinctly remember concerned passers-by stopping to inquire if I needed assistance. Amidst my despair, I noticed an apple lying on the ground. It had a bite mark and was covered in sand from where it had been recently dropped. In survival mode, I picked up the apple and wiped off the untouched portion of the skin. Carefully avoiding the bitten area, I savoured each bite. It was, without a doubt, one of the most delicious apples I had ever tasted. The energy it provided injected me with renewed strength to carry on. I didn't know at that moment, but I was surprisingly close to the finish line.

After receiving directions, I struggled my way towards the finish line. Although I was provided with instructions to find a car park near the finish line and other details, my deteriorated state made it difficult for me to register much of the information. Eventually, I arrived at the carpark but couldn't spot any fellow competitors or signs indicating the finish line. Frustrated and upset, I aimlessly ran and walked back and forth in a desperate attempt to find my way. I felt stuck and hopeless.

I later found out the event organisers had been monitoring my tracker and had initially sent someone to guide me back on track. However, upon noticing my progress towards them, they decided to call their helper back, causing me to unintentionally change directions once again. Interestingly, this 24-hour race had no official cut-off time, which turned out to be fortunate for me, since it took me over 26 hours to complete.

After what felt like an eternity of back and forth, I stumbled upon Paul, one of the participants I had been cycling alongside throughout the night. He was the guy who had decided to take a break at the transition area, indulging in sausage sandwiches before commencing the run. Despite leaving the transition area long before he did and having a considerable head start, he managed to make up for all the lost time by maintaining a steady pace and staying on course. I couldn't avoid feeling foolish in comparison. "Finish with me," he said, recognising my physical exhaustion and emotional drainage. Perhaps he had even overheard me shouting in anger at myself. "It's just this way," he reassured me. Paul had a crew of local runners accompanying him from the run transition, all of whom were familiar with the route from their collective experiences.

Together, we made our way towards the finish line, which was merely a kilometre away from where I had encountered Paul and his crew. The final stretch took us along a promenade, providing a pleasant backdrop for the triumphant finish. As we approached the finish line, Paul's crew slowed down to allow both of us to cross together. In a heartfelt gesture, Paul grabbed my hand and raised it in the air. I was immensely grateful to have met him on that momentous day. We crossed the finish line together in joint second-to-last place. Though we finished just over 26 hours, there was no cut-off time, so we officially completed the race and earned our finisher medals.

Dingle Triathlon (2014)

Race : Dingle Triathlon	Type: Olympic Triathlon	Length: 1.5k Swim 40K Bike 10K Run
Date: September, 2014	Where: Dingle, Kerry	Notes: My first Olympic Triathlon

I have only participated in two Olympic Triathlons to date. The first of them was the Dingle triathlon, which took place in the beautiful town of Dingle in co. Kerry, also known as the home of Fungie the Dingle Dolphin.

Trev, who is Miriam's best friend Sue's husband, had competed in the same event the year before (2013). He and Sue had spent a weekend in Dingle and Trev decided to give the triathlon a try. I was impressed by Trev's ability to balance his academic pursuits (he had obtained three degrees) with his love for physical activity. He had achieved a personal best of 3h 12m in a marathon and was determined to break the 3-hour mark before I met him.

In school, I met Sue and Miriam around the same time. They had already been best friends for years. Trev, a few years older than Miriam, Sue, and me, struck me as much more mature when I first met him.

I immediately took a liking to Trev. Although we didn't initially have a lot in common, he was such a pleasant person to talk to. When Trev found out that I was getting involved in running and physical training after quitting football, he offered to train with me. Our friendship quickly grew to a point where we didn't need to go through Miriam and Sue to contact each other. We started training together regularly and became close friends due to the amount of time we spent together on the bike and running.

Trev was my first training partner, and we shared many misadventures on epic five-hour mountain rides in Wicklow. One day, as rain poured down like it was trying to break some kind of Guinness World Record, we stumbled upon a lesson in cycling we never thought we'd need.

We were hurtling down a Wicklow hill at about sixty kilometres per hour, raindrops bouncing off our helmets. The weather was so atrocious that even our rim brakes were like, "Nah, we're taking a break today." when we spotted a T-junction in the distance, and panic started pedalling faster than our legs ever could.

As we approached the junction, reality hit us like a ton of bricks. Our bikes are on autopilot and the brakes are on strike. I glanced at Trev, who's just as bewildered as I am – the T-junction was looming closer and our bikes were not showing any signs of slowing down.

With the junction fast approaching, I realised my only option is to go full throttle through it and pray for the best. Turning left or right at this speed would turn us into human-sized skittles for oncoming cars. I braced myself for impact and zoomed through the junction, crossing the road like a cycling daredevil on a mission and BAM! I smashed into a three-foot stone wall, parting ways with my bike in a spectacular and graceless display. One shoe was off, the other on the loose and my head had decided that it wanted a closer look at the scenery on the other side of the road, sending me headfirst through a hedge.

Miraculously, I bounced back up, laughing at the ridiculousness of it all. I climbed back through the hedge, contemplating how close I had come to starring in a roadside drama. Meanwhile, Trev, the cycling wizard, had somehow managed to finesse his way through the junction without smashing into the wall. To this day I still don't know how he did it.

We dusted ourselves off, our bikes a bit worse for wear, but we were laughing through the soggy Irish air. I turned to Trev and said "This is why we are the only two gobshites out cycling today".

Coming back to the Dingle Triathlon, as I said, Trev shared his Dingle experience with us and Sue posted some action shots of him on Facebook. In his account of the race, Trev described the challenging conditions he had faced. The fog was so thick that he could hardly see what was ahead of him. The pictures perfectly captured the atmosphere. Yet, the day after they returned from Dingle, Sue and Trev told us that they were willing to enter the race again since their experience had been so incredible. So we all decided to sign up for the 2014 Dingle Triathlon and booked a beautiful B&B near the town of Dingle.

At the time of the triathlon, Trev was driving a Ford Transit minibus, so we had planned to travel together as two couples. This would be Miriam and Sue's first triathlon and they had enrolled in the sprint triathlon that took place on the same day but started shortly after the Olympic event. Despite their lack of experience, both of them had trained well. Sue, with her background in team sports, had always maintained a good level of fitness. Miriam trained with me regularly, particularly focusing on swimming and it was gratifying to witness her progress. Trev and I were also training together every weekend.

However, when Sue and Trev arrived at our place to pick us up, they brought unfortunate news. Trev, who had recently recovered from a severe bout of flu, had decided it wouldn't be wise for him to participate in the race. He didn't want to risk falling ill again or potentially facing a worse outcome by taking part in a race that we had primarily entered for fun.

Trev's decision not to participate in the race under those conditions was a sensible one. I think he may have learned a lesson from witnessing my own struggles at the WAR earlier in the year.

The following day, we woke up and had breakfast together. At that time, I was not accustomed to eating before any physical activity. I have since changed this habit and now always eat before training sessions, especially when I'm cycling. For swimming, I generally don't eat beforehand, since I usually swim either at 6am or 10am and a cup of tea is enough to fuel me. Similarly, when it comes to running, I try to avoid eating for about three to four hours before a run. I don't follow any scientific reasoning for this choice; I simply feel that it works better for me. I understand that everyone is different, and some people might adopt different eating patterns while they train.

After breakfast, we packed up our gear and prepared ourselves for the race. Then, we made our way to the transition area.

As I racked my bike in the transition area, I realised with a sinking feeling that I had forgotten to pack my bike shoes. I had actually left them back in Dublin. Typical me. I was so annoyed with myself that I contemplated withdrawing from the race. As it happened, Trev's withdrawal from the race surprisingly worked to my advantage. He sprang into action and started asking around for spare shoes. A kind gentleman from a local bike shop offered me some. Unfortunately, the clips on the shoes didn't match my pedals.

With the race about to begin and swimmers called to the water, Trev urged me to go ahead and do the swim, assuring me that by the time I finished, he would have a solution for the bike shoe problem. If it wasn't for his determination, I would have probably just returned to the B&B. The swim went surprisingly well and I emerged from the water in fifth place. As I hurried to transition, ripping off my wetsuit, I saw Trev waiting at the transition barrier. He shouted, "That's the best we could do!" He had found me a bike equipped with pedals which meant I could use my running shoes - I would lose power without the usual cleats but at least I could finish the race. I decided to forget about racing and simply enjoy the day.

I swiftly slipped on my running shoes and helmet and pushed my bike through the transition area towards the bike mount line. Triathletes are barred from cycling through transition areas, preventing potential chaos. Imagine the mayhem that could ensue if this regulation were not in place.

Setting off on the 40 kilometre cycle I felt great despite the noticeable lack of pushing power. Other competitors passed me but I didn't mind. After the morning mishap, I was simply glad to be there soaking in the amazing weather. My plan was to complete the cycling leg and then focus on having a strong run.

I had lost a few positions on the bike leg, but I had a solid run and managed to reclaim some of those places. I crossed the finish line in 17th place out of 92 participants, which left me satisfied with my performance. It had been a fantastic day.

Miriam and Sue had also completed their race. Sue suffered from a headache during the race and had to take a break at one point, but she showed great resilience and determination to get back into the race and earn her finisher's medal. It was an excellent introduction to triathlon for both of them and they were motivated to take on another challenge at Challenge Galway, this time stepping up to the Olympic distance.

Ocean Lava (2014)

Race : Ocean Lava 2014	Type: ¾ Iron distance Triathlon	Length: 3k Swim 120k Bike 30k Run
Date: October, 2014	Where: Lanzarote, Spain	Notes: Longest triathlon to this point

eflow.ie

On October 1st, Ocean Lava 2014 Lanzarote took place on the same course used for the Ironman Lanzarote race. Miriam and I decided to turn it into a family and friends holiday and we were joined by our close friends and training partners, Trev and Sue. Originally, we had signed up for the half-iron distance triathlon, while Miriam and Sue opted for the Olympic distance.

However, a few weeks after we registered, it was announced that the half-iron distance was being extended to a ¾ distance. For that year only, it was upgraded to a national championship. I was thrilled with the news and jokingly teased the others about it not being extended enough for me.

On our Lanzarote trip, we were joined by my sister Jude and her husband Brian, although they were there to support us rather than participate in the race. It worked out perfectly because they were able to take care of our three sons, Jake, Reece and Ben, while we were out on the course.

Although it was October, the weather was still incredibly hot. I had some concerns about racing in such conditions, since I had never experienced racing in similar heat before. Fortunately, the heat wasn't much of an issue during the swim, as the water provided enough coolness. However, there was a tense half-hour before the swim started when rumours circulated that the swim might be non-wetsuit only. This would have meant losing the benefits of wearing a wetsuit, such as temperature control and buoyancy. Thankfully, this turned out to be false and the swim was wetsuit legal.

The heat didn't bother me too much during the bike leg, as the course was fairly open and there was a strong breeze that helped keep me cool. However, when it came time for the run, the heat became more noticeable, although not as intense as I had anticipated. I made sure to stay hydrated and took advantage of the numerous opportunities to refuel on the four-loop run course.

I had a great swim, a steady bike ride and a solid run, all without any major incidents or issues. Unfortunately, Trev didn't have the same luck. While on the bike course, he, along with a couple of other guys, missed a turn near a roundabout. It took them a while to realise they were off course. Fortunately, they stumbled upon some local cyclists who directed them back to the race route. This detour added an extra 50 kilometres to their total distance, including the toughest climb on the route at Femes, which they now had to tackle twice. The three of them managed to make it back just in time before the cycle cut off, but one of the guys decided not to continue on to the run.

Trev, on the other hand, had a different approach. He didn't let the setback discourage him and he decided to continue with the race. By the time I was nearing the end of my third lap of the run, I realised that I hadn't seen him on the course yet. This struck me as odd because Trev was typically a stronger cyclist than me and had a strong mental game as well. I was truly amazed at his composure and determination. He remained calm and kept pushing forward, as if nothing had gone wrong.

Throughout the day, I faced numerous challenges as an inexperienced triathlete. My nutrition wasn't ideal; I lacked physical strength and my mental toughness was still developing. However, what kept me going during those tough moments was the knowledge that my family was eagerly awaiting my arrival at the finish line. I knew that my kids were experiencing the incredible atmosphere, surrounded by elite athletes embarking on the monumental challenge of completing three distinct events in one seamless race. Being a part of that experience ignited my determination and grit.

When the sweltering heat weighed me down on the bike, I visualised my family and instantly gained a surge of energy. Every pedal rotation brought me closer to reuniting with them. When I began the run, their excitement was palpable. I drew strength from their presence, propelling me forward. Crossing the finish line and being greeted and congratulated by my family was an indescribable feeling. Sharing that moment with them was truly incredible and I wished it could last forever. We also captured the moment in some photographs and replenished our depleted bodies with fluids. I felt Miriam now truly understood the challenges I faced throughout my training and races and why I pursued these endeavours. She had completed her race earlier in the scorching heat of Lanzarote, experiencing her own struggles and now she could relate to mine. We exchanged stories about our races and took a leisurely stroll with the kids and the rest of our group, eagerly awaiting Trev's arrival.

We managed to find a table at a pizza restaurant that had a clear view of the road leading to the finish line. As we sat there, we watched countless competitors pass by, giving it their all to reach the end. Suddenly, Trev appeared and, in jest, shouted out to us, "Order me some pizza, I'm famished!" He wasn't joking; he was genuinely hungry.

At the next table, there was a couple who had already finished the event and were now basking in their accomplishment. They had their food served while we anxiously awaited ours. Understanding Trev's struggle, the man turned to Sue and asked, "Would you like a slice of this pizza for him?" With his own firsthand experience of the race, his offer felt sincere and genuine. Sue graciously accepted. We all expressed our gratitude to this generous fellow participant. Grabbing the substantial slice of pizza, she swiftly made her way down the road to find Trev. Grateful, he accepted the delicious slice and continued on his way. When he completed another lap and passed by our tables, he shouted his heartfelt thanks, exclaiming that it was the best pizza he had ever tasted.

Trev pressed on with two more laps to go. After about an hour or so, he reappeared, a wide grin spreading across his face. "Last lap!" he shouted triumphantly. With renewed determination, he embarked on his final lap; as he thought anyway.

When the course approached the finishing gantry, a switchback took runners off the main path. However, as Trev passed by this section, he was stopped and

CHINA

informed that he had already completed his last lap. All he had to do was run down the gantry to finish. He took us all by surprise when we saw him walking back towards us, having just crossed the finish line.

I couldn't help but be impressed once again by Trev's unwavering resilience. Despite unknowingly adding an extra 50 kilometres to his bike and almost starting another lap on the run course, he appeared to have no worries or concerns. His mental strength in the face of adversity was truly remarkable. Witnessing someone I knew so well respond in such a positive and composed manner served as a tremendous source of inspiration for me. It became an example of how I could also handle similar obstacles if they arose.

The Race, Donegal (2015)

Race : The Race, Donegal	Type: Adventure Race Run, Kayak, Cycle, Hike, Cycle, Run.	Length: 250 Km
Date: March, 2015	Where: Donegal	Notes: Extreme weather conditions

In 2015, my focus shifted towards the most significant event of my life–my wedding. As a result, I didn't race much that year.

In the earlier part of the year, I decided to, once again, take on The Race in Donegal, having faced a setback during my previous attempt.

I had a clear understanding of what the day entailed and the preparations needed. While I always believed that my running would be strong, I was aware that my weakness lay in biking. However, I believed that I had grown stronger since my failure in 2014, especially considering that it was a mechanical issue that had caused me to withdraw from the race back then.

This time I was fortunate to have my friend Chris join me as a crew member. After hearing about my previous experience, he volunteered to drive my van to Donegal on Friday, with the race set to begin on Saturday at 5am. I picked up Chris in the van and took on most of the driving myself, mainly because it was a straightforward motorway and we didn't see the need to stop and switch drivers. Looking back, I don't think this decision benefited either of us, as I ended up fatigued from the long drive and Chris hadn't had much practice driving the van for the day that lay ahead.

On the morning of the race, I allowed myself to sleep in a bit longer than the other competitors. I have never been a fan of eating before any activity and given that I felt more tired than usual after the drive, I believed that the extra rest would benefit me. Eventually, I got out of bed and prepared myself for the day ahead. Stepping outside, I was greeted with the typical cold, wet and windy weather that Donegal is known for. At the start line the organisers had already gathered and before I knew it, the starting gun had fired and I found myself running into the darkness, surrounded by fellow competitors with flashing, illuminated gear. Although it was mandatory to bring head torches and lights for dark portions of the course, I made the decision not to wear mine that morning. Carrying it with me all day for less than an hour of darkness didn't seem practical. Additionally, as I anticipated being surrounded by competitors with ample light, I felt confident that I would be okay without it. I stored my lights in my transition boxes, saving them for when I truly needed them.

The run was dark, cold and wet; additionally, it was upgraded from a half-marathon to a run that was closer to a full marathon because of the unsafe weather conditions, which prevented the kayak section from taking place. This change favoured me, since I was a stronger runner than a kayaker. By the end of the run section, I was among the top 5 places, according to Chris. My main goal was simply to finish the race and after taking my time to ensure I had the right equipment, I started the first bike section.

This covered one hundred kilometres, although it felt much longer due to its difficulty and the weather was even more extreme than in 2014. The wind was relentless, always either blowing in my face or trying to knock me off the bike. It took a toll on my energy and I struggled to keep the bike straight and on the road. I was not strong enough to battle against this wind, which significantly slowed me down. As a consequence, I spent much more time in the freezing rain and my slow pace prevented me from generating enough heat to keep my body temperature high enough.

By the time I reached Muckish Mountain, I was literally in a delirious state. Chris later informed me that I was rambling and mentioning something like " ...my friend Chris is looking after my bike." I have no recollection of this. What I did know was that I was in a terrible condition and half an hour later I found myself in the changing tent, with several people trying to help raise my body temperature. My race was over. I spent another hour in the ambulance as a precautionary measure. An hour later, I found myself sitting in a café in Letterkenny, trying to make sense of what had happened. Deep down, I knew that I simply didn't have the physical strength required.

I repeatedly expressed my desire to enter The Race again in 2016 but Miriam and Chris attempted to dissuade me from this decision. "It's not worth compromising your health," they said. However, I was determined to conquer the race and knew deep down that I would not let it go without a fight. So, without hesitation, I registered for The Race 2016 when I returned home. I made a promise to myself that this time, the challenging weather in Donegal would not stop me and that I would not fail for a third and final attempt.

Ironman Wales (2015)

Race : Ironman Wales	Type: Triathlon	Length: Ironman 140.6 (miles)
Date: September, 2015	Where: Tenby, Wales	Notes: First attempt at Ironman

Having completed a three-quarter length triathlon in Lanzarote, I decided that Ironman Wales would be my first full-distance triathlon. Not only was it an Ironman brand race, to run one of which was a personal goal, it was also known as the toughest Ironman on the race schedule. For triathletes, finishing an Ironman branded race is the ultimate achievement, since only a tiny proportion of the world's population have accomplished this feat. The reputation of Ironman Wales as the toughest event on the planet was widely believed and its challenging course, including a zigzag walkway transition from the sea in Tenby, and a hilly bike route, made it the obvious choice for my inaugural attempt at the full distance.

One of the reasons I chose Ironman Wales (also known as 'To Slay the Dragon') was its location. Since there was no full-distance Ironman event in Ireland, it wasn't possible for me to compete on home soil. Thankfully, Wales was just a few hours away via ferry across the Irish sea, and after arriving in Wales, it was only a short half-hour drive to Tenby. To make things even more convenient, I could drive over in my LDV Convoy van, which I had purchased for camping trips. It was perfect for transporting my bike and all the necessary equipment, including my pre- and post-race food. LDV vans have a funny-looking shape, but that's what initially attracted me to the van.

My triathlon training partner, Trev, was also eager to take on the Ironman Wales run, so he and Sue decided to drive over via the ferry as well. In Tenby, we were fortunate to find a lovely apartment that overlooked a section of the bike course. Our balcony provided a perfect vantage point for the road where the athletes would pass twice during the race. This news was great for me and Trev, as we knew that catching a glimpse of our supportive wives as we passed by would provide a tremendous boost.

On the day before the race, I registered and prepared my bike, feeling a mix of nerves and excitement. It was reminiscent of the anticipation I had felt before facing a major exam—that anxious feeling of not knowing exactly what to expect but just wanting to get started and put an end to the uncertainty. Ironman Wales was my ultimate triathlon test and I had dedicated myself to extensive preparation during the previous nine months.

Before the race began, the Welsh national anthem was sung. The atmosphere was absolutely electric; like nothing I had experienced before and I still get bumps when I recall it. The air was thick with pride and emotion. I felt incredibly privileged to be in the presence of such determined and like-minded athletes. There was an extraordinary sense of camaraderie, knowing that we were all embarking on this challenging journey which would take us between ten and seventeen hours.

The swim start was staggered into groups or waves. When you initially sign up, you're asked your estimated swim time and your answer will determine where you place yourself on the beach, before starting. Faster swimmers enter the water first followed by the next fastest group and so on until all groups or waves have started. I had opted to start with the one-hour and ten-minute group, since I felt I could swim at that pace. I attempted to make my way towards that group, but before I could reach them, the starting hooter echoed through the morning sky, signalling the beginning of the age group start. From the sandy beach, a multitude of participants surged into the sea. Although I was just behind the group that I planned to start with, I found myself in a favourable enough position.

With determination, I sprinted towards the sea, navigating my way through the rolling waves that crashed one after the other. As the waves approached, I leapt over them, determined to maintain my progress. When the water reached waist-deep, I swiftly dived under the next oncoming wave. Emerging on the other side, I propelled myself forward, using a powerful combination of arm strokes and vigorous leg kicks to navigate the swells.

The 3.8 km swim leg was incredible. I had to complete two large laps to cover the distance. I managed to finish in just one hour and twelve minutes, experiencing only a few accidental kicks and slaps from fellow competitors, which was to be expected in such a crowded event.

Leaving the water, I made my way up the beach towards the walkway that led to the streets of Tenby and the transition area where my bike was waiting for the 180 kilometre cycle. The transition from the swim to the bike in Ironman Wales is truly unique. The walkway leading from the beach to the streets has multiple zigzag switchbacks. Even after navigating this walkway, there was still roughly a mile to go before reaching the transition area. Some participants left their running shoes in a tied plastic bag attached to the fence, as they found running a mile barefoot to be too challenging. However, the majority of competitors, including myself, braved the mile-long run without any footwear.

I took off my goggles and hat, followed by peeling my wetsuit down to my waist. Despite the chill in the air, I felt more comfortable running without the top half of my wetsuit on, avoiding the risk of overheating that may occur from running with it fully on. Instead of focusing on beating a specific time, I decided to fully immerse myself in the experience. The atmosphere created by the athletes, organisers and spectators was truly special, filling me with a sense of inspiration. A wide grin spread across my face as I absorbed the excitement.

Reaching my bike, I quickly removed my wetsuit completely before donning my helmet, sunglasses and a cycling jacket for added warmth. With my shoes already clipped into the pedals, I ran out of the transition area towards the bike mount line. Stepping onto my bike, I set off for the long cycling leg.

The bike route took us through picturesque countryside and quaint Welsh villages. The sunshine graced us throughout the ride, enhancing the beauty of our surroundings. In the latter stages of the bike course, I couldn't help but think, "Thank goodness it isn't raining because this would be quite challenging in wet conditions."

Ironman Wales is renowned for its challenging bike course, which naturally gave me some anxiety. However, when I started riding, I realised that it wasn't much more difficult than the training I had done back home. That was before I reached Saundersfoot, the location of the notorious 'Heartbreak Hill.' As I approached, I noticed numerous participants walking up the hill, pushing their bikes. My ego kicked in and I made a decision to give it my all and keep pedalling. It was an effort of epic proportions, but I managed to conquer the hill while still on my bike. Whenever I witness people pushing their bikes up hills during races, I embrace it as a personal challenge not to let the course overcome me. This mindset has driven me during races like The Race in Donegal and Ocean Lava in Lanzarote.

After just a couple of minutes, I encountered another hill; this one on a whole other level of insanity. On each side of the road, spectators swarmed, lining up at least ten bodies deep and the raucous noise overwhelmed me. Cowbells jingled, air horns blared and the crowd cheered, screamed and whistled. The sheer difficulty of the climb was forgotten, replaced by an infectious smile as the passionate spectators propelled me forward. To this day, I have yet to encounter anything that compares to that moment. It was as if we were given a taste of what it feels like for professional athletes competing in elite races like the Tour de France.

After spending a gruelling six hours and fifty-three minutes on my bike, I dismounted and made my way back to the transition area. Despite an unremarkable time, I was thrilled with my performance, considering the challenging course. I rushed into transition, leaving my shoes behind and throwing on my running kicks, ready to embark on the final stretch of this extraordinary event—a full 42-kilometre marathon.

As I left transition and began my run through the streets of Tenby, an unfamiliar sensation washed over me—my legs felt completely lifeless. The fatigue from pushing myself to the limit on the bike, covering a distance I had never tackled before on such an unforgiving course, had caught up with me. I resorted to walking mere moments after leaving transition, attempting to regain enough strength to run once more. Unfortunately, my legs simply lacked the power to continue.

B2R
BASE2RACE
IRONMAN

My spirits were low as I continued down the road, only about four hundred metres from the transition area. However, a glimmer of hope emerged when I spotted Miriam and Sue who had cleverly manoeuvred their way to the front of the crowd. I couldn't help but share my doubts with Miriam, confessing that I might be ready to throw in the towel.

Their encouraging words echoed in my ears: "Keep going, you're doing great." But deep down, I didn't feel great at all. I knew completing the marathon was going to be a long, eight-hour walk, especially after conquering the earlier swim and bike sections. I was determined not to let exhaustion defeat me.

Despite my fatigue, I refused to surrender. Every now and then, I mustered the energy to attempt running or shuffling my gait into something resembling a run. However, my legs quickly rebuffed my efforts, refusing to cooperate. It was a frustrating setback, but I didn't let it deter me from trying.

Befitting its reputation as the toughest of them all, the run course at ironman Wales presented its own challenges. The first five kilometres were an uphill grind. With each step, I stuttered my way towards the first turnaround at the 5k mark. Thankfully, it was a coned turnaround that led back down the same road I had just come up. The downhill stretch provided a small respite for my weary legs.

As I resumed my run, something miraculous happened–it was as if my legs had awoken from a deep slumber. They no longer resisted my movements and instead eagerly embraced the rhythm of my stride. I found myself running effortlessly, overtaking fellow participants as if I had just entered the race, completely skipping the swim and bike portions. The transformation was remarkable, and apparently unjustified.

For about an hour, I had trudged along on weary legs, resigned to a slow walk. But suddenly, aided by the gradual descent of the road, my legs came alive. They propelled me forward with new-found energy, defying my expectations. I had anticipated a grinding walk back up the long, challenging 5k stretch after completing the downhill section back into Tenby. However, my legs seemed determined not to miss out on the excitement of the event.

On the bustling streets, enthusiastic spectators cheered us on. Their energy was contagious and I couldn't help but smile as I soaked it all in. Their support invigorated me as I pushed forward.

Despite a challenging start on the run course, I managed to complete the marathon in a satisfying four hours and seventeen minutes. Considering the obstacles I faced earlier, this time was a confirmation of my perseverance and determination.

Ultimately, my total time for Ironman Wales was twelve hours and forty-three minutes. They say you should add an hour to your personal best in order to estimate your finish time at Ironman Wales, given its formidable difficulty level. This statement proved to be true, as the race truly pushed me to my limits, both physically and mentally.

I was euphoric when I crossed the finish line, completing my first Ironman. Miriam and Sue were there, sharing in the joy and anticipation as we eagerly awaited Trev's arrival. He arrived about half an hour later, finishing with a time of thirteen hours and sixteen minutes.

Trev is an impressive cyclist, much stronger than me in that discipline. On the other hand, I have a natural advantage when it comes to running due to our different body types. Trev, being a muscular powerhouse, can generate immense power on the pedals. However, he struggles to maintain the same level of performance when it comes to the run, as his bulky frame can make it more challenging to sustain his pace over the full marathon distance.

Given our contrasting strengths and weaknesses, it was always intriguing to see how our performances would compare. The outcome would reveal how our different attributes translated to our overall finishes in the race.

The following day, the true extent of our fortune with the weather became evident. It was as though the universe had aligned perfectly for our event. On this particular day, however, Mother Nature had a different plan in mind. The weather was absolutely dreadful, with fierce winds and torrential rain sweeping through Tenby. Trees were swaying, seemingly ready to be uprooted and the conditions were enough to keep most people huddled within the comfort of their homes.

As I looked out of the apartment window with my friends, I couldn't help but comment on how impossible it would have been to complete the race under such harsh conditions. "If the race had been held today, there's no way we could have crossed that finish line," I remarked. But Miriam, ever the optimist, responded with unwavering belief in our abilities. "You guys would have found a way," she said, instilling a newfound confidence in our resilience and determination.

The Race, Donegal (2016)

Race : The Race, Donegal	Type: Adventure Race Run, Kayak, Cycle, Hike, Cycle, Run.	Length: 250 Km
Date: March, 2016	Where: Donegal	Notes: Extreme weather conditions

I had never been so well prepared for a race as I was for The Race 2016 - my third attempt at the event. Countless hours had been dedicated to building my strength on the bike, running and hitting the gym during the winter. All those efforts had one ultimate goal: to conquer The Race. Joining me this time were Chris, who had returned again to support my effort and Miriam, who came along as well-needed extra support. Failure was not an option and we were determined to secure our finishers medal before leaving Donegal.

As the morning of the race dawned, I was ready to go to battle. Although the weather outside was unforgivingly cold and wet, I had anticipated it and prepared accordingly. To keep myself warm and dry during the initial run, I draped a poncho over my body. It proved to be an effective shield against the elements. With the sound of the gun, I shot off into the darkness of Donegal, just as I had done in the previous two editions of The Race.

The wind howled mercilessly and the rain slashed against my face with stinging force. Wincing in discomfort, I hastily pulled up the hood of my poncho, partially covering my face. The rain relentlessly blew in from the left, but I used the poncho's hood to shield the full left side of my face. Being blind in one eye had its small advantages, after all. With the poncho's hood, I could simultaneously block the rain from stinging my face while still maintaining visibility.

This year, the kayak section was reinstated, spanning a challenging fifteen kilometres from the harbour at Ramelton across the sea to the harbour at Rathmullan. I had heard fellow competitors describe it as the most difficult part of the entire race and some had even been forced to withdraw because they couldn't finish this section. Personally, I faced a tough patch for around thirty minutes when a particularly harsh weather system passed through, but aside from that, I found it quite enjoyable.

Next on the agenda was the first significant test: the initial bike section, one of two in the event. It was hard not to feel a surge of anxiety, especially regarding this first 98-kilometre bike leg, which had utterly battered me in the previous year. However, conditions this time around were not as challenging and I had grown much stronger both physically and mentally. I powered through this first bike section, gaining a newfound confidence by the time I reached Mount Muckish. Don't misunderstand me, this section was still incredibly tough—it remained the most challenging part of the entire race.

Next up was the run and in less than an hour I conquered the steep slopes of Muckish Mountain, navigating my way through the treacherous terrain. Despite the challenging conditions underfoot, I felt an incredible sense of strength. As I made my way back to the transition area, I felt relatively good and prepared for the next leg of the race—back on the bike.

I had initially decided not to race, focusing solely on reaching the end of each section and I remained committed to this strategy. Instead of rushing through each transition area, I took the time to prepare myself mentally and physically for the upcoming challenges before diving into them. This approach allowed me to ensure that I would be as ready as possible for the next leg of the race.

After completing the first cycling section, I took forty-seven minutes to refuel and recharge. At subsequent transitions, I allowed myself over forty minutes to rest and prepare. Speed was not my priority; my sole focus was on reaching the

finish line of this arduous race. While I do not recommend my strategy for those seeking a fast time, it was essential for me at this point in my racing journey. Having previously been defeated by the course on two occasions, my primary goal was simply to complete each section of the race. I treated each part as its own individual challenge within the larger challenge, understanding that if I could conquer them one by one, I would ultimately achieve the desired finish.
Miriam and Chris played crucial roles, providing invaluable support and meeting me at each transition point. While they expressed some concern about the duration of my transitions, I assured them that I was managing well. We would take the opportunity to chat and ensure that I was taking proper care of myself before I resumed in the section that followed. With each passing moment, my confidence grew stronger and I became increasingly certain that I would successfully complete the race that very night.
As the sun dipped below the horizon, I completed a rough-surfaced 75-kilometre cycling stage. With darkness shrouding the landscape, I mentally prepared myself for the final stage: a marathon to be conquered in the cover of night.
The marathon stage involved traversing both roads and trails, some of which had steep inclines. Unfortunately, I had made the mistake of putting my running leggings in the wrong transition box, leaving me with no choice but to tackle the marathon stage in my cycling bib, which is a tight pair of shorts with a padded insert in the undercarriage area to protect from saddle sore. This made the marathon run even more challenging as the cycling bib caused me to waddle instead of my usual running style. The discomfort and chafing were hard to ignore, but I pushed it aside and pressed on. To combat the sudden drop in temperature, I borrowed Chris's jumper.
Despite the discomfort and cold, the run went remarkably well. I found myself constantly overtaking fellow competitors throughout the entire distance. With the finish line in sight, I began to embrace my competitive side and focused on chasing down and passing others. As I neared the end, I spotted two lights ahead, around a kilometre or two away, intermittently visible as the terrain allowed. I closed in on them gradually, making steady progress. Eventually, I noticed that they had come to a standstill, surrounded by a group of supporters offering encouragement and sustenance. Suddenly, the lights shone brightly in my direction—I had been noticed.
As the figures up ahead sprinted forward, an exhilarating chase ensued. When it dawned on me that they were keeping an eye on my head torch, I made the decision to use it only when absolutely necessary. Additionally, I glanced over my shoulder to ensure no one was gaining ground on me, switching off the light each time. Despite my efforts, the guys ahead managed to maintain their lead and crossed the finish line before me. Nevertheless, it was an invigorating chase, propelling me to persist until the end, and I'm certain it had the same effect on them.

One of the individuals I was chasing turned out to be Gerrit Durnin, whom I had come to know as a fellow competitor in the two years. When I finally crossed the finish line, I felt a huge sense of accomplishment combined with a sense of relief knowing that I had finally put this challenge to rest.

Following a well-deserved break, Miriam guided me indoors to change my clothes and take a much needed shower. As I settled down, a sudden rush of uncontrollable shaking overwhelmed me. I couldn't comprehend what was happening, but the sensation was far from pleasant. Minute after minute ticked by as I struggled to regain control over my body, but eventually, the unsettling episode subsided. Understandably alarmed by the unsettling occurrence, Miriam was visibly shaken expressing her profound concern for my well-being; an experience entirely foreign to me previously. Yet it was simply my body's process of restabilising after a long endeavour encompassing running, kayaking, and cycling. Within minutes, any lingering effects had dissipated, leaving me in high spirits to revel in my achievement alongside fellow finishers, and I have not encountered anything similar since that day.

The support of my dedicated crew played a pivotal role in my success. Their unwavering support, even in the face of their own challenges, made me realise the importance of having a dependable team by your side in big endurance events like 'The Race.'

In the end, our journey in "The Race" took us 20 hours and 19 minutes to complete. It was an enormous test of physical and mental strength, resilience and determination. The race itself was a transformative experience, pushing me to my limits and teaching me valuable lessons about myself and my capabilities.

Challenge Galway (2016)

Race : Challenge Galway	Type: Iron distance triathlon.	Length: 3.8K Swim 180K Bike 42K Run
Date: June, 2016	Where: Galway	Notes: Huge turning point.

While Ironman holds a dominant position in the triathlon world, Challenge Triathlon offers a compelling alternative.

Challenge Galway in June 2016 marked my first foray into the world of Challenge Triathlon. This particular race was a full-distance triathlon, encompassing the swim, bike and run disciplines. While not as widely recognised as Ironman, Challenge races have gained popularity and are becoming increasingly popular among triathletes. While I was signing up to tackle the full-distance triathlon,

Challenge Galway also offered competitors the option of doing a half iron-distance triathlon and an Olympic distance triathlon.

One of the most renowned events under the Challenge banner is Challenge Roth, which race draws top professional triathletes from around the world and has consistently sold out within minutes from the subscription opening time. The allure and prestige surrounding Challenge Roth make it a highlight on the triathlon calendar.

As I ventured into Challenge Triathlon with the Galway race, I became aware of the brand's distinct approach and the strong following it has garnered. With events like Challenge Roth capturing the imagination of both professionals and age group competitors, the Challenge brand continues to make its mark in the triathlon world, carving out its own identity alongside the well-established Ironman races.

In the earlier part of 2016, I had decided I needed a coach and went online to find one. That's when I came across Bjorn Ludick, who became my coach. As it happened, Bjorn had entered the Galway half-marathon on the same day as my full-distance race. Prior to working together, I had come across Bjorn at various Triathlon Ireland events, where his reputation as one of the country's top triathletes preceded him; indeed, he had won the Irish National Series Champion in 2011. Despite his achievements, Bjorn was incredibly approachable and easy to talk to.

What drew me to Bjorn's coaching style was the perfect blend of support and understanding he offered. While he maintained constant contact with me to ensure I stayed on track with my training, when life's demands made it impossible to complete a session, Bjorn would reassure me and suggest focusing on the next session instead. The communication between us flowed effortlessly, allowing me to share my progress and any concerns I had along the way.

It was a pleasant surprise when Bjorn decided to take part in Challenge Galway half Iron distance triathlon. It demonstrated his genuine interest in the events I was taking part in and underlined the support he was willing to provide.

I vividly remember when I said to Bjorn that I wanted to tackle the DecaUK race in Windsor. His initial response was a simple, "Okay, sounds good, I'll check it out." Later that day, my phone rang and it was Bjorn on the other end of the line. He excitedly exclaimed, "You know this event is ten full iron distance triathlons in ten days, right?" I couldn't help but laugh and replied, "Yep, I'm fully aware." It was at that moment that I realised Bjorn's enthusiasm matched mine and he was just as excited as I was to embark on this incredible journey.

With a firm goal in mind, I dedicated myself to achieving a finish time of under eleven hours at Challenge Galway. I knew that my bike training would play a crucial role in accomplishing this feat, so I poured considerable effort into honing my skills on the bike. My hard work had paid off when I finally completed The Race in Donegal, gaining valuable confidence that would propel me towards my sub-eleven-hour target in a full-distance triathlon.

Miriam, Sue and Trev also signed up to Challenge Galway races, each of us determined to achieve our respective goals. While Trev and I were preparing to tackle the full-distance triathlon, Miriam and Sue were gearing up for another Olympic-distance race (1.5k swim, 40k bike, 10k run).

Sue sustained a severe hand injury before the Challenge Galway event, making it impossible for her to operate her bike brakes. Prioritising her safety, she chose not to participate, allowing her hand to heal.

The race weekend began with the Olympic distance event on Saturday, and the half and full distances on Sunday. Miriam was the first of us to participate in the Olympic triathlon, with the rest of us her enthusiastic supporters. Prior to her start, I provided her with essential equipment like my pump, levers and spare tubes. I made sure her wheels were properly pumped and I helped her organise her nutrition.

After the race began, Miriam swam exceptionally well, surpassing our expectations. Her speed on the bike leg was impressive, also catching us by surprise. Unfortunately, we temporarily lost sight of her when she completed her bike lap and transitioned into the run. However, we did manage to reunite with her during the run section.

Recognising our oversight, Sue joined Miriam for her last two run laps, offering her support and companionship on the challenging journey.

Miriam's outstanding performance set the bar high for Trev and I. Her impressive display of strength and resilience inspired us to push ourselves to our limits and give our best effort in pursuit of our own racing goals.

On the morning of the race, rough water conditions forced the organisers to reduce the swim distance by nearly 200m. This news was a relief to me, as it meant that I could possibly achieve a great swim time with the shortened distance. After swiftly transitioning to the biking portion, I was maintaining a steady speed of 32 kilometres per hour and feeling fantastic. I even started considering the possibility of finishing the race in under eleven hours, especially now that I had gained a few minutes due to the altered swim length.

However, my excitement quickly turned to dismay when I heard the dreaded hissing noise of my tyre losing air. This happened when I was already 65 kilometres into the course and making good progress. I promptly pulled over to the side of the road and dismounted my bike. Realising that it was a front wheel puncture, I knew that I could change it quickly. After removing the wheel and checking the tyre for any sharp objects that could have caused the puncture, I found nothing obvious. I reached into my saddlebag for one of my spare tubes, but to my disappointment, my pump was missing.

It turned out to be a major oversight on my part. The previous day, I had lent my pump and levers to Miriam for her triathlon and I hadn't got them back. I should have checked my equipment thoroughly on the morning of the race. As time went by, more and more competitors began to pass me. I desperately asked anyone if they had a spare pump, but no one seemed willing to stop and help. I was losing valuable time and couldn't blame those who didn't stop. They had their own race to focus on and it was ultimately my own mistake that put me in this unfortunate situation.

It felt like an eternity before a kind-hearted guy finally came to my aid and handed me a CO2 canister. Although I had never used one before, I was grateful for anything at this point and thanked him numerous times. With my tube already in place, I attempted to connect the canister to the valve, only to have the tube explode. I insisted that the guy continue with his race, as he had already done more than enough for me and I thanked him once again for his assistance. Now I found myself in need of a pump once more. Retrieving my second and final spare tube from my saddlebag, I anxiously waited for another few minutes until another empathetic individual stopped to offer me his pump. Once again, I expressed my immense gratitude before he swiftly took off.

I quickly started pumping air into the tube, determined to get back into the race as soon as possible.

I turned around and heard Trev's reassuring voice behind me: "All OK, Ger?" "All sorted now; you go ahead, go, go, go!" I shouted back at him, urging him to continue on his race. With Trev out of sight, I continued pumping air into the tube, determined to get it inflated enough to continue. The pump I had been given didn't have a gauge, so it was challenging to estimate when the tube reached around 100–120 PSI. Nevertheless, I didn't complain; I just focused on getting enough air into the tube.

Despite the chaos and frustration of the situation, I remember feeling surprisingly calm. It was as if all my past experiences with race crises had prepared me for this moment. I recalled the disappointment I had felt after things went awry at The Race in Donegal and the resilience demonstrated by Trev at Ocean Lava 2014 when he had mistakenly cycled an extra 50 kilometres on top of the expected 120 kilometres. Drawing on those memories, I found the determination to keep going.

Once the tyre was inflated, I jumped back on my bike. I couldn't be certain how much time I had lost during this ordeal, but it was likely at least twenty to thirty minutes. Most of that time was spent pleading with passing cyclists to stop and help me.

After only a short distance down the road, I was infuriated to hear that dreaded hissing sound once again. I couldn't believe this was happening for the second time. I meticulously inspected the tyre for any signs of glass or other sharp objects, but found nothing. To make matters worse, I had run out of spare tubes. I found myself in the same position of having to ask other athletes for assistance, knowing that I couldn't blame those who passed by without stopping.

Fortunately, I was able to get a tube from a fellow athlete, swiftly change it and continue with renewed determination. However, my luck ran out as my tube deflated for the third time after a few more kilometres. At this point, I felt completely lost and unsure of what to do next. The tube wasn't completely flat, so I tried my best to pump it up, hoping to reach an aid station where I could find help. I repeated this process until I reached the Corkscrew Road in Clare, known for its steep gradient and challenging switchbacks that forced some cyclists to dismount and walk.

At the top of the hill, I noticed a group of supporters cheering on the participants. Spotting a track pump amongst them, I approached and asked if I could borrow it to inflate my tube. I explained my situation and to my relief, they not only offered to help me with the pump but also provided a spare tube and assistance in changing it. It was a breath of fresh air to receive such support, especially after my previous struggles. The man who changed the tube for me was named Koe Whelan, and with his wife he was following a number of clubmates and offering support along the way. I expressed my sincerest gratitude to everyone for their kindness and continued on my journey, feeling a renewed sense of determination.

This tube did last a minute or two longer than the others that had been put in, but it did, after a few kilometres, meet the same fate. Again, it wasn't a complete puncture, so I was back to pumping the tube up every couple of minutes, cycling a few kilometres and repeating the process. Eventually, a van pulled up and out stepped Koe and his wife. They knew the situation, so I saved time by not having to explain it all to them from the start. We changed the tube and I continued on, but again, we got the same result.

I met Koe again down the road and he offered me his last tube. I knew I was inconveniencing them greatly, but what else could I do? We put this last tube in, but we all knew what the outcome was going to be and sure enough, I was back to pumping and cycling and pumping and cycling. This strategy only got me so far before the tube would not inflate any more, so at this stage I was out of tubes and there was nobody around to help.

By now, the number of punctures had reached a staggering six. Despite my attempts to salvage some air and continue on, this time the tube was completely flat. With no spare tubes left and no one in sight to lend a helping hand, I didn't hesitate to make my next decision. I began running, pushing my bike with one hand, while still wearing my bike shoes. I had already completed 120 kilometres with another 60 kilometres to go and, at that moment, I was determined to run every single one of those kilometres, if necessary. The thought of giving up simply didn't exist in my mind.

Although I couldn't control the misfortune that had befallen me, I had complete control over my reaction to it. The race was testing me, challenging me and pushing me to my limits to see if I would break. It had erected a psychological barrier right in my path, attempting to fill me with doubt and disbelief. But instead of allowing it to defeat me, I made a choice. I faced that wall head-on, ready to take on the challenge. The wall pushed against me with all its might, but now I pushed back, defying it in every way.

After approximately ten minutes of running, I suddenly realised that I was still wearing my cycling shoes. Without hesitation, I stopped, took them off and continued running barefoot while pushing my bike. There was a sense of instinctual survival driving me forward. I managed to run for another ten to fifteen minutes before a car pulled up alongside me.

"Do you need anything?" the driver asked. "Do you happen to have a spare wheel?" I inquired, having reached the point where I was done with changing tubes. To my surprise, the driver responded, "Front or back?" Initially, I thought he was joking, but it turned out that he had another competitor's bike in the back seat. The competitor had unfortunately fallen off his bike and was unable to continue. In this case, one person's Did Not Finish (DNF) became another person's saving grace. As I conversed further with the driver, I discovered that he owned a cycle shop near Galway city centre. I eagerly accepted the offer and swiftly replaced the wheel. Then, with newfound energy, I propelled myself forward. Over the final 60 kilometres, I passed countless fellow athletes, feeling unstoppable and confident that I would indeed finish this race.

As I approached transition, I could see Miriam and Sue waiting for me. Trev had already finished the bike portion and had been out on the run course for quite some time. The girls appeared concerned, knowing that something had gone wrong. Pointing at the unconventional wheel on my bike, I shouted, "Six punctures!" Despite the setback, I couldn't help but smile. There wasn't time to elaborate on the details. I hurried into the changing tent, quickly snacked on a Trek bar, changed into my running gear and eagerly set off on the run course.

By this point, the weather had taken a turn for the better. The city was bathed in beautiful sunshine, a stark contrast to the atrocious conditions experienced near the coast while on the bike during the race. It felt as if we were experiencing two completely different days. The vibrant atmosphere in the city added to the excitement as competitors made their way along the looped course. Adding to the buzz, a big screen near the finish line was broadcasting the World Cup game between the Irish national soccer team and France. As I embarked on the run, Ireland had taken an early lead with a one-nil advantage. However, by the time I completed one lap, they had unfortunately fallen behind, trailing two goals to one.

Earlier, Tri Coach Bjorn had completed the half-distance of the race. However, he stayed behind to encourage me and waited patiently until I crossed the finish line. As I tried to explain what had occurred during the bike portion of the race, I felt like my story sounded fabricated. Nevertheless, I recounted the six punctures I experienced, the challenging weather conditions and the constant need to inflate my tyres. Despite the adversity, I confidently told Coach Bjorn that this race had been my best one yet. Emotion welled up within me as I spoke, for I felt a profound sense of pride in conquering numerous obstacles throughout the day without ever giving up. After finishing the marathon in just under four hours and completing the race in a total of twelve hours and twenty minutes, I knew I had grown as an athlete. Whenever things go awry for me now, my mind drifts back to the unforgettable Challenge Galway 2016 and the strength I discovered within myself on that remarkable day.

Challenge Galway stood out as my most significant race up to that point. It wasn't my greatest race time-wise, as I didn't achieve a personal best. In fact, I had fallen short of my intended goal by an hour and a half. However, this race held a significance that surpassed mere timing. It marked a pivotal moment for me, particularly in terms of mental resilience and strength. The lessons and experiences gained from this race have been unmatched.

Wicklow 200 (2017)

Race : Wicklow 200	Type: Sportif (non- competitive)	Length: 200 Km
Date: June, 2017	Where: Co. Wicklow	Notes: Farthest I had cycled

Before taking on the Wicklow 200 in June 2017, I had never cycled such a long distance in one go. My previous longest stand alone cycling event was the Wicklow 100, which was only half the distance and which I completed 2010, just a week after purchasing my first road bike from Rob Cummins at Wheelworx. It took me six and a half hours to finish the Wicklow 100 and I likened the challenge to running a marathon with zero training, a feat I had foolishly attempted as an 18-year-old senior school student in 1998.

During the Wicklow 100, the faster cyclists who were racing the full 200 kilometres, were passing me by effortlessly as we approached the finish line. It served as a stark reminder of the significant difference in fitness levels and experience.

When I made the decision to enter in the Wicklow 200, I was well aware that the course would pose significant challenges. The route was technical, with numerous steep hills that demanded both physical and mental resilience. Adding to the challenge was the typical Irish weather, which couldn't decide if it wanted to give us sun, rain, wind or snow. Nonetheless, I was determined to push myself further and knew that additional time in the saddle was essential.

Since I wanted to minimise the chance of any setbacks, I opted to use my time trial bike for the Wicklow 200 instead of my old road bike. Perhaps not the wisest choice, as a road bike would have been more suitable for the demanding

climbs. However, I was up for the challenge and knew I had to work extra hard to overcome the disadvantages of using a TT bike on steep, hilly sections.
Throughout the event, I focused on pacing myself and avoiding overexertion. It was important to gauge my energy levels effectively, ensuring I had enough left in the tank to conquer each long, steep hill. Time seemed to blur as I pushed through the challenging terrain, constantly shifting between wet and dry conditions.

After 7 hours and 44 minutes of hard work and perseverance, I crossed the finish line of the Wicklow 200. The sense of accomplishment mingled with deep satisfaction at my performance on the day. Despite the difficulties posed by the technical course and my unconventional choice of bike, I had managed to complete the event with a sense of pride and fulfilment.

Reflecting on the Wicklow 200, I recognised the profound impact it had on my cycling. The event stood as proof of my growth, pushing me beyond what I once thought was impossible. It wasn't just a physical challenge; it became a mental battle that tested my grit and determination.

This experience fueled my confidence and motivation, igniting a passion for cycling that surpassed anything I had felt before. The Wicklow 200 wasn't merely a cycling event; it symbolised personal growth and achievement. It revealed my ability to overcome obstacles, instilling resilience and a strong belief in my capabilities.

From that day onward, I embraced new challenges, continually pushing myself further. I learned the importance of proper preparation, dedicating time to enhancing my cycling skills, to building endurance, and to ensuring I had suitable equipment. Success in cycling, as in any endeavour, extends beyond physical strength—it requires mental fortitude and strategic planning.

The Wicklow 200 is an incredible event. To me it was a reminder that with passion, perseverance, and a willingness to face challenges, there are no limits to what I can achieve in my cycling.

Celtic Warrior (2017)

Race: Celtic Warrior	Type: Iron distance triathlon (Double)	Length: 3.8k Swim 180k Cycle 42k Run (One a day double)
Date: August, 2017	Where: Mullingar, Co. Westmeath	Notes: First time doing a back-to-back

During the year of 2017, I fully immersed myself in a rigorous training plan for DecaUK. Undoubtedly, the most significant and daunting challenge of my life was now almost upon me. At that time, there were no ultra-endurance triathlon events in Ireland that surpassed the magnitude of a single-day iron distance triathlon, except one: Celtic Warrior, held at the Lilliput Adventure Centre on the shores of Lough Ennell in Co. Westmeath on the August Bank Holiday weekend each year.

Organised by the formidable Franky Wright, a great athlete himself, this multi-day event was the pinnacle of endurance, bringing together a festival of swim, bike and run events. It entailed a full-distance triathlon on Saturday, followed by another on Sunday, with multiple other events running simultaneously. The mere thought of participating in such an extraordinary undertaking sent shivers of excitement and anticipation down my spine.

On the Saturday of the Celtic Warrior weekend, the heavens seemed to be smiling upon us. The weather was an absolute dream—the sun radiated its warm rays, filling the atmosphere with a sense of vibrancy and boundless energy. It was a day filled with endless possibilities, both exhilarating and humbling.

With my eyes set firmly on the ultimate goal, I was committed to pacing myself diligently throughout that first day. Understanding the arduous nature of the two-day challenge, I made a conscious effort to nourish and refuel my body effectively. What faced me was a battle of endurance, not only within the race itself but also in preparing my body for the daunting task of repeating the entire process the next day.

As the day progressed, I was satisfied that I was executing my race plan flawlessly. Each stroke, pedal and stride propelled me closer to my ultimate objective. Propelled by determination and fortified by discipline, I meticulously managed my energy reserves. ensuring that I would have enough left in the tank for the following day.

With the day's race behind me, I sought the comfort of my bed, retiring early in hopes of a peaceful night's rest. As I lay there, wrapped in the serenity of anticipation, my mind brimmed with visions of conquering the trials of the next day with the same fortitude and tenacity displayed in the previous day's triumph.

The upcoming day promised another chance at accomplishment, another opportunity to test my limits and relish in the marvels of the human spirit. I drifted off to sleep, my body poised for the dawn of yet another day of intense determination and exhilaration at the Celtic Warrior event.

All too quickly, the next morning arrived. I lay in my bunk bed feeling extremely tired from the efforts of the previous day's efforts. "Do we just stay in bed?" I muttered through the stillness of the room, unsure if Miriam was already awake. From the top bunk came her response, which was reassuring and motivating. "No, you have to get up and give it a go." I had anticipated her answer, but I needed that extra nudge, that reminder of the commitment I had made to myself.

If I couldn't conquer the back-to-back Celtic Warrior, my ambitions of tackling the Deca in Windsor just over two months later in October would have been dashed. Miriam, too, reminded me of this pivotal goal. With her words resonating in my mind, I sprang out of bed, ready to prepare for the challenge that lay ahead.

I quickly donned my wetsuit and threw on some flip-flops, making my way to the kitchen en route to the lake. A cup of tea and some toast provided the nourishment I needed to sustain me through the day's rigours.

As I stepped outside, dreariness greeted me. The morning was enveloped in darkness, accompanied by a bone-chilling coldness and a relentless downpour. Even in the face of this inhospitable weather, my determination remained unwavering. Twenty-five brave souls had started the single-day event the previous day, but only about ten of us had dared to sign up to take part on the second day.

At the lakeshore, I discovered that Denzel Jacobs was the only other person joining me. We exchanged brief greetings and as the clock struck 6am, we plunged into the frigid waters, fully prepared for the numbing embrace. Despite the icy chill seeping into my extremities, my trusty wetsuit provided ample insulation and allowed me to forge ahead without distraction. The swim felt invigorating and I completed it in good time.

Emerging from the lake, the biting cold intensified and I was tempted to plunge back into the water momentarily, seeking refuge from the icy grasp of the morning. Miriam came to my aid, offering a warm towel and guiding me, shivering, to the adjacent shower block. As the hot water cascaded over me, I savoured the rejuvenating revival of my strength. Taking my time, I shed my wetsuit and put on my cycling gear, while eating warm toast to fuel my body for the impending bike leg.

With my bike in hand, ready to embark on the next phase of the Celtic Warrior, I searched for Denzel, hoping we could cycle together at the start. When I met him in the dorm kitchen, Denzel told me he had decided to call it quits. The biting cold had taken its toll and he felt unable to continue. Oddly enough, rather than disheartening me, his departure renewed my sense of determination. Driven by a surge of adrenaline, I silently reminded myself that if Denzel, for whom the cold had proven too formidable, couldn't muster the strength to begin the bike leg, then my own favourable condition boded well.

Without further hesitation, I hopped onto my bike, embarking on the first of six thirty-kilometre laps around the majestic Lough Ennell. The weather, unfortunately, showed no signs of improvement. In fact, it seemed to worsen with each passing moment. The wind howled, while the rain mercilessly pelted my face. Yet, rather than dampening my spirits, these adverse conditions contributed to my sense of exhilaration. I found myself locked in an epic battle against the elements, a clash that ignited a fire within me. The raindrops that stung my

face only served to fuel my determination, bringing a smile to my lips. Amid the raging storm and drenched surroundings, I felt an invincibility unlike any other. Doubt vanished, replaced by a resolute conviction that I would conquer the day's challenges, regardless of what lay ahead.

In this daunting weather, I pedalled onward, fully aware that each lap brought me closer to the realisation of my goal. The wind tugged at my every effort, challenging my progress, but I persevered. The rain-soaked roads became my arena and every rotation of my pedals affirmed my unwavering resolve. Despite the relentless tempest, I was unyielding in my pursuit of triumph.

With each passing lap, my conviction grew stronger. The daunting weather, instead of demoralising me, only served to stoke the fire of determination burning within. Navigating the treacherous conditions, I became one with the elements, embracing the struggle as evidence of my resilience. There was no doubt in my mind that I would complete the day's harsh challenges, surmounting every obstacle standing in my way.

After completing four laps, I took a break in the kitchen to enjoy a warm cup of tea and one of my favourite snacks, a falafel wrap with salad and hummus. Replenished and energised, I set out to finish the last two laps. The route around the lake presented a mix of flat and hilly terrain, which became more challenging with each lap. Nevertheless, I pushed through and finally concluded the bike leg.

Moving on to the run, my preferred discipline, I found satisfaction in the fact that running kept me warmer and boosted my mood, despite the ongoing unfavourable weather. Luckily, I had the company of Miriam, who joined me on a bike borrowed from Franky. Throughout the evening, we had fun chatting, laughing, and even shooting some entertaining videos.

Miriam and I were totally alone on the course all day and we were not expecting any others to wait for us at the finish line or anywhere else along the course. However, both Franky and Vincent, the race officials, insisted on being there to cheer me on when I completed the race. Vincent's wife, Catherine, herself an accomplished runner who represented Ireland in 24-hour running races through the years, also stayed at the finish line to show her support. It was an incredibly touching and emotional moment for me, one that will forever remain etched in my memory.

I had set a personal ultimatum for myself: if I couldn't finish the back-to-back race at Celtic Warrior, I wouldn't even consider travelling to Eton Dorney in Windsor to take on DecaUK. Celtic Warrior did give me a boost of confidence in my abilities, it also made me realise the immense difficulty of completing ten iron-distance triathlons in just ten days.

Celtic Warrior holds a special place in my heart now, as it played a significant role in my preparations for DecaUK. It's why I return to Lough Ennell every year on the bank holiday weekend in August.

Chapter 5: Mick

My wife Miriam's brother, Michael Lematy, was affectionately known as Mick by his friends and family. He was five years older than Miriam and the closest sibling to her in age. Growing up, Mick and Miriam spent a lot of time together. Their mother insisted that Mick take Miriam everywhere with him, even though he was a teenager and she was just a pre-teen. Though initially reluctant, Mick obliged and as a result, they formed a deep bond. Miriam looked up to Mick and thought he was the coolest big brother.

I had the pleasure of meeting Mick in 1999, just days after meeting Miriam. At the time, he was a few years older than us and worked as a self-employed carpenter and tradesman. Mick was a hard worker and had achieved a lot for himself. He owned a Honda Civic car, which was regarded as the ultimate status symbol in Ballymun at the time. While he initially lived in the family flat, shortly after we met, he purchased a house in Ashbourne, County Meath. During the house-warming, I had the chance to meet Mick's friends, who, like Miriam, adored him. He was the life of the party, the funny one in the group and everyone loved being around him.

Mick's presence in my life was significant. He would often stop by the family home on his way back from work. Seeing Mick's success and happiness, I was deeply inspired to strive for the same in my own life.

Mick had a mischievous side and loved playing pranks on people, myself included. One particular memory stands out to me. For Christmas in 2016, I surprised Miriam with a weekend trip to Amsterdam. As part of the gift, I had purchased an old tandem bike from Amsterdam that was shipped to us by its previous owner. The bike, originating from the 1970s, had a unique and vintage charm. My plan was to attach the tickets to the handlebars of the tandem bike on Christmas morning.

However, shortly after giving the bike to Miriam, we discovered that it had a puncture and needed attention. Determined to fix it before our first ride, I set out to replace the punctured tube under the watchful eyes of both Miriam and Mick.

Being a vintage model from the 1970s, the tandem bike did not have quick-release mechanisms for its wheels. To remove the wheel, I had to use two vice grips, which made the process more time-consuming. Since the bike was still inside our sitting room, where we were watching TV, I decided to change the tube right there, thinking it would be a quick fix.

I replaced the punctured tube with a new one, carefully put the tyre back in place, re-attached the wheel by tightening the nuts with the vice grips and then pumped up the new tube. The entire process took me approximately thirty minutes. Normally, changing a bike tube would only take about five minutes, but the tightness of the tyres and the absence of quick-release options made this particular task take a longer time to complete.

"Would you like a cup of tea?" I offered Miriam and Mick. They both replied with a resounding "Yes," as they always did. On my way to the kitchen, I prepared tea for all of us. After a few minutes, I returned to the sitting room, balancing the tray of steaming tea in my hands.

With the tea drunk, I decided to check the bike to see whether it was ready for a spin. Imagine my disappointment when I discovered that it had developed a flat tire. It seemed that either a shard of glass or something sharp had punctured the tube while inflating, or perhaps I had accidentally pinched the tube while putting the excessively tight tyre back on to the wheel. Frustrated but determined, I embarked on the process again, spending another arduous thirty minutes or more, forcing the tyre back onto the wheel.

Once I finally finished, my hands were exhausted from the effort. Undeterred, I asked Miriam and Mick once more, "Would you like a cup of tea?" They eagerly replied with "Please." Setting out on my journey to the kitchen once more, I prepared fresh cups of tea for all of us. Carefully carrying the tea back to the sitting room, I found myself experiencing a sense of déjà vu when I checked the tyre pressure on the bike and discovered, to my frustration, that it was completely flat once again.

I remembered the countless tubes I had wasted by accidentally puncturing them while attempting to replace them, whether it had been as a child trying to repair a puncture on my BMX bike or at Challenge Galway when I had used multiple tubes during that race just to try to get to T2. With only one tube left this time, I decided to give it one last try. The anticipation of taking Miriam out for a bike ride on this epic looking bike boosted my determination.

Once again, I began the tedious process of removing the wheel using vice grips, carefully taking off the tyre from the wheel, replacing the punctured tube with a new one and manoeuvring the tyre back onto the wheel. Finally, I tightened the wheel back onto the bike frame.

As I re-entered the room, carrying again fresh cups of tea, I noticed Mick in a squatting position by the bike, his fingers covering the air valve as he released the air from the tubes. It took me a few seconds to connect the dots and realise what had been happening. Anger quickly dissipated within seconds as Miriam and Mick burst into uncontrollable laughter. They had been having a good laugh at my expense, intentionally deflating the tyres and causing me to replace unpunctured tubes. I was in disbelief—he had really got me good! In hindsight, I should have realised sooner that Mick had some involvement in the prank.

This funny story took place during a period when Mick was living with Miriam, myself and our three sons. Unfortunately, Mick emerged from a dark period in his life. He began turning to alcohol as a coping mechanism. There were several contributing factors to this downward spiral. Growing up, Mick had a difficult time due to the absence of his father. Additionally, working as a self-employed carpenter brought its own set of challenges, as finding stable jobs was a constant. Add to that the responsibility of providing for his wife and three kids, along with the burden of a mortgage on a house purchased during the exorbitant housing prices of the Celtic Tiger years around 2000. It was an incredibly tough situation to deal with.

After the Celtic Tiger years, Ireland, like the rest of the world, was hit with a recession. This led to numerous job losses and people were no longer able to afford their inflated mortgages. Many were forced to relinquish their homes, plunging countless individuals into debt. As expected, these circumstances and he began taking a toll on Mick's relationship with his wife and he began drinking more. Being a carpenter, Mick took on jobs in different locations around Dublin and when the year drew to a close and Christmas approached, Mick decided to take a job in Limerick, which was 200km away from Dublin. This meant that he could only return home on weekends. Over the three months that the job lasted, Mick's relationship with his wife disintegrated, causing him to fall apart. He started drinking daily, and when he eventually returned to Dublin in December 2016, he found himself without a home.

Mick's life was in turmoil; he couldn't see his children and found himself homeless. Despite these challenges, he still loved his family and longed to be with them.

I became aware of Mick's situation when Miriam informed me that he was attempting to secure a bed at a hostel near Drogheda, an hour's drive from Dublin. Miriam asked if it would be possible for Mick to stay with us over Christmas. I was taken aback that she even felt the need to ask for permission. Without hesitation, we quickly got into the car and I drove to fetch Mick, bringing him home with us to stay for the Christmas period.

Mick remained with us not only for Christmas but also for the initial months of 2017. During this time, he took a break from work, striving to improve his situation in the hope of eventually returning to his own home and reuniting with his children in Ashbourne. Occasionally, I could catch glimpses of his underlying sadness and the deep longing he felt for his kids. It was difficult to witness, but for the most part, Mick maintained a positive and optimistic demeanour.

Of course, there was an element of Mick concealing his true feelings of sadness and depression. It is common for individuals, especially men, to hide their emotions, not wanting to appear vulnerable or burden others with their struggles. Given the challenges he faced, Mick adopted this policy, yet to his credit, he made an effort to stay positive. He would rise early in the mornings, preparing and planning for the day ahead, and often attending multiple AA (Alcoholics Anonymous) meetings throughout the day, sometimes as many as four meetings.

With a weekend getaway planned for April, Miriam and I faced the dilemma of what to do with the kids and Mick. Normally, the kids would stay with my sister Jude, but leaving Mick alone in the house while we were away didn't seem like the best idea. Considering Mick's progress with his meetings and his ongoing efforts to rebuild his life, we thought it might be beneficial for him to have some support and companionship during our absence.

However, I couldn't help but wonder if suggesting that he stay with his other sister, Trish, would inadvertently imply that we didn't trust him to be alone. I didn't want Mick to take it as a negative reflection on his progress or as a lack of faith in his ability to handle the situation.

Miriam suggested to Mick that he may be better off staying with his sister Trish while we were away and he agreed. However, I couldn't help but sense that he might have interpreted our request as a sign of us not wanting him around or that we didn't trust him to be alone. To dispel any misunderstanding, I made it a point to tell him that he was welcome to come back to our house once we returned and that we would prepare his favourite chickpea curry, complete with an extra kick of chilli, as he loved.

When we returned home after our break, I expected Mick to return as planned, but unfortunately, he didn't. I wasn't sure why he chose not to come back, as we had agreed on it when Miriam and I discussed our return. He never gave an explanation, but I had a feeling that he might have felt unwanted during our absence. I wanted to make sure he knew that this was not the case, so I made it a point to visit him at Trish's house where I extended a heartfelt invitation for him to come back to us. "I thought you were coming back," I said when I first saw him. Although I can't recall his exact reply, I sensed some hesitation, as if he felt like he was imposing on us. "Come back down and I'll make that curry you like," I said in an attempt to reassure him. He never did come back to us.

During Mick's time with us, he often expressed an interest in going running together. I would try to convince him that all he had to do was put on his running shoes and start. I emphasised that getting started was the hardest part and once he took that first step, he would realise that it wasn't as difficult as we often make it out to be, just like anything else in life. However, Mick would always respond with a hopeful "Next time, next time."

Mick had also made the decision to pursue rehabilitation. He believed it was the most effective means of demonstrating to himself and others that he was once again the person they knew and cared for. He reached out to his boss, Mark, to arrange funding for his admission to the Rutland Centre, a facility specialising in addiction treatment. Mark, displaying remarkable empathy and generosity, went above and beyond by providing Mick with the requested financial assistance, allowing him to enter the Rutland Centre.

The Rutland Centre has stringent guidelines that patients were expected to follow. These rules included abstaining from alcohol, drugs and aerosols and only limited visiting hours. The use of mobile phones was also prohibited. However, I was allowed to bring Mick essential items such as shower gel, food and cigarettes. Despite the numerous restrictions, Mick was determined to get his hands on cigarettes and he would contact me to arrange a meeting at the Rutland Centre outside visiting hours. He would keep a lookout for my car and quickly rush out to meet me whenever he spotted me driving into the car park through one of the windows at the centre with a view of the main gates. I had no qualms about this carefully orchestrated operation because it allowed me to spend time with him. Though Mick always seemed in good spirits, he did mention that his time at the centre was no easy feat. In total, Mick spent eight weeks at the Rutland Centre and before entering, he had amusingly marked the date on our kitchen wall planner as 'Mick's release back into the wild.'

In addition to the Rutland Centre's list of regulations, individuals enrolling in the programme were required to be clean from all substances, such as alcohol, drugs and even prescription medications. This meant that Mick had to stop taking the antidepressants that his doctor had prescribed for him.

After his release, Mick made the decision to stay with his other sister, Trish, who, like us, lived in Ballymun. It was a practical choice, as Trish had more space and it would be easier for Mick to have overnight visits with his three children. Although we didn't see Mick every day, we still had regular opportunities to spend time together. During one encounter, Mick jokingly mentioned that he wanted to come back to our place because he 'missed the food.' I chuckled and reassured him that he was always welcome.

With us, Trish shared concerning updates about Mick's mental state, revealing that he was experiencing a gradual deterioration and growing distress. His time at the rehab centre had taken a toll, leaving him feeling incredibly fragile. The programme was demanding and rigorous and although Mick had hoped it would help him rebuild his family, he soon discovered that this wouldn't be the case. Despite his mental struggles, he remained resolute in his decision to stay away from alcohol. Surprisingly, giving up alcohol proved relatively easy for him in the end, a feat that would have made his mother immensely proud. She had been a dedicated participant at Alcoholics Anonymous (AA) meetings for many years, having successfully battled her own addiction to alcohol. During her time in the programme, she had supported countless people on their journey to recovery. Being intimately familiar with the hardships facing Mick, she would undoubtedly have provided him with unwavering support, but unfortunately, she had passed away some years beforehand.

Mick's emotional vulnerability became increasingly apparent as he would describe himself as 'no good any more' 'ugly,' 'useless,' and believe that nobody would ever want him. His heartbreak was evident and these statements hinted at a deep sadness and despair. It was shocking to hear him utter these words, especially considering the positive and motivated demeanour he had displayed during his time with me, Miriam and our children.

Recognising the severity of Mick's emotional state, Trish arranged for him to consult his doctor, who prescribed him antidepressants. We hoped that this course of action would provide Mick with some relief.

Just two days after Mick started his medication, I received a phone call from his brother, Tom, which would significantly affect the trajectory of my own life. On May 11th, 2017, I was at work, covering a PE class for one of the teachers at Trinity Comp. I felt my phone vibrating in my pocket, as I kept it on silent mode during work and at night. It was rare for me to answer a call, but something compelled me to do so this time. I glanced at the screen and saw that it was Tom, Mick's brother, calling. I answered.

When Tom uttered the words, "Mick's gone," my heart sank. In that split second I knew what he meant. Deep in the pit of my stomach, I sensed that Mick had taken his own life. I couldn't explain why, but it felt like the accumulation of pain and suffering had become unbearable for him. Still hoping that I had misinterpreted Tom's words, I asked, "What do you mean, gone?" With a trembling voice, Tom replied, "He's dead," struggling to hold back his tears.

What strength it must have taken Tom, the eldest of the siblings, to share the devastating news of his younger brother's suicide. Tom had assumed the role of a father figure since their upbringing lacked a paternal presence. Trish was the first to learn of the tragic news while she was at work and she relied on Tom's to inform the rest of the family.

"We want you to tell Miriam," Tom pleaded, his voice filled with desperation.

"Of course," I replied, understanding the weight of his request. Tom believed it would be best if the news came from me. It was now my responsibility to do what Tom had done earlier that morning: deliver the devastating news to those closest to Mick, including Miriam, who held a special place in his life.

As I prepared myself to share the tragic news, my stomach twisted and a heavy feeling settled in my heart. Tom and I continued our conversation, discussing the hows and whys of surrounding Mick's untimely passing.

Mick had recently returned to work in an effort to regain a sense of normal life. He believed that by bringing structure back into his life, he would have a better chance of reuniting his family and providing for them. On that fateful morning, he left Trish's house at the usual time for work. However, instead of heading to work, he took a piece of cable from the house and made his way to Poppintree Park, which was just around the corner from the house. It was still early and the park had not yet opened to the public. Mick climbed over the high wall into the park and found a tree near the pond. There, he tied the cable to a branch and tragically took his own life. The peacefulness of the early morning, the isolation of the park and the weight of his inner turmoil led him to make this heart-wrenching decision.

I left work and began driving towards Miriam's workplace. I realised that this was the first time I had ever left her a voicemail asking her to call me back, which would undoubtedly raise concerns. When Miriam returned my call, I requested that she meet me outside. I had parked on the side of the road, unable to contain the weight of the news until she arrived.

"Why? What's wrong?" she anxiously inquired over the phone. At that moment, I believed it would be best to be direct and share the situation with her rather than let her speculate. Miriam's workplace had strict rules regarding phone usage, so she had to call me back from the toilets. It was far from an ideal scenario,

but at that moment, I felt that being upfront and delivering the news was the best course of action.

“Michael is gone, Miriam,” I informed her, the heavy weight of those words hanging heavily.

The sound of my wife’s cries and screams filled the air with unrelenting sorrow. It was an agonising experience, one that I wished I could shield her from. Miriam was escorted outside her workplace by a compassionate colleague, her shattered state of mind evident in her delirious state. She bombarded me with a torrent of questions, seeking answers that I myself did not have.

We made our way to Miriam’s sister’s house, the place where Mick had been staying in the days leading up to his tragic decision. The rest of the day was spent in a haze of anguish and confusion, desperately grappling to understand the ‘why’ behind Mick’s unfathomable act. Together, we sought a little relief in each other’s presence, attempting to process the unimaginable loss and find some semblance of closure.

During the first four days, I remained a source of strength for Miriam, offering her comfort and reassurance whenever she broke down. I assured her that we would face this difficult time together. However, on the fifth day, the burden of guilt had built up inside me like a reservoir ready to burst. After bringing Miriam home from her sister’s house, I found myself sitting alone at home, overcome with sadness as I contemplated the magnitude of the situation and the thoughts running through Mick’s mind that led him to such a final decision. Tears streamed down my face as I desperately tried to wipe them away, hoping to conceal my pain from Miriam. But she noticed, sat down beside me and tenderly asked, “Are you okay?” wrapping her arm around me. Instantly, I broke down, unable to contain my sobs. No matter how hard I tried to regain control, it seemed impossible. One of the driving forces behind my overwhelming guilt was the belief that Mick felt like a burden to us during his time with us, which is why he did not return home after finishing rehab at the Rutland Centre. This realisation weighed heavily on me.

Miriam pulled me close and hugged me tightly, reassuring me with her words. “He knew you loved him,” she whispered. Slowly, but surely, the tears and sobs began to subside. The ripple effect of Mick’s passing was enormous, permeating the lives of countless people. At the packed church in Ashbourne, Mick’s hometown, where his funeral was held, I couldn’t help but contemplate the tremendous impact his departure had on so many individuals. At that moment, a thought crossed my mind: “If only Mick could see how deeply his passing has affected all these people, perhaps he would have felt differently.” The room was filled with immense sadness, creating an atmosphere of profound sorrow that I had never before encountered.

It became clear to me that I needed to do something significant to help my family cope with the devastating loss. I also needed to address and process my own grief. Running, biking and swimming provided relief, allowing me to find moments of serenity amid the chaos of life. While thoughts of Mick would still surface while I exercised, they often brought about a sense of peace rather than a feeling of overwhelming sadness.

I had Mick's favourite song, "Moving" by Bugzy Malone, ingrained in my mind and embroidered into my customised cycling gear. Every time I felt tempted to skip a workout, I would recall the lyrics, "Gotta Keep It Movin'." During long runs or challenging rides, I would repeat the mantra to myself, "Gotta keep it movin', Gotta keep it movin'." Mick had become my internal motivation as I embarked on the greatest challenge of my life. When he passed away, I was overwhelmed with sorrow and regret, feeling that I had not done enough to help him overcome his mental struggles by encouraging him to exercise with me. It consumed my thoughts for a long time and I believed I had let him down.

It was Trish who reminded me that I couldn't have prevented his tragic choice. It was a decision he had made on his own. However, their words compelled me to find a way to honour him. I had signed up to take part in Deca UK 2017 months earlier and now I felt a deep need to dedicate my Deca attempt to him, using it as a means to navigate my own grief and the grief of my family. It also served as a message to others who may be struggling, demonstrating that with the determination to 'keep it moving' and support from those around us, there is always hope and someone to turn to.

I wanted to convey that no matter how dire the circumstances may seem, there are always people who are willing to provide support, lend an ear to listen and remind others that it's okay not to feel okay. I firmly believe in the sentiment, "Suicide does not end the chances of life getting worse; it eliminates the possibility of it ever getting better." There is no situation that is beyond repair or any scenario that cannot be turned around.

When Mick passed away, I experienced a range of emotions. Initially, I was shocked by the suddenness of it all. Overwhelming sadness washed over me, followed by anger, kindled by the circumstances surrounding his death. And then came the guilt. I noticed a sense of guilt for not doing more for him, as if I should have forcibly dragged him away from his struggles. That guilt lingered for months, weighing heavily on my heart. However, as time went on, I began to recognise and remember all the support and care Miriam and I had provided for Mick throughout our journey together. Gradually, that guilt started to fade, giving way to the understanding that I had done what I could with the knowledge and resources that I had at the time.

I still find myself pondering at times, "Could things have been different if I had convinced him to start running?" However, I have come to realise that this line of thinking is unfair to myself. As a personal trainer, I firmly believe that true change occurs only when individuals are genuinely ready and committed to making a change. You cannot force someone to go to the gym, train rigorously, or adopt a healthy diet against their will. They must feel a genuine desire to transform and possess a powerful 'why' that drives them. It is only then that they will maintain consistency and achieve their goals.

I firmly believe that people can only change when they reach a breaking point or when they are genuinely ready to change from within. While it is legitimate to make efforts and attempt to motivate others, there is nothing we can say or do that can possess the power to alter someone's mindset if they are not willing to embrace change themselves. Unfortunately, as much as we may wish it, we cannot force someone to change simply because we want them to.

Because of this understanding, I make a deliberate effort not to impose a healthier lifestyle on others. Instead, I strive to motivate them by showcasing my own actions and choices, demonstrating what is possible if they truly desire change. I can only do my part by carrying out my work and illuminating the path, serving as a beacon and setting an example for others to follow. Ultimately, the decision to embark on a healthier way of life lies within each individual and my role is to inspire and guide rather than push or demand.

And so, I embrace the powerful analogy that encapsulates my purpose: 'Be a lighthouse.' These words resonate within me every single day, empowering me to make better choices and live as a guiding light for others. I am proud to say, without hesitation, that I am a fucking lighthouse.

Chapter 6: Deca Destiny

Introduction to the Regulations and How DecaUK Works

	Super Sprint	Sprint	Olimpic	Half Ironman	Ironman	Deca
SWIM	400 m 0.2 miles	750 m 0.5 miles	1500 km 0.9 miles	1.9 km 1.2 miles	3.8 km 2.4 miles	38 km 24 miles
BIKE	10 km 6.2 miles	20 km 12.4 miles	40 km 24.8 miles	90 km 56 miles	180 km 112 miles	1800 km 1120 miles
RUN	2.5 km 1.6 miles	5 km 3.1 miles	10 km 6.2 miles	21 km 13.1 miles	42 km 26.2 miles	420 km 262 miles

Triathlon is like three sports in one; there is swimming, cycling and running. Triathlon competitions are held over four distances: sprint triathlon, Olympic triathlon, half Iron and Iron. A Deca is a full iron distance triathlon every day for ten consecutive days, following all the same rules as a single-day Iron event. In the table below the exact distances for each discipline of each event are displayed.

Triathlon offers various challenges for athletes at different levels, yet the Deca triathlon stands out as the ultimate test of physical and mental endurance, specifically designed for those who crave extreme challenges.

Not only does the Deca demand immense physical strength, but it also requires incredible mental fortitude. The sheer repetition of completing a full iron distance triathlon every day for ten consecutive days is an unparalleled test of resilience. It pushes athletes beyond physical exhaustion, forcing them to draw from the depths of their mental reserves to keep going.

The mental challenges of the Deca are multifaceted. Enduring the physical pain and fatigue becomes only one facet of the overall battle. Athletes must also navigate the mental obstacles that arise with each passing day. The mind becomes a battleground, where doubts, fears and uncertainties attempt to overshadow the desire to push forward.

In this insane event, athletes are forced to confront their inner demons and push beyond their perceived limits. The Deca becomes an exploration of human potential, where determination and mental toughness become the key ingredients for success.

Reserved only for the most dedicated and audacious athletes, the Deca represents the epitome of extreme triathlon challenges. It is not a race for the faint-hearted, but rather for those who seek to push themselves beyond what they previously thought possible.

The Deca stands as a tribute to human resilience and a showcase of the power of the human spirit. It requires an unwavering commitment and an unyielding belief in one's own abilities to conquer each day's daunting distances. But the reward of reaching the finish line after ten consecutive days of gruelling effort is unmatched.

Those who dare to take on the Deca are not just participants; they are pioneers, pushing the boundaries of what is considered achievable. They become part of an elite group of athletes who embrace the extreme nature of the challenge and emerge transformed, both physically and mentally.

Regardless of the distance, triathlons always follow a specific order: 1. Swim, 2. Bike and 3. Run. The goal is to complete each discipline as quickly as possible to emerge as the victor. To facilitate a smooth transition between the disciplines, there are two designated transition sections–T1 and T2.

T1, or transition 1, takes place after the swim portion. Athletes strive to make it to their bikes after leaving the water as swiftly as possible. They quickly shed their wetsuits and gear up in their cycling attire, which includes shoes and a helmet.

Triathletes often opt to wear a tri suit underneath their wetsuits to streamline their transition process. The Tri Suit serves as a versatile garment that allows them to save time by eliminating the need for extensive clothing changes during the race.

During T1, after completing the swim portion, triathletes aim to be as efficient as possible in transition. By wearing a tri suit, they can simply peel off their wetsuit and seamlessly transition to the bike leg. This not only saves valuable time but also eliminates the hassle of changing into cycling-specific clothing. Additionally, athletes employ various tips and tricks to optimise their transition efficiency.

Similarly, in T2, after completing the cycling section and before the run section, triathletes once again strive for quickness in changing from their bike shoes to their running shoes. Wearing a Tri Suit allows them to move swiftly through this transition, avoiding the need for even more clothing changes.

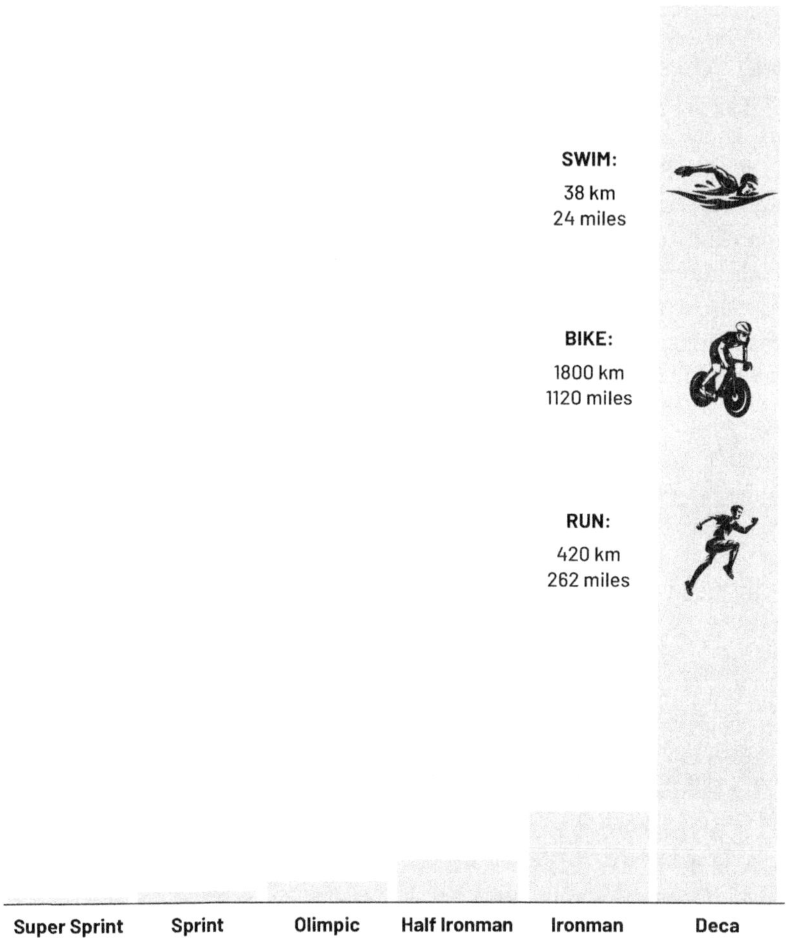

The innovative design of a tri suit encompasses features that cater to the unique demands of both cycling and running. It includes a protective pad that minimises saddle soreness during the bike leg. However, the pad is small enough to allow for comfortable running. This flexibility enables triathletes to wear the tri suit for the duration of the race, eliminating the need for additional clothing changes. This significant time-saving advantage allows them to stay focused on the race and maintain their momentum.

By utilising a tri suit, triathletes can optimise their performance by reducing transition times and streamlining their gear changes. The tri suit's dual-purpose design not only provides comfort and protection throughout all three disciplines but also eliminates the need for multiple outfit changes. Ultimately, the tri suit becomes an essential piece of equipment that enables triathletes to maximise their efficiency, shave off valuable seconds and give their best performance without any unnecessary distractions.

Transition areas in triathlons are often referred to as 'Free Time' because athletes don't need to use additional energy to make up for lost time. Instead, their goal is to pass through these areas as swiftly as possible. It's in these transition sections where races can be won or lost, making efficiency a key factor.
Triathletes employ numerous tips and tricks to enhance their transition speed. For instance, some athletes use rubber bands to secure their shoes in place before mounting their bikes. This prevents their shoes from rotating around with the pedals during the initial run out of transition. By avoiding the banging of shoes on the ground, this trick allows for a smoother transition and a more seamless bike mount as the shoes are ready in a horizontal position for the athlete to put their foot in more easily.

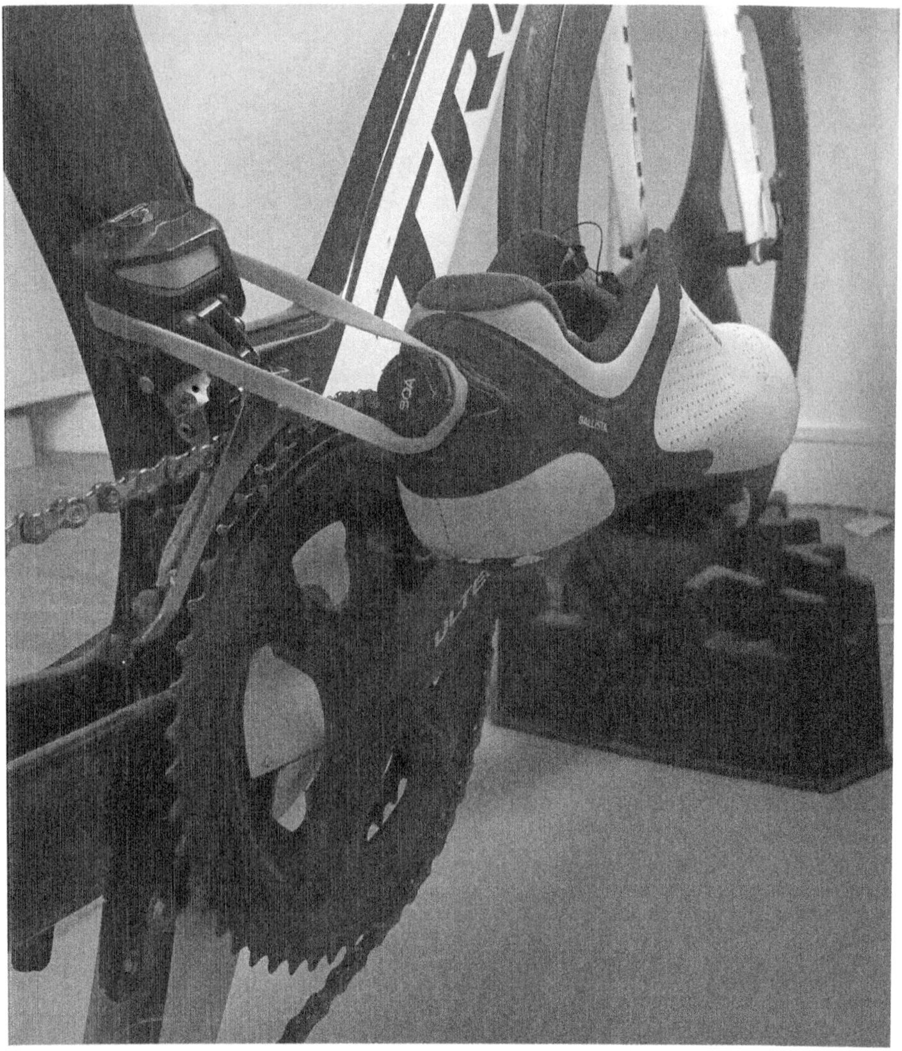

Another strategy used by triathletes is to prepare their socks and bike shoes in advance with talc. This helps facilitate a smoother and easier fitting when they put on their shoes during transition. Some triathletes even choose to forgo the use of socks altogether, further reducing the time spent on clothing changes. These small but effective tactics contribute to shaving off valuable seconds in transition. By streamlining their processes, triathletes can maintain their momentum and avoid any unnecessary hiccups during this critical phase of the race. It's through these strategic adjustments and attention to detail that triathletes aim to gain a competitive edge and optimise their overall race performance.

General triathlon Rules

- Competitors must have their helmet on and strapped before mounting the bike.
- Competitors must walk or run in the transition area; no riding is allowed until competitors have reached the mount line.
- Competitors must have their race number pinned on and visible, as well as additional numbers on their bike and helmet.
- Competitors must not follow the cyclist in front of them too closely. They must be at least two bike lengths behind them or 10 metres
- Competitors must ride their bikes as far to the left side (Ireland) of the lane as possible. They can only pass on the right (within the lane) and then must immediately return to the left. The violation of this rule is blocking, so you must let the faster riders pass by.
- Competitors must rack their bikes properly and respect their fellow competitors' equipment.
- Competitors must follow the directions of the Race Officials and Marshals without question.
- Competitors must not wear headphones while biking. They must be alert and aware and must know the course.
- Competitors must wear their timing chip throughout the race. After crossing the finish line, they must hand it to a race official to receive an official time.

Throughout this gruelling challenge, I was supported by an exceptional team whose roles were crucial to my performance. For detailed information about each team member and their contributions, please refer to 'DecaUK 2017 Team Members' in the Appendix.

During each day of DecaUK, the rules for the full distance triathlon remained consistent. The day would commence at the lakeside, where both competitors and crew members gathered for a brief race day instruction from the organising crew. While these briefings usually covered the same information, they served as a reminder of the cut-off times - this is the official Ironman cut-off times. Swim: 2hrs 20mins after the start, Bike 10hrs 30mins after the start, Run: 17hrs after the start. This is the DecaUK cut-off times: 23 hours after the start - and

any potential changes from the previous day, although changes were rare.
Following the briefing, competitors were instructed to enter the lake and proceed towards the first buoy. The race began with a floating start, meaning that once the starting sound was heard, participants could commence the race from their designated starting position. This differed from other triathlon starts, such as wave starts or beach starts, commonly used in Ironman races. In these starts, competitors rush into the water upon hearing an air horn, hooter, or even a cannon, as witnessed at the Ironman World Championships in Kona, Hawaii.
The consistent race day routine and start of the DecaUK triathlon provided competitors with a familiar and predictable environment as they embarked on the challenging journey each day.
Every triathlon competition can be uniquely designed, with varying routes and configurations. One approach is to have a singular, extensive loop that encompasses the bike, run and swim courses. Alternatively, the distances may be broken down into smaller loops.
A prime example is my participation in Ironman Lanzarote, where the swim course consisted of two laps. After finishing the initial lap, competitors left the water and ran a short distance up the beach, circling a cone before re-entering the water to commence the second lap. This technique is referred to as an Australian exit.
Another event I took part in was Ironman Wales, with a bike course divided into two loops and a run course divided into four loops. These loops were meticulously designed to reach the standard distances of a full-length triathlon, consisting of a 3.8 km swim, a 180 km bike ride and a 42 km run.

Contributor: Maurice Savage / Alamy Stock Photo

Each day of the competition was organised as a standalone race. As soon as the air horn was sounded at 7 am, the swim began and the clock started running for each athlete. The race continued until every participant crossed the finish line after completing the required distances. The duration varied, ranging from 12 to 23 hours.

To accurately track laps completed, officials counted the laps swum in the lake. Additionally, chip timing technology was used to count the laps on the bike course and during the run. This ensured that each competitor's distances were officially recorded and validated by the chip timing system.

As per the competition regulations, each athlete received a chip during the pre-race briefing, which was then attached to their ankle strap. This process took place the day prior to the first race of the ten-day event. It was the responsibility of both the athletes and their support crew to ensure that the chip was worn throughout the entire duration of the competition. This allowed the organising crew to accurately track the number of laps completed by the athletes in the bike and run sections. However, the chip was not necessary for the swim section due to its incompatibility with water.

To monitor the swim section, race officials were in charge of manually counting the six loops completed by athletes in the 3.8 km swim each day. To track the bike and run distances, chip timing mats were strategically placed at the turn-around points at the ends of both bike and run courses. Whenever an athlete crossed these points, a radio signal was transmitted from their ankle strap to the mats, indicating the completion of a lap.

The chip used in the competition did not function like a GPS watch, thus there were no visual maps available to track the laps. However, participants knew the number of laps completed because the radio signal transmitted from the chip was received by the timing mats each time they crossed the mat closest to the race headquarters. This information was immediately sent online to a website called 'Race Results,' which the race organisers could access on their laptop. They could then inform each athlete or their crew members about the number of laps completed.

Counting bike laps individually could be challenging, especially when fatigued and prone to losing focus. Fortunately, the race officials were readily available to provide lap count updates whenever requested. Moreover, they made it a point to notify participants when they were about to begin their final lap to ensure they did not exceed the required 180 km on the bike or 42 km on the run.

One of the noteworthy members of the race organising crew at DecaUK was Matt Brown.

Throughout the ten-day event, Matt was consistently helpful and always willing to assist. We developed a good rapport, having bonded over the uncanny similarity of our cycling jerseys. One day, while he was surveying the bike course for any potential obstacles that could impact the athletes, I noticed Matt's jersey. It

predominantly featured a yellow colour with black trim, adorned with a striking black skull and crossbones logo. Interestingly, my own jersey had a primarily black design with yellow trim and a yellow skull and crossbones. Lightheartedly, I joked to Matt, "Clearly, mine is the better-looking one."
One of Matt's responsibilities each day was to inform competitors when they were approaching their final lap in the bike section. He seemed to thoroughly

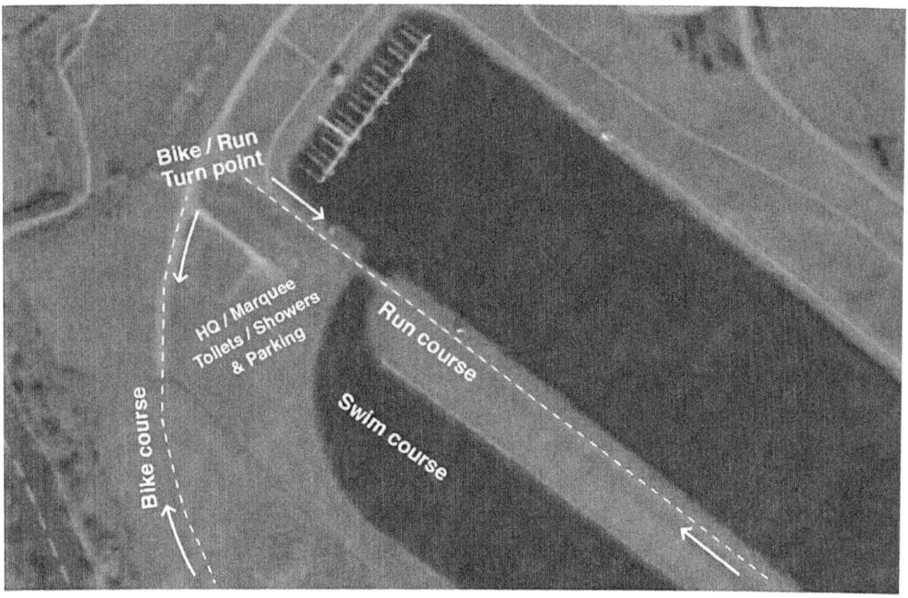

Fig. 1 shows an overview of DecaUK HQ in relation to the swim, bike and run course starting areas; they were all in close proximity to each other.

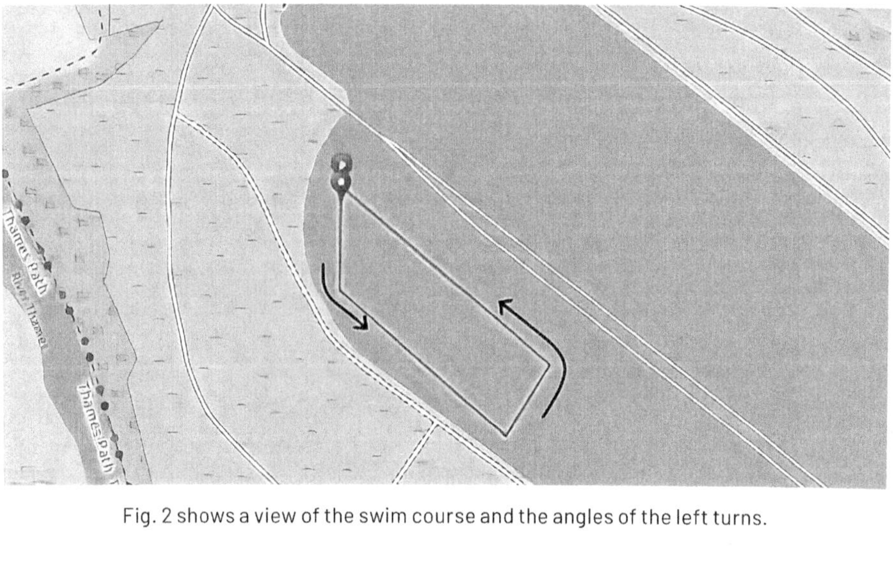

Fig. 2 shows a view of the swim course and the angles of the left turns.

enjoy this task, which earned him the biggest smiles and cheers of the day from both participants and crew members. It was a heart-warming sight to see Matt holding a yellow board with bold black text that proudly proclaimed "LAST LAP."

The period between completing one discipline and commencing the next, such as between swimming and biking or biking and running, is known as transition time. This duration is added to your overall time and contributes to your total race duration. Unlike traditional stopwatch timing, the clock does not halt when you finish one discipline and resume when you start the next. Instead, it continues to run continuously throughout the race.

Only when you complete all the required disciplines and distances at the end of each day does the clock stop for you. These times then accumulate over the course of the ten-day event. For example, if you consistently finish a full-distance triathlon in 10 hours each day over ten days, your cumulative finishing time would amount to 100 hours. The athlete who completes the ten-day event with the fewest hours recorded will rightfully claim victory as the fastest competitor.

As you now know, a Deca consists of completing an iron distance triathlon repeatedly over the span of ten days. Throughout this extended period, a multitude of events can occur, including accidents or incidents resulting from exhaustion or unforeseen circumstances. Therefore, ensuring the welfare and safety of the competitors is of utmost importance.

In previous instances of the Deca, participants have experienced extreme fatigue, sometimes leading to falling asleep while cycling. Such is the toll the event takes on their bodies. To mitigate potential risks and provide prompt response to any incidents, Deca events are held in a single, controlled location. This allows the organisers to maintain complete oversight of the athletes and promptly address any issues that may arise at any given time.

During DecaUK 2017, we held our race at Eton Dorney practice lake, which ran parallel to the competition lake used in the London 2012 Olympics. The race course was marked by various points, including the start buoy indicated as 'FIG.2 Point A,' where we gathered each day, eagerly awaiting the sound of the air horn to signal the race commencement. From there, we swam towards the first buoy mentioned as 'FIG.2 Point B,' then proceeded to the second buoy known as 'FIG.2 Point C,' which marked the first 90-degree turn. Following that, we made another 90-degree turn at 'FIG.2 Point D,' leading us back to the starting buoy, where we began the next lap. To complete the full 3.8k swim, we needed to swim a total of 8 laps.

Drafting is permitted in the swim section of all triathlons, allowing athletes to closely follow a competitor in front of them without facing penalties. This strategy is commonly adopted by swimmers to conserve their energy for the remaining disciplines. Similarly, drafting is permitted during the run section,

as it can help athletes maintain a faster pace and conserve energy.
However, drafting is not allowed in the bike section of triathlons. The advantage gained from drafting on the bike leg can be significant, providing a substantial boost in speed and efficiency. To maintain fairness and preserve the integrity of the competition, drafting is prohibited during the bike section.
A wetsuit is required for participants in a full-distance triathlon, such as an Ironman event, if the water temperature is 16 degrees Celsius or below. However, it is prohibited to wear a wetsuit if the water temperature exceeds 24 degrees, as it can lead to overheating, which can be dangerous for the athlete. At Dorney Lake, the water temperature typically ranged from 14 to 16 degrees Celsius, sometimes feeling even colder. Therefore, it was an obvious choice to wear a wetsuit. In addition, participants were allowed to wear gloves and booties in these colder temperatures. The lake at Dorney was well-maintained by the staff and had exceptionally clear water, allowing you to see the small blackfish swimming at the bottom. Although it was not very deep, with a maximum depth of around 15 feet, it was still a stunning lake to swim in. Despite the confined space for such a long event, I found great enjoyment in the beautiful scenery.
On October 4th, 2017, the Deca race was not the only event taking place. Alongside the Deca competitors, there were other athletes preparing to race on the same course. These athletes were participating in various other endurance triathlons, including the Quin Ultra Endurance triathlon (comprising 5 iron dis-

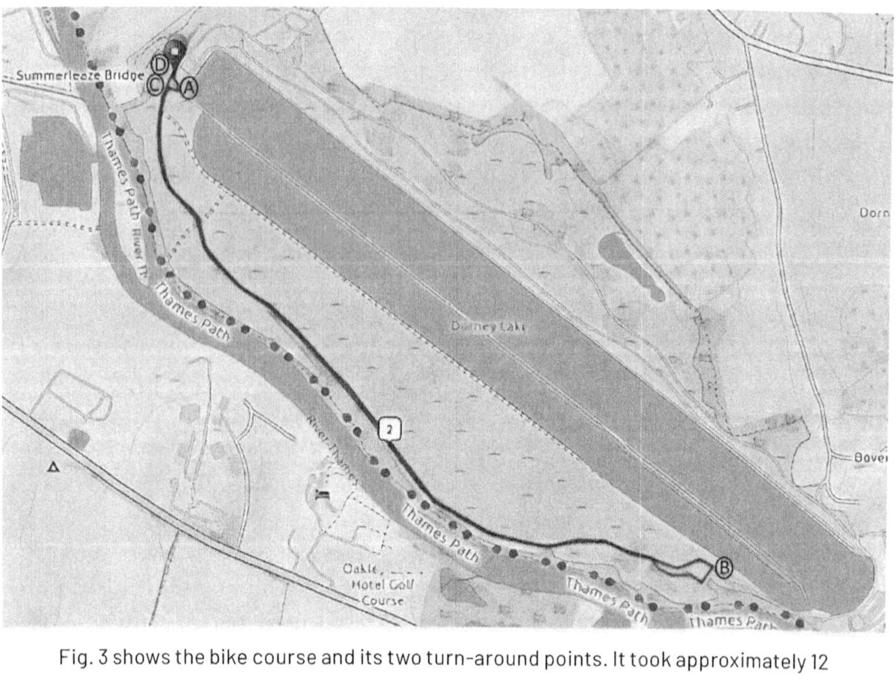

Fig. 3 shows the bike course and its two turn-around points. It took approximately 12 minutes to complete one lap of the required 39 laps.

tance triathlons in 5 days), the Treble Ultra Endurance triathlon (consisting of 3 iron distance triathlons in 3 days), the Double Ultra Endurance triathlon (involving 2 iron distance triathlons in 2 days) and a single iron distance triathlon. Just like the Deca participants, these athletes were required to complete the standard distances of a 3.8k swim, a 180k bike and 42k run. Additionally, there was one individual tackling the ten swims over the ten-day period, while others were challenging themselves by running ten marathons in ten consecutive days.
The starting point of the bike course was situated around 100 metres away from the lakeside. To begin the bike leg of the triathlon, participants were required to collect their bikes from the race organisers' headquarters (Fig. 1 A). The support crew members were allowed to retrieve the bikes on behalf of the athletes and bring them to the starting area. Once the athletes were prepared, they could mount their bikes and ride over the chip timing mat (Fig. 3 A) to signify the beginning of their bike leg.

The cyclists were then directed to pedal towards the far end of the bike course, located at the opposite end of the lake. Here, they needed to manoeuvre around a cone and ride over the second chip timing mat (Fig. 3 B) to record the distance covered. After completing this section, they would return to the starting area and race headquarters (Fig. 3 C), where a cone was set up for them to round (Fig. 3 D). This marked the completion of a full lap of the bike course.

In order to cover the required distance of 180 kilometres, we had to complete a total of 39 laps on the bike course. It was important to note that drafting, where cyclists closely follow one another to reduce wind resistance, was strictly prohibited. To maintain a fair and safe race, we were obliged to maintain a minimum distance of 10 metres between our front wheels and the rear wheel of any cyclist ahead of us.

However, in the specific case of DecaUK, there was a slightly more relaxed approach. We were allowed to ride alongside each other for brief periods of time if we wanted to chat, as long as this privilege was not abused. Additionally, if a fellow competitor required assistance, such as in the case of a flat tyre or the need for food, we were permitted to lend a helping hand.

One important rule to note was that only registered competitors were allowed to cycle on the route. This meant that no outside assistance from family or friends was permitted on the bike course. This ensured that all participants competed under the same conditions.

One of the highlights of the bike route, especially for me, was the picturesque scenery and wildlife as it passed through a nature reserve. I observed the shelters that birdwatchers would use and I was amazed by the presence of hawks and kites, some of which were remarkably large. The bike course provided a pleasant and serene environment, further enhancing the overall experience of the race.
The bike route didn't just offer stunning views of cranes and herons but also provided glimpses of a geese-filled field and various vibrantly coloured birds.

On occasion, I found myself slowing down to observe birds of prey effortlessly gliding overhead, eagerly anticipating the possibility of seeing them dive and emerge with their prey. These majestic creatures offered a delightful and captivating distraction from the race.
However, the true daredevils on the route were the squirrels. These mischievous critters would dart out in front of the bikes, almost as if they were intentionally testing their luck, like a gang of adrenaline junkies. One day, I came dangerously close to accidentally running one over, prompting me to come to a halt to ensure its safety. A fellow cyclist, Martin Curran, had a clever technique to avoid the unsettling feeling of squashing the squirrels. Whenever he spotted one emerging from the grass at the roadside, he would let out a loud, booming scream in his deep Scottish accent. Instantly, the squirrels would retreat as if they had hit an impenetrable glass barrier, returning to the safety of the grass. It was a hilarious sight to witness and it added a touch of humour to the race experience.

The Run

The run portion of the triathlon took place on a smooth tarmac (Fig. 4) pedestrian road that stretched alongside the man-made lake. To signify the start of the run section, each triathlete had to cross a timing mat located near the turnaround point of the cycling route, next to race headquarters. The road had a length of 1.75 kilometres, requiring athletes to run its entire length to reach the turnaround

thatcameraman.com

point (Fig. 4 B), cross the chip timing mat and then return to the starting point by running back up the road to the first chip timing mat (Fig. 4 A). This completed one 3.5 kilometre lap and participants had to complete 12 laps in total to cover the full 42.2 kilometre distance. This distance is the same as that of the Dublin marathon, the London marathon, the Boston marathon and other famous marathons. To put it into perspective, imagine running a 5k race almost 8.5 times. It is already challenging to run this distance as a standalone race, but when combined with a 3.8 kilometre swim and a 180 kilometre bike ride, it becomes even more demanding. Now, envision doing this every day for ten consecutive days.

The run course consisted mostly of flat terrain, with the exception of six inclines in the form of humpback bridges. These bridges were strategically placed along the route to facilitate the flow of water from the competition lake to the practice lake. Athletes who desired to swim, kayak, or row from one lake to the other, had the opportunity to do so by passing under these bridges. As the event progressed, the inclines of these bridges would begin to have a noticeable impact on the participants. Every day, I would commence the run section under the radiant October sun, but as I completed a lap or two, darkness would gradually engulf the surroundings. With no street lights available, we had to rely on head torches to navigate through the darkness.

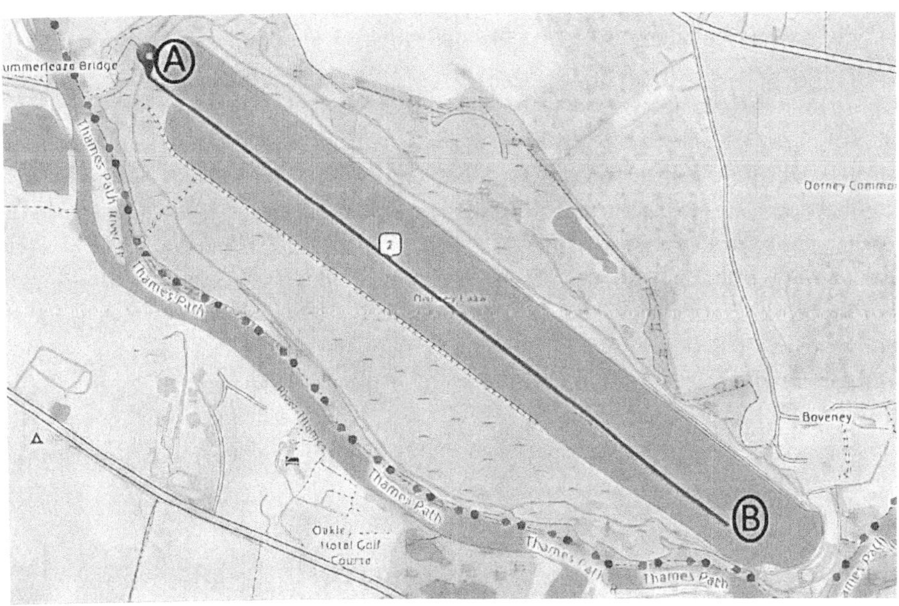

In Fig. 4, we can observe the run section of the triathlon, which dissects the two lakes, one designated for rowing competition and the other for practice sessions, with the latter being where we swam. The run course featured six humpback bridges, which gradually became more prominent and noticeable as the event progressed, especially after around 6-7 days.

For a detailed list of the equipment I used during DecaUK and its associated costs, see the 'Equipment and Costs' section in Resources.

The Journey to DecaUK Begins

Monday 2nd, October, 2017

Two days before the start of DecaUK, I woke up at 7:20 am, to drop off Miriam at work. Afterwards, I drove back home to get the kids ready for school, feeling emotional because I knew it would be ten days until I would see them again. It was the longest time I had ever been away from them. Returning home, I made a final check on the equipment I needed for my upcoming trip. We then collected the camper van we had decided to rent and brought it back to my house, loading it with all the necessary gear, food and everything else I would need for this incredible adventure that was about to unfold. Driving the van was my sister Paula who would stay with me for the entire event and then drive me home. Also with us for the first few days was Paula's husband Paddy.

As we approached Irish Ferries, the toll booth attendant greeted us by our first names, recognising us from the information we registered when we made our booking. After confirming our names, we boarded the boat for a two and a half hour journey.

Unfortunately, the sea was choppy, which made the journey less enjoyable. Although it didn't bother me personally, it was a challenge for many elderly passengers who found it unsafe to leave their seats. Walking to the toilet felt like navigating a zig-zag agility drill, with the waves constantly shifting my balance. At one point, the ship leaned one way, causing me to head straight towards an elderly gentleman who was seated. His eyes filled with fear as he braced himself for an imminent painful collision. Fortunately, the boat suddenly swayed in the opposite direction, propelling me in a completely different trajectory. Paddy and Paula witnessed the man's panic and the unexpected change in my direction. We all had a good laugh.

After reaching Holyhead, we embarked on a six-hour drive to Windsor, arriving at the campsite after 11pm.

Meeting competitors and registration

Tuesday 3rd, October, 2017

The following morning, I had the opportunity to meet three fellow competitors at the campsite. I walked up to Rob Duddington's camping area, where he and his crew member, Mark Padley, were inspecting Rob's bike. I introduced myself and we had a chat. Rob mentioned that Mark had participated in two previous Deca events himself. Little did I know at the time that there had only been two other Decas in the UK up to 2017; Mark had finished second in the 2011 Deca and fourth in 2012, when Gerry Duffy was also competing. It was an impressive achievement.

I was impressed by the high calibre of Rob's crew members. In contrast, I felt like the odd one out, thinking, "Shit, we are out of our league here." The most extreme challenge I had ever undertaken was the double iron distance in two days I had completed at Lough Ennell two months earlier. Before that, I had only done three individual Iron distance events. I was struck by a wave of uncertainty about what lay ahead.

Later on, I had the opportunity to meet Graham Smedley, who turned out to be a genuinely nice guy. We had a lengthy conversation, during which I assumed that he was another vegan participant. Graham explained that he followed a vegetarian diet because some of the supplements he took were not vegan.

Indeed, he worked for a company called Herbalife 24 Nutrition. In contrast, I told him that I did not take supplements and that I strove to obtain all my necessary vitamins, minerals and macronutrients from natural food sources. While this approach has worked well for me, I would later realise that my video promoting the use of natural foods over supplements received a few disapproving looks from others in the community.

I also had the pleasure of meeting Chris James and learned that he had accomplished an incredible feat in 2011: completing three Iron distance triathlons in three consecutive days at the same event where Gerry Duffy undertook his Deca challenge. Chris was not only an impressive athlete but also a kind and pleasant individual. What amazed me was that he had only his daughter as his crew, which must have been incredibly tough for both of them since the average number of members for a race crew is two to four.

Registration for the event was scheduled for 4:00 pm at the race headquarters, followed by a race briefing at 5:00 pm. The registration process involved checking in to confirm your participation in the event and receiving a bag containing items such as your race number, swim hat and race chip as well as other merchandise from Brutal Events, the organising company behind the race. I had been in contact with Claire Smith, the owner of Brutal Events, in the eighteen months leading up to the event. Claire preferred to work behind the scenes, trusting Jim Page, her right-hand man, to conduct the race briefing while she sat nearby, diligently working on her laptop.

Jim, or James Page, an incredibly helpful and empathetic individual who had a genuine enthusiasm for assisting all the competitors and proved to be an invaluable asset to the event. Rules and regulations were standard for a triathlon, which means there were no surprises for us in the race briefing.

Wednesday 4th, October, 2017 - Day 1: Once More into the Fray...

Strategy

On the first day of the Deca, my goal was to approach each section—the swim, bike and run—conservatively. I wanted to take it one lap at a time, without pushing myself too hard, in order to conserve energy and reduce the risk of injury.
I had a nutrition strategy in place, which you can read more about in the recipe

section: "The Secret Recipes from DecaUK". For day one, my plan was to consume half of a brown smoothie, saving the other half for the initial laps of the bike section. After the swim, when I might feel cold, I would make a pit stop at the showers on my way to the camper. Standing under the hot water would help me warm up. Once dressed, I would eat a generous bowl of porridge before getting on my bike to start the cycling portion.

During the first five bike laps, I would consume the second half of my smoothie. After completing these laps, I would return to the camper for some food, typically toast initially, followed by soup, rice and other whole foods later in the day. After every five laps on the bike, I would take a break, getting off the bike and returning to the camper to eat once again.

Following the bike section, I would take a moment to stretch and avoid eating too much solid food in order to prevent digestive issues during the run. My focus on the run was to run as much as possible and minimise walking while maintaining enough energy and freshness to continue the next day.
During the run, my strategy for day one was to run at a steady pace for five minutes, followed by a one-minute walk, repeating this pattern until I completed a lap. At the end of each lap, I would take on fluids and fuel up with some fruits to replenish my energy stores.
For after the race, we had a recovery plan in place. My first step was to jump straight into the cold lake as a form of cryotherapy. I believed this would help with the post-race inflammation and aid in the recovery process.

Next, I planned to get a quick massage. As a qualified sports massage therapist, I understood the benefits of a good massage. Even if someone was not qualified, they could still perform basic strokes like effleurage without causing harm. Effleurage involves using long, two-handed strokes with oil to reduce friction on the skin. The strokes start off light and can then become deeper by applying more pressure. This technique can promote relaxation, and relieve stress as well as removing toxins from the muscles. I was confident that I could guide anyone through giving an effective massage and in my exhausted state, I welcomed any attempt at relaxation, unless it involved falling off the massage table. I'll explain how that happened later. Finally, I wanted to ensure I replenished my body with solid nutritious food before getting as much sleep as possible. With another race scheduled for the next

morning at 7:30am, I knew I needed to maximise my rest. (For details on the nutrition plan I used during DecaUK, see the 'DecaUK Nutritional Daily Schedule' in the Resources section.)

Diary of the Day

I can still vividly remember the sound of the air horn, a loud blast that signalled the start of the race on the first day. As everyone took off from the floating start, I intentionally positioned myself at the back of the pack. I didn't want to appear foolish by being left behind by the experienced enduroman champions and top-class athletes in the field. I already had doubts about my place among the competitors and I certainly didn't want to confirm those doubts by getting in their way right from the start. I had learned that lesson the hard way during one of my earliest races in 2012 at the Fingal 10k.

However, it didn't take long for me to face my first challenge. As I swam from the starting buoy to the first buoy, my goggles suddenly filled with water. I had been using the same pair of goggles for months without any issues, but I hadn't had the opportunity to practise in the lake beforehand. The cold water seemed to catch me off guard and It was hard not to feel like a novice at that moment.

Fortunately, I always carry a spare pair of goggles during races and this proved to be a lifesaver. I stopped swimming, removed the leaking goggles from my face and retrieved the spare goggles from my leg. It's a tip I learned when I first started competing in triathlons and it has come in handy on multiple occasions.

In order to secure the goggles on my leg, I wear them around my thigh. The lenses face outward, towards the right side of my body. To put them on, I step into the elastic band of the goggles, just like slipping into a pair of pants. I pull them up high, ensuring a snug fit on my thigh, so there is no chance of them coming off while I'm swimming. This trick has proven to be incredibly useful and has saved me from many unforeseen obstacles during races.

The second pair I brought as a spare turned out to be even worse than the original ones. They leaked even more during the swim, making it clear that the first pair was the better option. I quickly switched back to the original goggles, made sure they were tightened securely and continued with the swim. Luckily, this adjustment seemed to do the trick and I was able to complete the swim without any further issues. In fact, it was a great confidence boost to find myself overtaking other swimmers during the swim leg.

I couldn't help but notice that many of the other swimmers were wearing gloves and booties to combat the cold water. At the time, I didn't feel they were necessary. The water temperature felt pleasant enough for swimming and I didn't want any additional gear that could potentially hinder my performance.

In preparation for the race, I had also bought an extra layer to wear under my wetsuit. It was a long-sleeved, 1 mm thick neoprene layer designed to provide additional warmth in colder conditions. On the first day of the race, I decided not to use it. The water temperature didn't feel cold enough to warrant wearing the extra layer. I wanted to gauge the conditions before deciding if to use the extra layer.

Despite the goggles malfunctioning, I managed to complete the swim in one hour and seventeen minutes. Overall, I felt satisfied with my performance in the water.

After emerging from the lake, I immediately felt the chill of the morning air. It was a beautiful day, with clear skies and bright sunshine, but the temperature was quite cold. To warm up, my plan was to make a quick pit stop at the competitors' shower on my way to the camper. I hoped that a thirty-second burst of warm water would help raise my body temperature. As I stood in the shower, shivering, I could feel the heat gradually seep into my skin.

After the brief shower, I braved the cold air and sprinted fifty metres to my camper. Once inside, I quickly stripped off my wet gear and began drying myself off. I was grateful to have the assistance of my crew members, who helped me get dressed as efficiently as possible.

I took my time getting changed, enjoying a relaxed pace as I powered up with a hearty bowl of porridge. When I felt ready, I hopped on my bike and started the first lap, making sure to pace myself conservatively. As expected, there were already a few competitors ahead of me in the bike section. They might have had a faster swim or been quicker in transition.

About halfway through my second lap, near the turnaround point (Fig. 3B), I heard a hissing sound coming from my back tyre. It was a puncture and I couldn't believe my luck. To make matters worse, I had made the foolish decision not to bring my saddlebag, which would have contained spare tubes. I couldn't remember why I left it behind, as there was no good reason for it.

In a state of panic, I began running back towards the start line instead of making a rational decision. I was so close to the turnaround mat that, had I been thinking clearly, I could have at least registered that lap on the system by running over the mat. However, my panicked state led me straight back to the camper, like a homing pigeon seeking refuge, in search of a new wheel. If I had been more composed, I would have used my phone to contact Paddy, who was back at the camper and asked him to bring my spare bike to me. This would have allowed me to continue the race from where I had my mechanical problem. Carrying a phone was permitted and even mandatory in some instances, primarily for safety reasons given the challenging nature of the event. The organisers were aware of the potential risks, such as crashes or participants falling asleep on their bikes, which can occur in ultra-endurance events like DecaUK.

Unfortunately, in my highly stressed state, I completely forgot that I had my phone with me. It was a disastrous oversight. I sprinted back to the camper still wearing my cycling shoes, which meant an additional two-kilometre run from where I experienced the puncture. I can only imagine what the other participants must have been thinking as they witnessed my predicament. 'Look at this fool,' they might have said. 'Only two laps into the race and already in trouble.'

Graham Smedley, a fellow participant, stopped and offered me a CO2 cartridge to temporarily fix my punctured tube and help me get back on the road to the camper. Although the canister he provided should have worked fine, I made a mess of it. I had never successfully used one before and wasn't familiar with the process. A CO2 cartridge is a small metal container filled with liquefied CO2, that releases gas into a punctured tube when connected to the tube's valve. This rapidly inflates the tube. I attached it to the valve on my tube and activated it, but instead of filling the tube with air, it sprayed the liquified CO2 everywhere else. My hand and wheel were covered in the white liquid released by the canister.

Not wanting to waste any more time, I quickly stuffed the small canister into my back pocket, intending to replace it for Graham later. I asked my crew to try and purchase the same canisters in the local bike shop to fulfil my promise, but unfortunately, they were not available there. However, just like the Lannisters always pay their debts, the Prendergast's crew always keeps their word.

Skipping ahead for a moment in the story, a few months after returning home, I managed to find the same canisters online and promptly sent five of them to Graham in the UK as a gesture of gratitude and repayment for his assistance.

As I made my way back to the camper, running while pushing my bike, I was met with concerned inquiries from fellow racers on the course. Understanding the need to regroup, retrieve my spare bike and get back on track, I focused on reaching the camper. It took me a good fifteen minutes to cover the distance and as soon as I arrived, I requested my crew to assess and resolve the issue with the back wheel while I proceeded with the race using my backup bike.

I had begun the race with a time trial bike, a superior choice compared to my backup bike. I was determined to have it back in my possession as soon as possible. TT bikes are specifically designed for faster speeds, making them specially suitable for triathlon or time trial events. Since all my training had been done on my TT bike, my body was well-adjusted to its unique features. Switching to any other bike mid-race was far from ideal, especially considering that my old road bike, the only alternative available, was not particularly fast.

My road bike, a 2010 Giant Defy, is an old and basic model and as soon as I started cycling on it, I could feel the strain on my back. I rarely trained on this bike and only brought it along as a last resort. Unfortunately, on the first day, during the second lap, I found myself relying on my last resort.

Despite the discomfort, I tried to remain focused and not let it affect my mindset. My goal was to complete each lap, one by one, until I could get my hands on my TT bike again. However, to my disappointment, I was unable to retrieve my TT bike that day and had to complete the 180-kilometre bike course on my road bike.

It turned out that the puncture was a consequence of a much bigger issue, caused by ruptured spokes. The damage to the back wheel of my TT bike was severe, requiring the expertise of a bike shop to fix it. Several spokes had ruptured, rendering my bike unrideable. Cycling on my spare bike proved to be a struggle. I made a conscious decision not to push the pace since my road bike simply couldn't support such efforts.

I maintained a reasonable pace, avoiding over-exertion and conserving energy. As other competitors passed me, I reminded myself that my objective was to complete the race and not to compete against them. My mantra became, "You're not here to race these guys; you're here to try and finish this thing." My focus shifted to finishing day one and ensuring I was healthy enough to start day two. Despite being overtaken by others, I resisted the temptation to chase after them and instead prioritised my own well-being and the long-term goal of completing the race. 'Play the long game.'

The bike course consisted of 38 laps and my plan was to do five laps before taking a break in the camper to refuel. Although we managed to stick to this plan on the first day, my road bike was causing significant discomfort to my back. Determined to push through, I persevered and finally completed the bike section after a gruelling nine hours.

During my training, I had decided to try an endurance drink supplement that had been recommended by a well-known Irish triathlete. He claimed it worked well for him without causing any gastrointestinal problems, so I thought I would give it a shot. I had used it for a few weeks at home and although it tasted stale and was difficult to swallow, it did not upset my stomach during training sessions and helped me get through without needing to carry excessive amounts of food.

On the first day of the race, I had started with this drink in my bottle. I managed to finish a full bottle, which was something I had never achieved even during a

four-hour ride at home. However, the consequences of consuming it became evident in the following days. I experienced ongoing stomach issues until day six and I firmly believe it was due to my mistake of taking too much of this drink. It didn't work for me, possibly because I used it incorrectly. However, I am aware that it works for other people. After feeling sick immediately after using it on day one, I decided not to use it again.

As I moved on to the run section, I felt a sense of relief, knowing that running was my strong suit. Despite being the last competitor to complete the bike course that day, I made a conscious decision to pace myself and focus on reaching the finish line in good condition.

Throughout the marathon, I strategically took breaks and refuelled with water and fruit at every lap. This allowed me to replenish my energy and stay hydrated, ensuring that I could maintain a steady pace and continue running comfortably.

Martin Curran, one of the two Scottish competitors in the race, showcased his strength in cycling but faced challenges during the run section. As the first night came to a close, Martin and I were the last two competitors remaining on the run course, determined to finish the day strong.

Although I had started my marathon run over an hour after Martin, I managed to catch him when the finish line was just twenty metres away. Faced with a choice, I contemplated whether to pass him or simply follow him in. Considering the respect and camaraderie that had developed between us throughout the first day, I believed it would be more fitting to show him respect by staying a few metres behind and crossing the finish line just after him. We both congratulated each other on successfully completing day one.

In truth, if I had known Martin as well back then as I came to know him over the next few days, I may have sneaked ahead of him for a bit of banter. Our friendship grew during the event and I enjoyed our connection. Being the last finisher on day one didn't bother me. Given the challenges I faced with my bike, I was grateful to have completed the day without any injuries. Little did I know what adventures awaited us in the days that followed.

Out of the fourteen participants who began day one of the Deca Ironman event, all fourteen successfully completed it. However, William Price, although participating in the event, was not eligible to compete for the overall title of DecaUK 2017 champion. This was due to his decision not to run the marathon on any of the ten days. William had been dealing with a knee injury that prevented him from running. Instead, he opted to complete a marathon distance each day for ten days on a rowing machine. While this presented a unique triathlon-like challenge, it was not recognised as an official part of the event and therefore, William could not be considered for the chance of winning it.

After crossing the finish line, I followed my post-race recovery plan, which included soaking my legs in the cold lake for ten minutes. This technique, suggested to me by Gerry Duffy during our meeting in Mullingar earlier in the year, provided the benefits of muscle soothing and cooldown without risking the onset of hypothermia. The cold water worked wonders in easing the strain and trauma my muscles had endured during the difficult full-distance triathlon. In the camper van, my crew had my clothes and comforting hot water bottles ready to warm me up after my dip in the icy waters. We then made our way back to the campsite in our camper, where excellent facilities awaited, including the luxury of hot showers. I relished the opportunity to indulge in a nice, hot shower, allowing the steam and warm water to wash away the remnants of salt, sweat and dirt from my body, leaving me feeling revitalised and refreshed, ready to start my recovery journey.

After enjoying a satisfying, protein-rich meal like my chickpea curry, I continued my recovery with a nice massage from Paddy and took a moment to update Miriam on my progress through a series of text messages before finally settling into bed and drifting off to sleep. Having the luxury of a full six hours of sleep played a crucial role in my recovery. It allowed me to experience the deep stages of sleep, where optimal recovery occurs. As the competition progressed, the significance of this became increasingly apparent.

Day 1	14 started - 14 finished				
Name	**Position**	**Total**	**Swim**	**Bike**	**Run**
William Price		12:53:44	1:20:07	7:13:11	4:20:11
Graham Smedley	1	13:39:10	1:14:16	7:10:30	5:14:25
Paul Machin	2	13:47:15	1:17:36	6:53:41	5:35:59
Anthony Gerundini	3	14:35:23	1:33:38	8:12:09	4:49:37
Tiernan Simmons	4	14:43:42	1:36:53	7:23:47	5:43:02
Rob Duddington	5	14:43:50	1:08:28	7:49:47	5:55:37
Ziv Navon	6	14:48:02	1:20:21	7:11:32	6:16:11
Graeme Allan	7	15:04:19	1:48:08	7:09:05	6:07:07
Simon Bayman	8	15:10:29	1:21:58	7:05:38	6:42:54
Chris James	9	15:33:48	1:34:13	7:54:32	6:05:05
Dave Kershaw	10	15:36:55	1:24:59	8:14:18	5:57:39
Simon Jacob	11	15:47:23	1:12:35	8:05:53	6:28:56
Martin Curran	12	16:02:32	1:21:14	7:33:29	7:07:50
Gerard Prendergast	13	16:02:40	1:17:20	8:55:17	5:50:04

Race Commentary

All fourteen athletes who participated in the first Iron distance triathlon at DecaUK 2017 successfully completed the race. However, it is worth noting that William Price, who had not officially entered the event due to a knee injury preventing him from partaking in the run section, would row instead. As a result, he could not be considered for the overall title even if he were to win the event.
On the first day, Graham Smedley, one of the favourites, emerged victorious with a remarkable performance. Anthony Gerundini, the overall favourite for the event title, came in second place, closely followed by Paul Machin, who secured the final spot on the podium. Notably, Paul's bike split was two hours faster than Ger Prendergast in last place, who finished just eight seconds behind Martin Curran.
As the event unfolded, the competitors' strategies became a subject of intrigue. Who was following a long-term plan? Who may have started too aggressively? With nine more full distance triathlons scheduled for the next nine days, the answers to these questions would surely reveal themselves.

Thursday 5th, October, 2017 - Day 2: Dealing with Setbacks

Strategy

For day two, our plan was to replicate our strategy from day one. After completing every five laps of the bike course, I would dismount and take a break in the camper to enjoy the nutritious meals prepared by our crew, Paula and Paddy, just like we did on the first day. This approach had proved to be successful in ensuring that I finished day one within a reasonable time frame.
Despite finishing last on day one, I felt physically and mentally strong at the start of day two. This reinforced my belief in the effectiveness of the strategy I had adopted, which was to 'play the long game' as I had learned from TC (Anthony Gerundini).
On the first day, my intention was to maintain an easy pace during the run to prevent any potential injuries. However, in the excitement of the event, I lost focus on that plan and ended up running slightly faster than intended.
For day two, I decided to stick to the same plan that I had set for day one. This time, my determination to adhere to it was strong. While I knew that I was slower on the bike compared to some of my competitors, I was confident in my running abilities, knowing that I was faster than most in that discipline. To avoid injuries, I deliberately aimed to run at a slower pace, resisting the urge to

get caught up in the excitement of the event or attempting to make up for lost time during the bike section.
My strategy involved running for three minutes followed by two minutes of walking, making sure to begin each lap by walking.
For the swim, my plan was to continue using my original goggles despite the problems I had with them on the first day.

Diary of the Day

Although it was October, the sun beat down relentlessly, casting a strong and intense light on the dry road. As the days progressed, I couldn't help but observe the subtle changes in nature. The evenings seemed to arrive earlier and the ground became covered with an increasing number of fallen leaves. It was a clear indication that winter was approaching, bringing with it colder and harsher days.

thatcameraman.com

During the race, I recall one of the dedicated crew members of the organising team taking the time to sweep away the fallen leaves at the turnaround point (Fig. 3 B) on the far end of the bike course. This was to prevent accidents. Thankfully, their diligence ensured that no incidents occurred.

Unfortunately, we encountered some issues with our rented camper van. One of the challenges we faced was running out of gas for cooking. Typically, I would start my day with a serving of porridge right after completing my swim in the lake.

With the camper van, we had been provided with two gas cylinders, one of which was supposedly two-thirds full and the other one-third full. Although they were meant to last for three weeks, both cylinders gave out after a day. Despite this inconvenient setback, I tried not to let it affect my focus. We resorted to making toast in the HQ tent and made the best of the situation.

Replacing the gas cylinder became a challenge especially when we discovered that the connections in England were different from the ones we had brought along. It took us two days to finally resolve the issue. Additionally, we experienced problems with the leisure battery which only provided power to the lights, preventing us from using a toaster. As a result, the crew had to make trips back and forth to the HQ tent throughout the day.

On top of these logistical challenges, I had to contend with unexpected saddle sores. This was surprising, as I had completed numerous long rides leading up to DecaUK without experiencing any such issues. I had washed thoroughly and used cream after day one to prevent me getting saddle sores so I was very surprised to find that they were an issue on day two.

On the morning of day two, we had our first competitor drop out. The individual who had set up camp next to us had crashed off his bike during the second lap. It was evident that he required medical attention and later on, I received word from another competitor, as he passed by me, that the injured participant, whose name was Paul, would be unable to continue. From my perspective, it seemed that he had exerted tremendous effort on the first day, pushing himself to his physical limits.

Sadly, Paul's race came to an end due to his crash. He went to a local hospital for scans and fortunately, was not badly injured. Later that evening, he returned to Dorney Lake and chatted to my crew giving them salt tablets for my use before departing for home. We were incredibly grateful for his generosity and made good use of the tablets.

Given the challenging nature of the event, it was my priority to ensure that my crew members took care of themselves and enjoyed the experience as much as possible.

I was thoroughly enjoying the weather and my spirit remained high. The swim portion of day two went exceptionally well. Surprisingly, my goggles, which had caused me trouble with fogging up during the first few strokes on day one, held up perfectly for the swim on day two. Although I occasionally had to stop and wipe them clear, at times the fog cleared on its own.

I still found myself without my TT bike and I was hoping that my crew could arrange to have it delivered to me at some point during the bike section. The bike was still at the local bike shop, undergoing repairs to replace the spokes on its back wheel but I was promised that it would be back with me very soon.

During the bike section, around halfway through, TC, the hot favourite, cycled up beside me. TC, whose real name is Anthony Gerundini, earned his nickname due to his love for Toyota Corollas. Prior to DecaUK, TC had already participated in various ultra endurance events, including a Quin (five Iron distance triathlons in 5 days) in 2011, where he emerged as the winner. The following year, TC entered the Deca, also organised by Enduroman and once again claimed victory. Not only is he a remarkable competitor, but TC is also known for his humility and his generosity in sharing advice.

I was eagerly anticipating meeting TC before travelling to England. Our email correspondences had proved invaluable, with his advice convincing me to enter DecaUK and his race tips helping me formulate my race plan. Just two weeks earlier, TC had achieved an incredible feat by winning a treble continuous Iron distance triathlon. This type of competitive triathlon combines the distances of three Ironmans into one race, including a 11.4k swim, a 540k bike and a 126k run. Astonishingly, TC had entered another race the weekend before the Deca. The level of dedication and accomplishment he demonstrated was truly awe-inspiring.

With a friendly gesture, TC rode up beside me. “Do I need to point out the obvious?” he asked. Curious, I responded, “What’s that?” TC then pointed out that my chain had no oil and that it was squeaking. I hadn’t noticed the noise, because I was wearing a thick hat under my helmet that muffled the sound. He advised me to pull over when I returned and apply some oil to the chain. Given TC’s experience and success, I knew it would be wise to follow his advice. I quickly applied oil to the chain and resumed my ride.

On the next lap, I was handed my TT bike, freshly tuned and in perfect condition with the exception of my back wheel which had been replaced with a spare wheel from Miriam’s road bike that I had brought along for spares. I swiftly swapped my back-up road bike for the rejuvenated time trial machine. The improvement was incredible.

Every morning I made sure to bring my phone along on the bike course to record a video log. I had two reasons for doing this. Firstly, I wanted to update everyone back home on my progress and how I was faring in the race. Secondly, I knew that as the days unfolded, I would forget much of what was happening, so I wanted to have this footage as a personal record. Typically, I would record the video after completing the first five laps, although occasionally I would forget my phone and record the vlog a bit later in the morning. After recording, I would post the video to my Facebook account. One day, on the vlog, I mentioned that I had applied oil to the bike and jokingly stated that it felt like having a motor attached. It was a light-hearted remark, but it served as a reminder of my sub-par bike maintenance skills.

During my training for the event, I had completed numerous miles on my bike, including a week of half distance triathlons and a week of full distance triathlons. Some of the bike rides during the second week even exceeded the standard 180k needed for a full iron distance triathlon, stretching up to 200k. Surprisingly, I had never experienced any issues with saddle sores, so it was disheartening to find myself dealing with very painful saddle sores during the full 180k ride on the second day of the event. Although it was uncomfortable, I tried my best not to let it distract me. On a pain scale of one to ten, I would have rated it at around six.

I successfully completed the marathon without encountering any issues. As I crossed the finish line, a new sense of possibility began to take shape in my mind. I contemplated ways to enhance my race times without exerting additional effort. With these ideas firmly in mind, I was eager to discuss them with the crew, who played a vital role in implementing our race strategy.

At the finish line, I was greeted by Paula and Paddy. I bent down to remove my timing chip and handed it to Paula who sprinted off like a hare towards the Race HQ, mistakenly believing that the race would only end once the timing chip was returned.

In her eagerness to return the timing chip, Paula sprinted past the organisers' tents, and tripped over one of the grounding wires of a tent falling face-first onto the ground. Quickly recovering, she flashed the chip at Paddy and me, wordlessly assuring us that she hadn't lost it and then turned and resumed her sprint towards the race HQ. Paddy and I couldn't help but burst into laughter, as these kinds of incidents were commonplace when Paula was around.

On day 2 of the Deca, Chris James, the gentleman I had met at the campsite on our arrival discovered that he had been locked out of his van, where his gear and bed were stored. His daughter had unintentionally taken the van keys home with her, leaving Chris without essential supplies and a place to sleep. Because of this, Chris's Deca attempt had come to an end.

It was some surprise then when Chris showed up the next day for the marathon on day 3. Instead of giving up, he had decided to take on a personal challenge of completing ten marathons in ten days. Despite the disappointment he faced, Chris took it in stride and tackled each day's marathon with a smile. He even arrived at the start of the marathon ahead of his own run, so he could cheer us on during the bike section. It was uplifting to see him there, not only for the support but also because when you saw him, you knew that the end of the bike section was approaching. Chris's indomitable spirit and positivity were truly inspiring.

Day 2	14 started - 13 finished			
Name	Total	Swim	Bike	Run
William Price	14:40:49	1:31:00	8:35:46	4:34:05
Anthony Gerundini	14:44:29	1:43:44	7:59:43	5:01:03
Graham Smedley	15:12:03	1:23:25	8:21:38	5:27:01
Tiernan Simmons	15:47:52	1:46:11	7:58:51	6:02:51
Dave Kershaw	15:51:00	1:34:57	8:31:51	5:44:13
Graeme Allan	15:52:40	1:42:35	8:11:00	5:59:06
Gerard Prendergast	16:00:25	1:19:59	9:14:45	5:25:42
Rob Duddington	16:02:00	1:14:58	9:00:07	5:46:57
Simon Jacob	16:29:54	1:19:59	9:05:00	6:04:55
Martin Curran	16:49:52	1:33:45	8:24:49	6:51:19
Chris James	16:50:29	1:47:33	8:46:28	6:16:29
Ziv Navon	16:57:27	1:31:25	8:49:13	6:36:50
Simon Bayman	17:25:38	1:32:21	8:14:54	7:38:25
Paul Machin	1:45:53	1:30:08	15:45:00	

Race Commentary

On day two of the event, Paul Machin became the first participant to withdraw from the race, choosing to stop after completing two laps on the bike course. The race favourite, TC (Anthony Gerundini), proved his prowess by securing first place with a remarkable twenty-six-minute lead over Graham Smedley, who was considered a strong contender for the overall win. Notably, Rob Duddington finished in eighth place, completing the course in sixteen hours and two minutes, the same time as Ger Prendergast's last-place finish on the previous day. Intriguingly, five other athletes finished with times longer than this.

Ger Prendergast experienced a significant jump from last place to mid-table in the standings, completing the race only two minutes faster than his finishing time on day one. This raises questions about the pacing strategies employed by some athletes on the first day. Perhaps Prendergast's mechanical issues on day one inadvertently served as a restraint, preventing him from making the same mistake. In hindsight, his last-place finish on the initial day may have been a blessing in disguise, enabling him to approach subsequent days with more caution and preserve his energy for improved results.

Friday 6th, October, 2017 - Day 3: Optimising Performance

Strategy

Upon completing day 2, I decided to change our strategy in order to finish the race earlier without exerting much additional effort. I realised that I had been sacrificing too much of my 'free time' or transition time and I wanted to find a way to minimise that.

In the previous two days, my strategy had been to complete five laps, take a break at the camper to refuel with the food prepared by my crew and then get back on the bike for another five laps. This pattern continued until I reached the required distance of 180k on the bike course. This approach was effective in showing respect to the course and distances, ensuring I could stay in the race until day 10. However, it was quite slow, which was acceptable for the ultimate goal of finishing. Yet, I believed I could improve upon it.

During a meeting with Gerry Duffy a week before the race, he had stressed the importance of continuously moving forward whenever possible. This idea resonated with me even before meeting Gerry, but hearing it from him reinforced my belief in its significance and I had been so motivated by this concept that I made it my motto months ago and had it printed on my custom cycling clothing. It was proudly displayed on my right arm: "Gotta Keep It Movin'." This motto was specially created for me by my brother-in-law Mick and became a constant reminder of the importance of pushing forward in every sense.

With newfound determination and Gerry's advice in mind, I decided to implement a revised strategy. I aimed to minimise my transition time and focus on maintaining a steady momentum throughout the race.

In addition to this, I would have my TT bike back for the full 180k, and I felt that with the combination of this and my new strategy, I could do much better.

To streamline my eating process, I instructed my support team to have my food ready and to hand it to me at the side of the road. I would not leave my bike and eat in the camper as I had done the first two days. Instead, I would stop my bike and put my feet on the ground while receiving the food, and then pedal off until the next food stop.

One of the food options that worked well for me was avocado on toast with Tamari sauce, a wheat-free soy sauce. The tamari sauce added a tasty touch. Another reliable choice was peanut butter and banana on either spelt or sourdough bread.

As for the run, I aimed to keep moving forward without causing excessive strain to my body by running for three minutes and then walking for two minutes.

Previously, I had run for five minutes and walked for one, but I wanted to be more cautious, considering that the run often causes the most physical impact on the body. By continuing the three-minute run and two-minute walk intervals that worked well on day two, I hoped to strike a balance between progressing and minimising potential damage. Additionally, I made the decision to avoid stopping at the end of each lap and instead keep a continuous rhythm. This strategy seemed promising and I believed it would give me a solid chance at achieving my goal.

Diary

In my morning vlog on day 3, I discussed how the swim went well overall, but I began to notice the effects of the cold during the last two laps. To combat this, I started using the neoprene gloves that I had purchased for kayaking during the next swim and for the remainder of the swims. During those final two laps, my fingers became numb and the lack of sensation and strength caused my baby and ring fingers to push backward against the water during each stroke. Normally, when swimming, your hands act as paddles, providing firm resistance in the water. However, with the loss of feeling and strength, my smaller two fingers were simply flailing as I attempted to propel my body forward. This resulted in reduced power and became another obstacle to overcome.

The combination of the cold water and the prolonged time spent on the bike likely contributed to the weakening of my hands. The cold had numbed my fingers, making it extremely difficult to achieve the necessary grip and propulsion in the water. This particular issue was just one of many challenges that I would encounter during the ten-day race. While it did impede my progress, it did not completely hinder my ability to finish.

The first two laps on the bike will forever be etched in my memory; they felt never-ending. I was in a terrible state, overcome with weakness and a complete lack of energy. In my vlog, I even described those initial laps as 'horrendous.' The energy supplement drink I had consumed on day one was still wreaking havoc on my stomach, causing significant concerns for both myself and my team.

To add to my discomfort, my saddle sore had escalated on the pain scale from a six to an excruciating eight. It posed an even greater challenge on this particular day.

However, as I pushed through and completed the first five laps on day three, I started to feel a glimmer of improvement. The sun had emerged, casting its warm glow upon Eton Dorney. The bike course took me through a picturesque nature reserve that was simply breathtaking. I had the pleasure of encountering various incredible creatures along the way, including kites, hawks, squirrels, pheasants, gees and more. At one point, my fellow competitor Graham Smedley spotted a deer and tried to point it out to me, but I'm unsure whether my partial blindness or his state of delirium was the reason I couldn't see it clearly.

Our new strategy, as previously mentioned, was a simple one: eat on the go. However, we still adhered to a block of five laps. The first lap was designated as a 'free' lap, meaning free from food, consuming nothing except a salt tablet on occasion to maintain balanced blood sodium levels.

During prolonged endurance events like marathons or any activity lasting over 3–4 hours, there is a risk of sodium levels in the blood dropping. When we sweat, we lose salt from our bodies and this can be visibly observed on our skin and clothing during training sessions, particularly on hot days. It becomes crucial to replenish sodium levels to ensure optimal bodily function. Athletes who neglect to replace sodium while hydrating solely with water run the risk of over-hydrating their bodies, leading to a condition called hyponatremia–characterised by dangerously low sodium levels. In severe cases, hyponatremia can result in brain swelling, seizures, or, in rare instances, fatality.

This is precisely why events like Ironman provide energy bars containing salt or items like salt-coated pretzels at aid stations. These sodium-rich options help athletes maintain proper electrolyte balance and mitigate the risks associated with hyponatremia.

During the designated 'free' lap, my main focus was to stay hydrated and maintain balanced electrolyte levels. I would make sure to consume water and salt during this time to prevent dehydration and support my body's needs. Additionally, I saw this lap as an opportunity for my digestive system to recuperate, allowing the previously eaten foods to be digested. Or at least give my digestive system a break.

For the first five laps on the bike, I had a specific routine. I would always drink the remaining half of my Savage Smoothie (the smoothie recipe is available in the section 'The Secret Recipes from DecaUK'), with the first half consumed before the swim. I preferred the smoothie to be thick in consistency, almost like wet cement but still pourable. After completing these five laps, I would hand over the blender beaker to my support crew and use the sixth lap as a rest lap to aid in digestion.

The next four rounds consisted of toast topped with avocado and a chargrilled aubergine pesto. To streamline the process, I initially pulled over at the side of the road to receive the toast from my crew. Then, while cycling, I would eat the toast, allowing me to continue moving forward even at a slower pace. This method proved to be more efficient, as I was still making progress while nourishing myself.

For the next set of five laps, I decided to incorporate soup into my nutrition plan. I had packed around 15 tins of organic soup specifically for this purpose. I had two flavours available: organic lentil soup and organic vegetable soup. To make it more convenient for consumption while cycling, I asked my support team to blend the soup after heating it. This way, I could easily drink it like a hot beverage without the need to stop during the next five laps. Additionally, the blended soup required less digestion, allowing my digestive system to rest and reducing the amount of blood needed for digestion. As a result, I could conserve energy. Compared to the food stops, which required me to slow down and consume the food at a reduced pace, using the soup in a beaker allowed me to maintain my stride. I simply had to reach for the beaker from the bottle cage that is usually used to hold a cyclist's water bottle, take a sip of the highly nutritious soup and place it back in the cage, the same way a cyclist would for a bottle of water. This practice could be applied to any long ride and the soup could even be taken cold if desired. Similarly, this approach could be extended to include other wet meals like curries or dhals, providing a practical and efficient way to fuel during cycling.

The crew also incorporated spinach into the soup at my request to enhance its nutritional value. The soup was served in a 700ml beaker, which proved to be more than sufficient in keeping me energised and satisfied for the entire five laps, lasting approximately an hour.

After completing the soup round, we generally switched back to having avocado on toast with Tamari sauce for the next five laps. Tamari sauce, being a soy sauce without wheat, was an excellent source of sodium and worked perfectly for the event. Seeking some variety, I opted for a change from savoury to sweet. It was crucial to avoid monotony in my diet and having something sweet to look forward to provided an extra boost. I had brought boxes of Nakd and TREK bars from my local Tesco in Dublin, as I didn't expect to find them near Dorney Lake. However, I was pleasantly surprised to discover a Tesco supermarket just ten minutes away from our location that also stocked the same bars. Prior to the race, I had been informed that there was only a local Sainsbury's nearby, so I packed as much food as possible based on that information.

The bars are made exclusively from dates and nuts, without any artificial sugars or sweeteners. I always prefer using them at home, unless I opt for making my own homemade version. These bars are simply created by pressing together all the natural ingredients. In terms of nutritional value, they surpass random cereal bars as they lack added sugars. Notably, Nakd bars not only taste delicious, but they also feel like proper food. Unlike artificial sugars that provide an immediate energy boost that quickly diminishes, the natural sugars in these bars offer a more gradual release of energy, avoiding a subsequent crash. As a vegan-friendly option, these bars are highly appealing to me.

By 2pm, the race organiser's provided meals would arrive at race HQ for crew members to collect for their athletes. Before the event, Claire Smith had sent out a form to gather information on athletes' nutrition requirements. As a vegan, I had mentioned my dietary needs, although I didn't have high expectations for the race crew to provide vegan meals. I knew from past experiences that finding suitable food options outside of home can be challenging, as many people are not well-versed in veganism. To ensure I was covered, I brought a significant amount of my own food. However, to my surprise, I was handed some delicious and healthy vegan options. The dinners included dishes like rice, couscous, chickpea salad and baked potatoes. One day, they even served me Linda McCartney sausages, which I had never tried before. Despite my hunger at the time, I didn't bother asking what they were; I simply devoured them because they were incredibly tasty. Normally, I don't consume many processed foods, but on that particular day, they hit the spot. I had a fun exchange with Justin, one of the race organising crew members, who had delivered the food. He was a big guy with a thick Devon accent and he jokingly referred to the Linda McCartney sausages as "Ooohh Linda McCartneys," which sparked some banter between us. He even playfully named my smoothies and soups "Linda McCartney milkshakes."

Initially, the plan was for Paula and Paddy to stay for three days, covering the day before the event, the first full day and leaving in the evening of the second race day. They had booked a flight that coincided with the time I would be running the marathon on the second day. Consequently, I would be on my own for most of the race on day 3, until my brother Kevin was scheduled to arrive later in the day. I knew this would pose a significant challenge, as I would have to take care of my recovery, prepare my own food, get my bed ready, organise my clothing and supplies for the following day and handle all the other tasks that the crew had been assisting me with. Additionally, I would have to muster the motivation to get out of bed and put on my wetsuit for the cold immersion on the morning of day three.

Luckily, Paula was able to secure time off from work. Surprisingly, my brother Kevin arrived earlier than I had anticipated. Kevin is a highly skilled osteopath based at Barney Flannery's clinic in Drogheda. Known for his direct and professional approach, Kevin brought his expertise and experience from the clinic to our crew. He is so good at what he does that I willingly drive for two hours for a session with him at his clinic.

As soon as Kevin arrived, he wasted no time in diving into action. He called me into our gazebo, located beside the camper, for some quick stretching and spinal manipulations. The immediate benefits were incredible, and I felt a significant reduction in overall body stiffness.

Later that day, my sister-in-law, Linda, joined us. She is a passionate sports enthusiast, actively participating in GAA and attending my fitness classes. With a strong passion for soccer, she never misses a home or away match of St. Patrick's Athletic Football Club during the Irish League season. Linda has also successfully completed a couple of marathons, including the Dublin City Marathon. With Kevin and Linda added to the existing crew, we formed an unbeatable team.

During their presence, our pit stops became like those of an F1 racing team—quick and efficient. At times, I jokingly compared myself to Marvel's Ironman, as I would simply walk into the transition area after completing a section of the race and stand there while the crew effortlessly dressed me in the appropriate clothing for the next section, whether it be for biking or running. Everything was taken care of by the crew and all I had to do was walk into the changing area in our gazebo, stand still and within a minute or two, I would be fully dressed and ready to go for the next leg of the race.

The night run followed a similar pattern; the pit stops for refuelling were executed with efficiency and effectiveness. I stuck to my strategy of running for three minutes and then walking for two minutes.

During the marathon section on day one, I initially followed a pattern of running for five minutes and walking for one minute. The brief walk breaks were intended to relieve some pressure on my legs and allow them to recover momentarily. However, I began to feel that this approach didn't fully respect the event. So, I made a switch from running consistently for five minutes and only slowing down for one minute to running for three minutes and slowing down for two minutes instead. By implementing this new strategy and pacing myself, I would finish the marathon in a longer time, but it would put less strain and stress on my body. I believed I could sustain this strategy for the remaining days of the ten-day event, but as I would soon discover, that wasn't exactly the case.

As I approached my fifth lap, darkness was descending. I was running towards TC, who was headed in the opposite direction back to the far turnaround point. "Hey bud!" I greeted him. In a playful manner, he responded, "Don't you bud me, you fucking Dark Horse," while giving me a high five. It was an incredible boost to receive recognition from someone like TC, whom I deeply respected and admired.

After a gruelling fifteen hours of swimming, cycling and running, I unexpectedly crossed the finish line in first place. It was an astonishing achievement, considering my primary goal was still to reach the end of the ten-day event. I couldn't believe that I had surpassed some amazing endurance athletes. Notably, my finishing time was a whole hour faster than both day one and day two, with the majority of that time gained during the bike segment thanks to our new strategy.

I didn't have much time to celebrate. My focus immediately shifted to preparing my mind and body for the challenges of the following day. Following my customary recovery routine, I stood in the cold water of the lake up to my hips to aid in my recovery. I then received a quick massage back at the campsite, took a hot shower and made sure to fuel my body with nourishing food. Finally, it was time to climb up the ladder into my bunk bed. Since we returned to the campsite earlier on day three, I had a bit more time to complete these essential recovery tasks.

Day 3				
Name	**Total**	**Swim**	**Bike**	**Run**
Gerard Prendergast	15:00:01	1:17:54	8:24:45	5:17:23
Dave Kershaw	15:43:08	1:33:59	8:14:30	5:54:39
Rob Duddington	15:47:52	1:11:56	8:45:13	5:50:44
Graham Smedley	15:53:16	1:19:39	8:35:58	5:57:40
Anthony Gerundini	16:18:51	1:44:49	8:57:36	5:36:27
Tiernan Simmons	16:54:24	1:40:39	7:50:32	7:23:14
Martin Curran	17:04:19	1:28:31	8:12:05	7:23:44
Graeme Allan	17:07:17	1:42:57	8:52:08	6:32:12
Simon Jacob	17:17:44	1:20:07	9:05:26	6:52:12
Ziv Navon	17:24:52	1:22:19	8:36:54	7:25:40
William Price (Retired after bike lap 23)	9:21:19	1:21:58	7:59:22	0:00:00

Race Commentary

There has been a major shake-up in the leaderboard after day three of the event. Ger Prendergast emerged as the victor, finishing a remarkable forty-three minutes ahead of the second-place contender, attributing his success to a 'change in strategy.' Joining him on the podium are Dave Kershaw in second place and Rob Duddington in third, both representing the UK. Duddington continues to excel, consistently leading the pack out of the lake and on the bike course.

However, there are notable absences in the race, as Chris James and Simon Bayman did not participate on day three, thinning out the field of athletes. Unfortunately, another competitor, William Price, decided to call it quits after enduring twenty-three gruelling laps on the bike course.

Interestingly, the presumed favourite, TC, has dropped down to fifth place, reminding us that even the best can face challenges. With Gerundini showcasing patience, has Prendergast discovered a winning rhythm and strategy to dominate the event? The question now is whether Graham Smedley will stage a comeback and reclaim his position.

Saturday 7th, October, 2017 - Day 4: Fine-tuning the Strategy

Strategy

After the successful day three, my aim was to carry on in the same manner. We had implemented effective strategies on the bike, but I believed there was room for improvement. While stopping to grab food from the guys didn't waste much time, it disrupted our momentum and required more energy to restart from a standstill. So, I suggested a change to the team. I asked them to have the food ready for me as I passed by, allowing me to grab it on the go. This small tactic would help conserve energy and maintain our momentum.

My plan was that as I cycled by, my team would hand me half of the toast, typically using my left hand since they lined up on the left side of the road and I would continue cycling while eating. This allowed me to slow down slightly while eating, all the while making progress. After finishing the toast, I would increase my pace to complete the lap, return to the camper and crew and repeat this process for three more laps. For the fifth lap, I decided not to eat but instead focused on hydrating by drinking water, electrolytes, or taking a salt tablet. I believed this strategy would work well, but I knew that putting it into action was the only way to find out for sure.

At this point, Graham Smedley was leading the overall race. Graham was a highly accomplished athlete who had previously won the endurance triathlon, Enduroman Treble, in the UK. Recognising his superior experience, I decided not to engage in a head-to-head race with him. Racing against Graham would only decrease my chances of finishing the event. Instead, my plan was to remain consistent and focus on my own performance.

Diary

Following the successful strategy change on day three, the rest of the field began to see me as a potential contender. However, the weather the next day was cold and wet, making the swim one of the coldest I had yet experienced. It was during this swim that I first came into contact with Simon Jacob. Simon was a strong swimmer, cyclist and runner and I believed he had great potential in the event.

Simon and I were both strong swimmers, which meant that we often found ourselves swimming near each other in the lake. While we hadn't spoken yet, I could always spot him in the yellow swim hat, always in close proximity to me.

On day four, I found myself just behind Simon at one point and made an effort to overtake him. However, after passing Simon he stayed close to me by swimming in my slip stream. No matter how much effort I put into pulling away from him, I realised that he was right behind me. It seemed that we had both realised that trying to overtake or lose each other was only wasting precious energy.

We emerged from the lake seconds apart and I felt the immense effort I had put into the swim that day trying to distance myself from Simon. It was a challenging experience that I didn't want to find myself in again.

I started the bike course in a haze of rain. It was a cold and damp day, but I had prepared myself by wearing several layers of clothing. The plan remained the same - stick to the food strategy and maintain consistent lap times. Although I didn't use a watch to time my laps, I had made a conscious decision before day one not to let data control my pace. Instead, I relied on my own instincts and intuition. I focused on how my body felt and adjusted my pace accordingly.

To gauge my effort level, I used the concept of RPE, or rate of perceived effort. On a scale of one to ten, with one representing the easiest effort and ten indicating maximum exertion, I aimed to work at around five or six on the scale. This meant maintaining a moderate and challenging pace that pushed me just enough without exhausting myself.

During my training sessions, I experienced various issues with my GPS watches and I didn't want these distractions to affect me during the race. Additionally, I wanted to have the flexibility to adjust my pacing as needed. If I felt tired or unwell at any point during the ten days of the race, I didn't want the pressure of adhering to a specific pace dictated by a watch.

I did find one useful function on my Casio G-shock watch. I used the stopwatch feature to time my 3-minute runs and 2-minute walks during the marathon section of the race. In general, though, I had discovered that using data watches had a negative impact on me. Every time I wore one, I would try to run faster than my previous session, without considering whether I might be fatigued or not feeling my best. It also served as a constant distraction, since I would find myself checking my speed, distance and constantly calculating how much further or faster I needed to go. Overall, I felt that relying on data watches hindered my performance rather than improving it at ultra events.

In a conversation with my new friend Martin Curran from Scotland, he confidently said to me, 'If you just keep doing what you did yesterday, you're going to win it.' I appreciated his encouragement and replied, 'It was a good day, but there's still a long way to go. Right now, I just want to focus on finishing.' And it was the truth. My main goal was to complete the 10-day event and proudly call myself a Deca finisher. However, there were numerous challenges and obstacles that awaited me before that dream could become a reality.

Martin had a mental strategy that involved ticking a box for each section he completed every day. He had three boxes to tick daily, amounting to 30 boxes overall. I thought it was an excellent approach, but the sheer number of stages still seemed overwhelming. Personally, I preferred to take it one lap at a time, whether it was in the swim, bike, or run. This allowed me to stay focused and fully present in each moment without getting ahead of myself.

As I transitioned to the run course, the sun shone brightly and there was a calmness in the air as the wind seemed to have disappeared. To keep me company and provide support, I had Linda ride alongside me on one of the two yellow fold-up bikes I had brought for the crew.

To my surprise, I completed a full lap of the run course before crossing paths with any of the other competitors. Graham Smedley had completed the bike leg before me, indicating that he had likely taken a brief break. With no issues to speak of, I continued ticking off the laps during the run. In hindsight, I realised that it would have been a better choice to run on the grass beside the asphalt road, whenever possible. However, I had made the decision from day one to run on the asphalt surface. My reasoning was that all my training had been done on a 500m asphalt loop around the school where my gym is located. I believed that this would have provided me with enough resilience and strength to complete all the run sections at Dorney Lake on a similar surface, even though I was aware of the option to run on grass. My issue with running on the grass was that I felt sluggish and slow anytime I did run on grass so I wanted to avoid that. However, the benefit of running on grass is that it is softer and less harsh on your muscles and joints.

The final two laps of the day proved to be a significant challenge due to digestive issues. The endurance drink I had used on day one continued to affect me, causing discomfort and affecting my performance. I had not been able to have a proper bowel movement for a couple of days and the situation was becoming more concerning. Normally, at home, I would have been on the toilet like clockwork right after my morning cup of tea. This new experience left me feeling worried and out-of-sorts.

Despite the pain and struggle, I pushed through, running and hunching over as the discomfort increased. My main focus was to complete those final two laps. Time seemed to move at a snail's pace, but I persisted, putting one foot in front of the other, determined to reach the finish line. Finally, the moment arrived and I crossed the finish line, overwhelmed with relief and happiness. Finishing the race meant that I could finally begin my post-race routine and address my physical challenges.

After finishing day four in second place, behind Graham Smedley, we began with our nightly routine. I spent ten minutes in the cold lake, which helped with my recovery. We then drove back to the campsite, where I enjoyed a hot shower. Whoever was available, in this case, it was Kev, provided a much-needed rubdown to ease any muscle tension or soreness. Finally, I settled into bed to rest. Despite the physical exertion, I didn't feel a strong desire to eat. Although it probably would have been beneficial, my exhaustion and ongoing stomach troubles made the thought of eating unappealing. However, I remained confident in our nutrition plan, which had proved effective throughout the early mornings.

Day 4				
Name	Total	Swim	Bike	Run
Graham Smedley	14:48:31	1:19:20	8:00:57	5:28:14
Gerard Prendergast	14:58:34	1:16:00	8:44:32	4:58:03
Dave Kershaw	16:11:19	1:29:40	8:48:19	5:53:21
Rob Duddington	16:37:13	1:08:08	9:46:10	5:42:57
Anthony Gerundini	17:02:20	1:46:33	9:45:56	5:29:52
Simon Jacob	17:29:18	1:15:52	9:21:18	6:52:09
Graeme Allan	17:47:02	1:38:55	8:32:54	7:35:14
Ziv Navon	17:48:13	1:26:58	9:02:04	7:19:12
Martin Curran	20:48:55	1:26:56	9:07:27	10:14:32
Tiernan Simmons (Retired after bike lap 16)	6:08:06	1:40:58	4:27:08	0:00:00

Race Commentary

On day four, all athletes who completed day three were present at the lake. Graham Smedley made a comeback, securing his position as the overall leader. Ger Prendergast finished ten minutes behind Graham in second place, while Dave Kershaw had another strong performance, coming in third. Former Deca winner TC finished in fifth place once again, making his chances of another Deca win seem increasingly unlikely with each passing day. The question remains: is TC waiting for the opportune moment to strike on day five? However, this strategy carries a risk as he continues to lose time to the leaders. Initially, the other competitors thought he was being conservative, but now they sense an opportunity as his times slow down and their leads expand. Unfortunately, Tiernan Simmons, also known as T, had to end his Deca aspirations during the bike course. The event is becoming even more unforgiving and we wonder who will be the next to face its challenges. Will Graham Smedley continue to push for victory? Can Ger Prendergast answer back on day five? Or will Dave Kershaw aim for the top spot?

Sunday 8th, October, 2017 - Day 5: Small Victories

Strategy

On day five, our strategy was to replicate the tactics from day three and four. However, as the day unfolded, we discovered some clever tricks to enhance our efficiency. While heading towards the lake just before the swim started, I came up with a strategy to improve efficiency. I approached Simon while we stood in the lake just before the start and proposed that we take turns drafting off each other for two laps each. This way, one of us would have the opportunity to take a break and conserve energy while benefiting from the drafting and then we would switch roles for the next two laps. We planned to repeat this cycle until we completed the eight-lap course. Considering that drafting is allowed in the triathlon swim, it seemed like a smart move to take advantage of this opportunity.

Diary

TC had started the swim late and after a few laps, he began to suffer from the cold due to a rip in his wetsuit. He had been dealing with this since day one so the negative effects from this would have accumulated over the previous four days. A wetsuit is designed to function as an artificial layer of skin, allowing a small amount of water to enter and be heated by the body's natural warmth. The wetsuit then traps and retains this warm water while preventing any additional cold water from entering. Unfortunately, with a rip in his wetsuit like TC experienced, too much water had entered, preventing his body from properly heating it. Despite the challenge, TC got back into the lake and completed the swim. However, it took him nearly two and a half hours to finish.

In the days leading up to the fifth day, I had been dealing with the distress of unresolved stomach issues. I was unable to have a bowel movement, which caused both physical discomfort and heightened stress for me. At times, the pain was so intense that I found myself hunched over, and it was a completely unfamiliar and worrisome situation.

My crew members were aware of the problem and had been trying various solutions over the past few days, including orange juice, Rennie tablets and other medications and foods. However, nothing seemed to alleviate the issue.

On the morning of the fifth triathlon, I finally felt the urgent need to use the toilet. We had an agreement amongst ourselves that nobody would use the camper toilet out of courtesy to the others sleeping in it. So, I quickly dashed to the toilets at the race headquarters.

When I returned to the campervan, there was a smile on my face. Linda noticed my expression and asked, "What are you smiling about?" I couldn't contain my excitement and shared the news with her and the rest of the crew. "I did it, I just went number two" I announced. To my surprise, they all cheered and celebrated this seemingly small victory. It was the first time I could recall being celebrated for something as basic as having a bowel movement. It felt like a collective moment of joy for our crew, considering the previous worry and concern surrounding this issue. Little did we know that there would be more obstacles for us to overcome on this challenging journey.

After the intense swimming race with Simon on day four, I decided not to exert as much energy in the lake on day five. It must have appeared to the spectators that we had a plan to draft off each other on day four, because before the swim started on day five, there was a surprising announcement made by Paul, the chief medic and crew member of the race organising team. He declared, 'There's to be no drafting on the swim.' Instantly, I sensed that it was directed at me and Simon. It felt like someone was closely monitoring our every move.

Though I didn't voice my thoughts, other athletes joined in, questioning the announcement since drafting is permitted during the triathlon swim section. It is during the bike section that drafting is not allowed. Claire Smith spoke up, approaching Paul to remind him that the rules clearly state that drafting is legal in the swim. Consequently, the announcement was revised to "No drafting on the bike."

On day four, Simon and I were competing against each other in the lake rather than working together. The announcement before day five's swim gave me the motivation to propose a partnership with Simon in order to conserve energy. As

thatcameraman.com

we walked into the lake to prepare for the swim start, I turned to Simon and asked, "Do you want to share laps? You do two, then I'll do two and see how it goes."
"Let's do it," he replied and we agreed to collaborate for the swim.
My ultimate goal was to reach day ten in one piece, if possible. If sharing a few swim laps could save even a minuscule amount of energy, it was a strategy I was willing to employ.
Starting from day five, Simon and I implemented our strategy of sharing laps in the swim. I would swim for two laps while Simon drafted off me and then we would switch roles without interrupting our strokes. While it was clear that drafting was allowed in the swim section of the race, we sensed some discontent among other athletes and their teams.
Our crew members relayed information about this dissatisfaction back to us athletes. Despite that, the swim portion went smoothly and I felt better physically compared to the previous four days when emerging from the lake. The invigorating powers of the cold, crystal-clear water seemed to revitalise me and I noticed that the lake didn't feel as cold as it had in previous days. It's possible that this was due to the effects of wearing my long-sleeved neoprene top underneath my wetsuit. This 1 mm thick, round-necked neoprene top was designed to provide extra insulation. I had chosen not to wear it during the first two days, wanting to experience its benefits during the latter stages of the race. However, after a conversation with TC, I decided to wear it every day.
By day five, our bike plan had really come together and I found my rhythm. To refine the plan even more, I decided to bring a beaker of soup with me for the next four laps. This allowed me to feed myself without the need to stop or slow down. Similarly, I had hydration bottles in bike cages for the duration of the cycle.
When it came to taking salt tablets, we devised a new strategy. Again, instead of stopping, I would try to grab a salt tablet as I cycled past. I would hold it in my hand and quickly swallow it while maintaining my pace. We were constantly coming up with creative ideas to improve our efficiency and speed. We even started joking around with silly concepts to keep the mood light. On one lap, I shouted to the guys, 'Can I have a salt tablet on my next round, please?' Their response was, 'Sure, no problem.' So I jokingly added, 'Just pop a few in a slingshot and shoot them at my face. Whatever sticks, I'll take!' As I raced by on my bike, I could hear the laughter behind me.
We were having a great time and I knew that this lighthearted approach would work in our favour. While the other competitors might be physically exhausted and worn out, we were laughing and enjoying ourselves. I was conscious that this positive mindset and camaraderie would give me a competitive advantage. So, despite the distress I was experiencing, I kept smiling, having fun and maintaining a positive attitude.
On the fifth day, I could feel a slight ache in my feet during the run. The asphalt from the previous four marathons had taken a toll on them. However, things

were off to a great start on this particular day. In my morning bike vlog, I discussed our efficient 'Formula 1 style pit stops,' or transitions from swimming to biking.

Kev and Linda were getting me in and out of transition quickly, stripping me down and dressing me up, while Paula made sure I had a quick energy boost by shoving spoonfuls of porridge down my throat. I couldn't help but laugh at their seriousness in performing these tasks. It gave me a tremendous boost, allowing me to get a couple of bike laps done before most of the other participants, except for Rob Duddington. Every morning, Rob would finish his swim and hop onto the bike just before me. For those couple of laps, Rob and I dominated the bike course.

Rob had a strategy similar to mine. While my crew members did not have much experience with triathlons, Rob had someone on his team who had completed two Decas. I believed that my crew had a greater influence on my final results than his. We had an incredible spirit that was hard to beat and we always aimed to have an enjoyable time. In fact, one of our inside jokes was quoting a line from the Jim Carrey movie 'The Cable Guy,' saying, "I'm having a super time."

The time had come for the 'dream team' to part ways. Kev and Linda were set to return home for work the next day. Setting off on my second lap of the run, there was still plenty of daylight left and I found myself enjoying the run course all to myself. Before bidding their farewells, Linda had a surprise in store for me. She revealed that she would be coming back for the last two days of the event. Linda's passion for sports had truly taken hold. She became my eyes and ears on day five, keeping me updated on my position in the race and also on Graham Smedley's progress. At the beginning of day five, Graham was leading by two and a half hours. By the end of day five, I had managed to turn that two and a half hour deficit into a two and a half hour lead. It wasn't my specific goal, but I had stuck to my game plan of maintaining consistent bike laps and run laps, which ultimately led to this significant turnaround in the race.

I felt overjoyed as I entered the camper after completing the marathon. It had been a fantastic day, filled with positives. At the start of the day I was two and a half hours behind Graham Smedley in the overall standings but, in a remarkable turn of events, we managed to completely flip the script and now we were two and a half hours in front of Graham and his team. Not only had we taken a substantial lead, but I was also relieved that my recurring digestive issue did not bother me that night. My spirits were high and day five felt like a collective victory for the entire team. Having completed the swim, bike and run we then went through our post-race routine. For my massage, we decided to try something different by setting up the massage table in the shower block to save me from walking all the way to the tent. After taking a shower and getting dressed, wearing my thermal socks, woolly hat and rugby bench coat, I lay on the massage table facing upward with my right leg exposed ready to be massaged. However, something felt off–the bed seemed more unstable than usual. I found myself suddenly flipped and landing on the back of my neck on the hard floor of the shower block.

The massage table had not been properly secured when set up, leading to the unexpected accident. Despite the pain I was experiencing, a tired laugh escaped from my lips. I could see tears welling up in Paula's eyes, but as soon as she saw my reaction, she too burst into laughter.

Fortunately, no injuries were sustained and I managed to regain my footing on my own.

Climbing into bed, I discovered three hot water bottles nestled in my sleeping bag, providing a comforting warmth that was incredibly pleasant. I was instructed to check my phone for a video message from Gerry Duffy, the only other Irish man to have completed the Deca. Gerry had taken the time to send me a personal message, mentioning that he had been closely following my progress via the race results page online. He emphasised the immense amount of time and effort I had dedicated to training, reflecting on the countless hours, days, weeks and months of hard work that had earned me the right to be where I was. Gerry encouraged me to remember that every step I took from the next morning onward would bring me closer to the finish line. Signing off with his well wishes, he expressed his strong support and mentioned that he was truly rooting for me. I was overcome with a surge of emotions. It had been a fantastic day, with everything going our way and culminating in our fastest overall time for the race, with a finish time of 14:46:35.

Day 5				
Name	Total	Swim	Bike	Run
Gerard Prendergast	14:46:35	1:14:40	8:21:03	5:10:53
Dave Kershaw	16:23:33	1:29:47	8:42:04	6:11:44
Rob Duddington	16:33:13	1:08:59	9:21:22	6:02:53
Simon Jacob	17:50:24	1:14:35	9:28:57	7:06:53
Graeme Allan (DNS Day 6)	19:02:22	1:39:34	9:44:30	7:38:20
Anthony Gerundini(DNS Day 6)	19:07:25	2:44:41	11:08:52	5:13:53
Martin Curran	20.04.33	1:29:06	9:08:14	9:27:14
Graham Smedley	20:25:13	1:20:28	9:06:20	9:58:26
Ziv Navon (DNS Day 6)	22:27:10	1:29:09	10:38:42	10:19:20

Race Commentary

Once again, all the athletes who had successfully completed day four gathered at the lake to commence day five of the event. Ger Prendergast demonstrated exceptional strength and determination, securing a well-deserved victory with an impressive time of 14 hours and 46 minutes.

His outstanding performance positioned him a staggering 1 hour and 37 minutes ahead of Dave Kershaw, solidifying his dominant position at the midway point of the overall competition.

Meanwhile, Rob Duddington quietly maintained his consistent performance and secured another podium finish.

However, the hopes of Graham Smedley, who had been vying for the overall title, were dealt a significant blow as he finished over five hours behind Prendergast. The pre-race favourite, TC, crossed the finish line in sixth place, leaving doubts about his strategy. Is TC too far behind to mount a comeback? Or is he strategically waiting for the second half of the event to make his move? Can Smedley recover from his devastating fifth day and regain his competitive edge, or has injury dashed his hopes of winning?

With these uncertainties lingering, all eyes are on Prendergast as he continues to assert his dominance and maintain his lead at the top of the leaderboard. The second half of the competition promises to be filled with anticipation and excitement.

Monday 9th, October, 2017 - Day 6: Surprising Revelations

Strategy

By day 6, we had developed a new tactic. I asked the team to add a portion of dinner into a child's plastic cup that fit perfectly in my hand.

This allowed me to still hold onto the handlebars with my right hand while holding the cup if necessary. As I cycled by, I would slow down to grab the cup, quickly consume the food as if it were a drink and then tuck the empty cup inside the collarbone area of my jersey then proceed to cycle the rest of the lap at a consistent speed.

On completing that lap, I would throw the empty cup back to the team and pick up another cup of food. My goal was to finish cycling earlier in order to maximise the time available for more running laps in daylight.

Diary

When I arrived at the lake on day six, I noticed that TC was missing. It wasn't unusual for him to arrive late to ultra races, so I didn't think much of it initially. During the bike section, I learned the reason behind his absence.

Martin Curran, informed me that TC had decided not to continue after he finished day five.

TC, who claimed to be a poor swimmer, struggled daily with the chilly lake temperature, not helped by the enormous tear in his wetsuit.

Although TC didn't start the swim, he still showed up to cheer on everyone. I was currently leading the race. Initially, I had believed that TC was patiently waiting for the other competitors to tire, so that he could surpass us all and take the lead. I felt a pang of sadness, as I respected him immensely. Nonetheless, a small part of me felt relieved that he wouldn't overtake me, which was quickly followed by guilt for harbouring such thoughts about a fellow competitor's exit from the event. That guilt soon shifted to concern for his well-being, since I knew TC was as resilient as they come and I thought it must have been something serious that forced him to withdraw from the race.

TC chose to stay for the rest of the event, offering support and encouragement to others instead of heading home. I found his decision remarkably courageous.

Day six introduced a new contender to the race, Dave Kershaw. Despite being thirty years old, Dave's gentle demeanour made him seem younger. Although his swimming was not particularly strong, I would often lap him in the water. However, beneath his unassuming exterior, Dave possessed a hidden toughness and competitiveness. One fascinating fact I discovered during our numerous con-

thatcameraman.com

versations was that he had successfully swum the English Channel. This achievement demonstrated just how resilient and unafraid of challenges Dave truly was. Furthermore, Dave's physical presence was also impressive, weighing over 16 stone and possessing a solid build, making him a force to be reckoned with on the bike. While he struggled slightly with the marathons due to his larger frame, Dave's unwavering determination allowed him to overcome these obstacles and complete them.

As Dave and I crossed paths during the run, he would comment, "You beat me again on the bike, Gerard." I could sense his surprise and perhaps even a hint of frustration, with each instance. Despite not considering myself a strong cyclist and feeling like the weakest among the participants, I reminded myself of my strategic approach. I maintained a consistent pace throughout each lap, avoiding the temptation to exert excessive energy by pushing the pedals forcefully. Meanwhile, I observed Dave and some others putting significant power into their pedalling, overtaking me in the process. However, as the race progressed, I would calmly sail past them using the same cadence and effort as I had been all day. I strongly believe that my nutrition plan played a crucial role in allowing me to sustain my pace and performance.

There was a peculiar atmosphere on day six of the race. It was Monday and competitors in the quin, quad, treble, double and single events had concluded their races. This meant that only the Deca athletes remained, totalling six individuals. Moreover, the finish rate for the other races had been disappointingly low, with few managing to complete their races. In the Quin event, three participants had entered, but none had finished. Furthermore, only one competitor had entered the triple event, and did not finish. As for the double Iron distance race, seven people had entered, but only three completed it. Lastly, in the single Iron distance event, three individuals initially entered, but only one managed to cross the finish line. The perplexing element was that the course, on paper, appeared to be flat and easily manageable. Why was the course so unexpectedly tough and slow?

On paper, the course seemed perfect. It was mostly flat, the tarmac was relatively smooth, with only a few rough patches on the bike section. Personally, I found the loop structure quite favourable, because it worked well with my nutrition plan. Some of my fellow competitors believed that the marathon loops were excessively long, although I didn't quite agree with that sentiment.

I do have a theory as to why the bike course ended up being much slower than expected. Analysing the times after the event concluded, it became clear that the bike leg took significantly longer than what is considered a decent bike split for a single-day iron distance race. Spending nine hours on a bike is two to three hours longer than the usual time it takes to cover such a distance. Although we were aware that we were maintaining a slower pace throughout the event, this discrepancy was still substantial. I believe the reason behind the slower pace lies in the sharp turnaround points along the course.

As we approached the far end of the course and reached the turnaround point, there was a short downhill slope that provided some relief. Although, we had to slow down to safely navigate the turn. This required us to decelerate for approximately 50 to 100 metres before making the turn. Although the downslope was brief and only lasted about 50 metres, it necessitated a significant reduction in speed as we approached the turnaround point.

This slow and disruptive process was repeated approximately seventy-six times over the course of thirty-eight laps, including the additional turn at the HQ end, which was slightly faster due to its less tight nature.

On the other hand, the run portion of the race was intentionally slow. Attempting to run at a sub-four hour marathon pace would significantly strain your body, hindering its ability to recover for the following day's events. Over the course of the ten days, your body would endure immense trauma, a sensation only truly understood by those who have experienced it.

There was a change in the crew on day 6 as my friend, Chris Fitzpatrick, who had previously supported me in The Race in Donegal, arrived to assist. Paula, who had been part of the crew, was exhausted from the past few days and needed to rest. As soon as Chris arrived, he had to manage things on his own, allowing Paula to get some well earned rest.

I had to stop cycling to explain our lap strategy to Chris myself, but I could only do so in small bits each time I passed for a lap. This arrangement didn't work as effectively as we had hoped and caused some stress. It was nobody's fault; it was simply the situation we found ourselves in. As a result, we lost around forty minutes on the bike, which was not a significant setback considering the lead we had already built up. I was aware of our lead, but it hadn't crossed my mind when I stopped to plan and discuss strategy with Chris in detail. I distinctly recall our first exchange at Eton Dorney, where Chris asked, "What's it like? Hard?" to which I confidently replied, "Man, this is easy." Little did I know that everything was about to change.

Halfway through the marathon, I started experiencing some discomfort in my hip and noticed tightness developing in my left tensor fasciae latae (TFL), which is a long tendon that runs from the outside of the hip to the outside of the knee. This area is prone to tightening up in runners and often contributes to a common injury known as 'Runner's knee.' Stretching this tendon can be challenging since it's not a muscle and doesn't respond to stretching as readily.

Foam rolling is a beneficial technique for addressing tightness around the TFL area, although it's important to avoid directly rolling over the tendon itself. Similar to stretching, direct pressure on the tendon can be extremely painful. In essence, foam rolling involves using a cylindrical hollow object, typically covered in a soft foam layer, for self-massage. These foam rollers come in various sizes and some are designed with grooves and nodules to help break down scar tissue and release tightness in the muscles. Foam rolling can be performed

on various parts of the body, offering relief and relaxation. Personally, I enjoy foam rolling, particularly on my quadriceps, as it provides a great release in that specific area.
Although I had to adjust my running pace to accommodate the hip pain and tightness in my TFL, we successfully completed the marathon leg with no significant issues. The expected soreness in my legs was present, as I had anticipated. I reassured myself and the crew that it was all part of the journey.
After finishing the run, I proceeded with my nightly cryotherapy session in the lake, providing some relief to my fatigued muscles. Once we returned to the campsite, I indulged in a hot shower to soothe my body, followed by a quick rub on my calves and quads to aid in recovery. Paula made sure that the plinth, which had caused some mishaps the previous night, was set up correctly. Feeling optimistic and satisfied with our performance, I went to bed, looking forward to waking up for day seven of the race.

Day 6				
Name	Total	Swim	Bike	Run
Gerard Prendergast	15:41:22	1:14:43	9:01:56	5:24:43
Dave Kershaw	16:34:26	1:29:41	9:06:01	5:58:45
Rob Duddington	16:35:32	1:07:29	9:30:24	5:57:40
Simon Jacob	18:43:06	1:14:45	10:27:49	7:00:33
Martin Curran	20:30:45	1:36:50	9:28:19	9:25:37
Graham Smedley	20:30:45	1:25:04	10:12:08	8:53:34

Race Commentary

Following the completion of day five at Eton Dorney, only six athletes remain in the event. To everyone's surprise, Ziv Navon, Graeme Allan and TC (Anthony Gerundini) did not join the competition on the morning of day six. As for Ger Prendergast, he once again dominated, achieving the fastest bike split and run split of the day.
Unfortunately, Graham Smedley's chances of winning the title now appear to be slim after finishing last alongside Martin Curran. Despite facing overwhelming adversity due to injuries they picked up, these two warriors continue to press on. Their finishing times grant them a three and a half-hour window from the day six finish line to plunge into the cold waters of the lake on day seven and begin the arduous challenge of completing an iron distance triathlon once more.
The pressing question remains: Can Smedley and Curran summon the physical

and mental strength to reach the start of day seven in time? Additionally, has the competition now turned into a two-horse race between Prendergast and Kershaw? Or could Rob Duddington manage to gain ground on the front-runners in the up-coming days?

Tuesday 10th, October, 2017 - Day 7: Embracing Grit

Strategy

I was pleased with how our bike strategy had developed since day one. My legs had endured a lot of stress over the past six days, so I knew I needed to adjust my running strategy.

Instead of sticking to a fixed interval, I modified the length of time I ran and focused more on how my legs felt. I would run when they felt good and walk when they needed rest. Using the six bridges on the course as markers, I chose to walk up the inclines of each bridge, knowing that the added gradient would only increase the strain. Whether running towards the turnaround point at the end of the lake or heading back towards HQ, I maintained this walking pattern. I only resumed running once I reached a flat surface.

Also, realising the importance of convenience and comfort, we decided to relocate the camper closer to the start/finish line of the run section. This allowed me to reach the camper easily for eating, changing clothes and a bit of comfort, after completing any of the run laps.

Diary

My performance on day seven may have been my slowest according to the finishing time chart, only forty minutes slower than before, although there's more to the story than meets the eye. Surprisingly, my swim was actually my best swim time throughout the ten days and my bike time was nearly ten minutes faster than the previous day.

Both the swim and the bike sections passed without any cause for concern. However, towards the end of the bike section, I started feeling discomfort in my quads. Despite this, I didn't allow it to affect my mindset too much. Chris, who had turned out to be an amazing addition to the team, assisted me in stretching my glutes and quads before I began the run. At this point, my friend Ciaran had joined us and immediately got to work. Together, Chris and Ciaran formed a great team.

As we started the run, I was well aware that it would be a struggle. The pain in my right quad, which had already bothered me slightly during the later part of the bike portion, was worsening. I persevered with my three-minute run strategy, which now resembled a limping effort, followed by a two-minute walk. Early on, I made the decision to try power walking in order to regain a few minutes.

As I reached the halfway point, the struggle became more intense. The pain had become unbearable and negative thoughts flooded my mind. Doubts like "What if I can't keep going?" "The pain is overpowering" and "How will I explain this if I have to quit?" consumed my thoughts.

After completing my sixth lap and returning to the start/finish line area, I knew that if I stopped for more than a few seconds, I might struggle to continue. So, without even pausing to communicate with any of the crew members, I simply rounded the cone at the start/finish line and pressed on.

"Do you want a drink or some food?" a voice called out from our camper. I couldn't even distinguish who it was, as I had my back turned at that moment, focused on embarking on my seventh lap. I just shook my head and kept going, determined to endure the pain and push forward.

As I persevered, my focus shifted to reaching the next bridge and then the one after that. However, the pain in my legs grew more intense, making it increasingly difficult to focus on anything else. The darkness engulfed the surroundings, accompanied by a strong gust of wind and heavy rain that intensified as time passed.

In an attempt to alleviate the continuous impact on my legs, I opted to run on the grass. My gait had transformed into a 'one-eye, zig-zag, zombie shuffle' as I struggled to maintain a steady and coordinated movement.

Approaching the bridge, exhaustion took its toll. Without warning, my legs gave way, causing me to collapse forward onto the wet and chilly grass beside the asphalt track. Kneeling on the grass while sitting on my heels, I hunched over with my face pressed against the ground. The excruciating pain in my legs and hips consumed my senses, while the damp surface instantly chilled my hands.

As I found myself on the ground, my initial relief that nobody was present to witness my fall. Reality quickly set in–I couldn't stay there for long as the harsh conditions posed a serious risk of hypothermia.

As the pain in my legs became unbearable tears welled up in my eyes. It was a sensation I had experienced before, reminding me of Donegal at The Race 2015. Memories flooded my mind, tempting me with the thought of surrender. I could easily return to the camper, inform the organisers that I was done and retreat to the comfort of my warm bed, allowing myself to sleep for days. The allure of this option was strong.

I contemplated the notion that reaching this point was an achievement in itself and therefore, there was no shame in quitting now. I imagined the sympathy I would receive in the coming days, with people reassuring me, "You've done so well to get this far," providing justification for my decision. Then again, my mind drifted back to The Race 2015 and the tumultuous emotions I experienced after withdrawing. I vividly remembered the frustration that shadowed me for the entire year until I finally conquered that challenge. A mere thirty minutes after pulling out, I found myself sitting in a café with Chris. We engaged in lighthearted banter, yet beneath the surface, regret gnawed at me. Even as we joked and laughed, the disappointment clung to me, a persistent whisper in the back of my mind. Those regrets became my relentless companions, haunting my thoughts and driving me to return with a fierce determination in 2016. It was as if a dark cloud had settled over my consciousness, constantly reminding me of my unfinished business and fueling my resolve to banish the anguish that had taken root within me.

As if all this was not torturing me enough, I suddenly heard the loud and profoundly irritating screaming noise of the geese in the lake, but it was like they were beside me shouting in my ears. "Are these geese laughing at me???" I thought. "Shut up, you arseholes!" I screamed at the geese as their laughter at my pain only seemed to intensify.

"Gotta keep it movin', gotta keep it movin'," I repeated Mick's motto in my head. It was emblazoned on the right arm of my customised kit, a constant reminder of the purpose behind my Deca challenge. "I am here to honour him," I reminded myself, "I need to get up and keep moving." But my legs felt completely depleted, aching and unresponsive.

Frustration and anger surged through me. "Get up, you fool! Don't let anyone see you like this," I scolded myself. Determined, I rose to my feet, pushing aside the pain and urged myself forward.

I managed to walk and limp for about 200 metres before my legs gave way once more, forcing me to collapse onto the grass. At that moment, it felt like my Deca journey was coming to an end.

Realising that I needed external assistance to push through this seemingly insurmountable obstacle, I knew exactly who to call.

With determination, I quickly regained my footing and reached for my phone. As I dialled the number, I started walking, knowing that I could cover a few hundred metres while engaged in conversation. The distraction would be a welcomed respite from the pain and solitude of the dark night.

I realised how isolated I was. There were no other runners in sight and my crew members were miles away in our camper. Thankfully, I still had my phone with me from earlier, when I recorded a vlog at the start of the run section. It was fortunate because I hadn't carried anything else with me during the previous days of running.

Amongst the darkness and solitude, there was one person whose voice I longed to hear—my wife, Miriam. I dialled her number and she answered, initially sounding happy to hear from me. Her tone quickly shifted to concern as I explained the challenging situation I found myself in.

I informed her of my belief that my race was over and that I was ready to give up. "Just reach the finish line tonight, take your time and assess how you feel then,"

Painting - Eamonn McEntee

she advised. Her words struck a chord, providing the reassurance I needed. She understood me better than anyone else - aware of my impulsive nature and tendency to be overly critical. This was precisely what I needed at that moment–to redirect my focus on getting back in the race. However, the pain I was experiencing made this a challenging task. "If I can just make it back to the camper," I encouraged myself, "I can take a break and allow my legs to recover."

After our conversation, Miriam immediately contacted Chris and Ciaran, who were waiting at the camper. Without wasting any time, they hopped on the fold-up bikes and pedalled towards the distant end of the run course, where they eventually came across me walking back towards the start/finish line. I shared my struggles and explained the situation to the guys. Thankfully, they had already devised a plan. Chris volunteered to cycle back and seek pain relief from the medic, who I hadn't needed until now, while Ciaran would accompany me on his bike as I continued walking towards the camper. Every now and then, I attempted to jog, but it only made the pain worse.

As we arrived back at the camper, the sight of Chris and the medic, Paul, my spirits. Paul assessed my situation and quickly handed me two Neurofen tablets, to be followed by two paracetamol after two hours and then another two Neurofen tablets two hours later. With a resilient mindset, I couldn't help but smile and say confidently, "I won't need that second round of two Neurofen. I'm determined not to stay out here for that much longer."

Feeling the effects of their support, I felt a surge of motivation. Their presence reminded me that I was not alone in this race. I was surrounded by a team that believed in me, willing to go the extra mile to ensure I could continue. It gave me strength to keep pushing forward, despite the pain that seemed to intensify with each step.

With renewed determination, I set my sights on the finish line, fully aware that the road ahead was not going to be easy. Armed with the support of my crew, I was ready to face the challenge head-on. Nothing would stop me from crossing that finish line.

I pressed on, despite the tablets not seeming to have much effect. We continued walking towards the turn at the end of the tenth lap when I mentioned to the guys that I might try lying down for a few minutes to give my legs some rest. Chris agreed, but Ciaran expressed concern that I might not be able to get back up if I stopped. My hesitation to take a break wasn't driven by a desire to maintain my lead; rather, it was spurred by my determination not to give up.

The guys tried to persuade me to shift my focus away from my race position and instead concentrate on the ultimate goal of simply finishing. I knew, deep down, that they were right. Taking a cue from what I had observed other participants doing throughout the past week, I decided to take a rest. I hobbled into the camper and settled on the makeshift bed, which was actually just the folded-down kitchen table. At a mere five feet long, it hardly accommodated my 6'2" frame, forcing me to curl up in a foetal position.

The plan was to rest for twenty minutes, but as time ticked by, I still didn't feel any relief from the painkillers. Restlessness took over and, after ten minutes, I couldn't bear lying still any longer. I jumped up and burst out of the camper door, determined to finish the remaining two laps and get them over with so that I could finally get some proper rest.

Ciaran volunteered to join me for the final two laps. It was a role reversal of sorts, I had trained Ciaran countless times in fitness classes and now he was stepping up to lead me. "Let's try smaller intervals," Ciaran suggested and I agreed fully. We began ticking off the miles, focusing intently on the stopwatch, which served as a welcomed distraction from the pain.

Implementing a strategy of 30 seconds running followed by 20 seconds walking, we found our rhythm and even managed to inject some fun into the process. It seemed that the paracetamol had kicked in just in time for these last two laps. Surprisingly, they turned out to be the two fastest run laps we had completed throughout the day.

Crossing the finish line, albeit in pieces, a decision had to be made. The guys proposed sticking to our post-race routine of heading to the lake for a refreshing swim, taking a shower and receiving a well-deserved massage. I knew that what I truly needed was to crawl into bed and give my body the rest it desperately craved. Paula, who was also exhausted, spent the entire evening in bed, leaving my bed unprepared and my hot water bottles the same. At that point, I couldn't be bothered. I had no energy left, only enough strength to undress from my running gear, climb into bed and throw a blanket over myself. It was the latest we had finished since the beginning of the race, with the time reading 12:40am. My finish time was 17:10.42 - third fastest on the day with only six left in the race.

During the night, I woke up a couple of times feeling cold; the blanket would slip off and to make matters worse, I didn't have any pyjamas on.

Instead of taking a quick drive back to the campsite, we decided to park the camper van at our gazebo and stay overnight at race HQ. It turned out to be a wise decision, because it meant I could wake up and be in the race starting area the next morning. Additionally, race HQ provided accessible toilets and a power supply, which allowed me to carry out my morning rituals of emptying my bowels, preparing a cup of tea and blending a breakfast smoothie.

Day 7				
Name	Total	Swim	Bike	Run
Dave Kershaw	16:07:25	1:21:57	8:43:10	6:02:19
Rob Duddington	16:36:25	1:05:25	9:21:39	6:09:23
Gerard Prendergast	17:10:42	1:12:22	8:48:52	7:09:28
Graham Smedley	18:04:38	1:16:29	8:41:53	8:06:17
Simon Jacob	18:27:24	1:12:41	9:17:55	7:56:49
Martin Curran	19:53:29	1:38:21	9:24:37	8:50:32

Race Commentary

On the seventh day, six exhausted and bruised participants ventured into the freezing waters of Dorney Lake, hoping for a revitalising experience akin to the miraculous waters of Lourdes. Despite their worn-out appearance, all six individuals somehow persevered and crossed the finish line on that chilly October evening.

However, Ger Prendergast, a contender for the overall title, faced a setback due to an injury, raising doubts about his ability to complete the entire event. Perhaps he can find motivation in the incredible achievements of Graham Smedley and Martin Curran, who have exceeded expectations thus far. Smedley has remained resilient despite the obstacles, as have Curran and Simon Jacob, who now find themselves walking a significant portion of the marathon. In fact, it appears that all the athletes are spending more time walking than they originally anticipated. Is Prendergast on the verge of experiencing similar struggles to Smedley's on day five? Could Dave Kershaw now be positioned to take the lead in the race? How much longer can these athletes continue pushing their minds and bodies to such extraordinary limits?

Wednesday 11th, October, 2017 - Day 8: Just Stay in the Game

Strategy

As day eight approached, my focus shifted towards managing the pain and staying in the race. Although I was determined to maintain my lead, I had to set that goal aside temporarily and simply focus on reaching the start and finish lines of the remaining three days.

My strategy remained unchanged, but I was aware that the true challenge would arise once I began the run. It would be during that time that I would determine whether I needed to walk for extended periods during the marathon, or if I had recovered sufficiently to stick to my plan of running and only walking over the bridges.

Diary

Day seven was nearly catastrophic. Midway through the marathon, my legs completely shut down, almost forcing me to exit the race. While sleep came easily after day seven, my thoughts were consumed by whether I could endure another full-distance triathlon with my legs in such a state. While I was confident about completing the swim and hoped a dip in the lake might even rejuvenate me, I was deeply concerned about the 180k bike ride and terrified at the prospect of running another marathon on battered legs.

In my morning vlog on day eight, I described the swim as being incredibly cold, the coldest so far. The air was also chilly, but my thoughts were focused on the arrival of my family later in the day, which helped distract me from the cold.

During the bike ride, I noticed a persistent squeaking coming from the front wheel with each rotation. It was difficult to identify the exact cause of the problem, so I asked the team for assistance. Since the second lap of the bike ride on day one, I had been relying on my spare bike and, when I got my TT bike back, it had a spare wheel on it since the original wheel was unusable. The spare wheel I was using belonged to Miriam's new road bike. Although it was only a basic wheel, it has proved to be dependable throughout the race, never puncturing or causing any trouble.

After a few laps to the camper, I was pleasantly surprised to find that the crew had managed to source a fantastic racing wheel. It turned out that TC had generously offered it to them, which was a truly kind gesture. Additionally, TC provided me with quad compressions to assist with the trouble I was experiencing in my quadriceps.

Quad compressions function in a similar manner to compression socks, which are often worn by individuals with blood circulation issues during long flights. In this case, the quad compressions aided in improving circulation in my quadriceps, the muscles located in the upper leg. By enhancing blood flow, the compressions helped alleviate the pain and the stiffness I was feeling.

After we replaced the front wheel I was eager to get back on the bike. It felt fantastic. The time had come for Ciaran and Chris, two lads who had been instrumental in keeping the Deca dream alive, to head home. They did an exceptional job and were invaluable members of the team. When we reached lap 30 on the bike, they bid farewell. Chris had earned the nickname 'Human Octopus' due to his remarkable multi-tasking abilities, making it seem as though he had eight arms. Ciaran, with his quick response times and fair complexion, had been affectionately dubbed 'White Lightning.'

Chris and Ciaran not only brought an exceptional work rate and their organisational skills to the team, but their humour also added a nice atmosphere. Surrounding myself with people like them proved to be immensely beneficial.

On day eight of the bike course, I was in excellent form when my wife Miriam and two of my three boys arrived. The sight of them triggered an overwhelming wave of emotion. Perhaps it was a mixture of pride and relief. As I cycled past them, my smile stretched from ear to ear. While taking the turnaround, the organising crew and some spectators showered me with tremendous cheers, causing my eyes to well up. The feeling was indescribable and one that I will forever cherish.

Completing the turnaround, I cycled back towards my family, who eagerly awaited me beside our camper, stationed about 40 metres from the turn.

I paused to embrace my wife and boys, exchanging hugs and kisses. We captured some precious moments in photographs before I resumed my cycle. Seeing them there filled me with confidence and determination. I felt invincible, knowing that with my family now by my side, my chances of completing the ten days had drastically improved.

Miriam played a crucial role in the transitions and joined me on the run section as my running companion. She had an uncanny understanding of my emotional reactions, surpassing anyone else. That day, as we conversed, I temporarily forgot my whereabouts and the magnitude of the challenge. It felt as though we were casually jogging a five-kilometre run back home during a training session. Miriam stayed with me for the first three laps before nightfall descended. After a break, she rejoined me on a bike, cycling alongside me for a few more laps.

Throughout the event, I remained highly attentive to the well-being of my crew. If they were struggling or fatigued, they wouldn't be in the proper state to assist me. I frequently encouraged them to take breaks, rest, or grab a meal. During those initial laps, Miriam and I discussed my decision to participate in the Deca event, about which she initially had reservations. "You proved us all wrong," she exclaimed. "You're definitely going to finish this now," she confidently declared. With a big smile, I playfully responded, "Can I have that in writing, please?" Internally, I cautioned myself not to make such definitive statements until day ten; after all, anything could happen. Nevertheless, a part of me truly believed that I would indeed complete the event. I just didn't want to tempt fate by saying it aloud.

On that day, my bike time amounted to nine hours, which, while not my best time of the week, was the second fastest for the day, trailing behind by a mere four minutes. My transition went smoothly as well. I was able to start the run before Dave Kershaw, who had the fastest bike time and had already completed half a lap by the time I spotted him on the run course.

The run proved to be challenging, although not as gruelling as the night before. My strategy was to run solely on grass. When forced to transition onto the pavement, such as at the bridges, I would walk up and over them due to the slight incline. Additionally, there were short tarmac sections, resembling car pull-in areas, situated halfway between the end of one bridge and the start of the next. I also chose to walk over them. While these sections only spanned ten to fifteen metres, they provided a reprieve for my feet and quads from the continuous pounding. My pace was not particularly fast, but it was still fifty minutes quicker than the previous night. I exercised caution with this newfound strategy, as I had a lingering fear that something could go seriously wrong with my legs if I pushed too hard. It felt as though I was treading on eggshells, constantly aware of the potential risks.

TC (Anthony Gerundini) had heard about my struggle with my quads and went above and beyond by offering me his HOKA running shoes, we both wore size 11. HOKA shoes are renowned in the running world, favoured by many elite endurance athletes for their superior cushioning and protection over long distances. Although, at that time, I was accustomed to running in minimalist shoes, I was immensely grateful for TC's kind gesture. Since then, I have shifted to wearing HOKA shoes for my long runs, recognising the excellent protection and comfort they provide.

During that phase of the race, I was on the run course, determined to push through the night, while TC was pacing Dave Kershaw, who held the second-place position. Learning about my injury motivated Dave to close the now three-hour gap between us. As TC and I ran towards each other from opposite sides of the track, he shouted, "Play the long game! Do you hear me? Play the long game!" It was evident that TC was there to support and uplift everyone. Although I didn't have the opportunity to run alongside TC, which is a shame, I did manage to have a chat with him later that same night as I walked towards the start of one of my marathon laps. I am certain that our paths will cross again in future races and I eagerly look forward to learning more from TC.

Dave wasn't far behind me, just twelve minutes back. He was really pushing himself now, attempting to narrow the distance between us. With only two laps to go, my legs were screaming for relief and I contemplated taking a break. "Maybe I should just let Dave pass and let him secure the win for the night" I thought to myself, considering I was still three and a half hours ahead overall. The thought of relinquishing the lead and escaping the pressure of being chased down seemed tempting. I quickly scolded myself for even entertaining such a foolish idea.

I approached the turnaround point signalling the end of another lap, my determination surged. Linda approached me with some form of sustenance, but in a sudden burst of emotion, I let out an outburst. "I'm not giving up the lead, fuck that. He's not going to take it from me." It was as if I was angry at Dave for daring to challenge my position, displaying an arrogant and petulant attitude. Linda looked at me in shock, surely thinking I sounded like a complete fool. Regardless, I kept going, refusing to pause to refuel. When it came to the final lap, I wasn't sure if Dave had closed the gap or not. I made the decision to run the entire last lap without stopping to walk. The pain was intense, but my drive to reach the finish line ahead of Dave pushed me forward.

Despite the fatigue and the upcoming double iron distance triathlon ahead of me in the next two days, I pushed forward, ignoring the pleas of my weary legs to walk. In hindsight, it may not have been the smartest decision.

I managed to complete the run in a time of 6 hours and 18 minutes, even with my battered legs. It was the fastest run of the day. Finally, I reached Dorney Lake, a place with seemingly magical powers to soothe my burning feet and legs. After a quick shower on-site, we hopped into the camper and headed back to the campsite.

Once we arrived, Miriam kindly gave me a rubdown on my quads. The tent felt like a refrigerator in the chilly night, but I bundled up with my woolly hat, fleece jumper and long rugby bench coat to keep warm. Exhausted, I climbed into bed and fell asleep within seconds of my head hitting the pillow.

Day 8				
Name	Total	Swim	Bike	Run
Gerard Prendergast	16:32:09	1:13:59	9:00:06	6:18:05
Dave Kershaw	16:50:15	1:22:48	8:56:45	6:30:43
Rob Duddington	18:44:00	1:08:22	10:05:40	7:29:59
Graham Smedley	19:56:10	1:16:00	9:09:14	9:30:58
Martin Curran	20:27:24	1:33:07	9:38:03	9:16:15
Simon Jacob (DNS Day 9)	22:29:50	1:15:53	11:23:05	9:50:52

Race Commentary

On the morning of day eight, the six ultra endurance participants, resembling zombies in their exhausted state, gathered once again at Lake Dorney, hoping for a miraculous transformation. Ger Prendergast, displaying a Lazarus-like comeback, claimed the victory for the day, closely followed by the ever-present Dave Kershaw. Simon Jacob, against all odds, managed to complete his day's challenge after enduring a savage twenty-two and a half hours. This meant he had a mere hour and a half to rest before plunging back into the water. It was truly madness. Despite a strong swim, Jacob's bike leg took an astounding eleven and a half hours and his marathon was nearly ten hours long. It seemed impossible for him to maintain such a demanding pace.

Remarkably, Smedley and Curran persevered once again, operating on just two to three hours of sleep for multiple consecutive days. These men demonstrated a remarkable level of grit as they returned to the lake day after day. Will Prendergast's recent victory be enough to prove that he cannot be denied, or will the toll on his body become too much to ignore? Can Kershaw mount a comeback? And with such limited sleep, will Smedley, Curran and Jacob be able to make it back to the lake in time to start day nine?

Thursday 12th, October, 2017 - Day 9: Accusations

Strategy

Our strategy for day nine was to maintain the status quo, we were just over three hours ahead of Dave Kershaw after day eight. Day eight turned out to be a remarkable improvement after the horrendous day seven and we knew that sticking to our current plan was crucial. Upon completing a lap of the run course on day eight, I could sense enough recovery to continue following the same pace and tactics on day nine, just as we had effectively executed the day before.

Diary

Day nine began with a sense of optimism for several reasons. Firstly, I was thrilled to still be in the race, persevering despite the challenges. Secondly, I held a substantial lead and it seemed likely that I would maintain that position unless a major setback occurred. Lastly, the presence of my family by my side provided an incredible boost of motivation and encouragement.

Yet the day started with a wave of sadness. We arrived at the lake on schedule, completing my usual morning routine of having a smoothie, using the restroom and making my way to the headquarters.

Putting on my wetsuit and brushing my teeth, I stood lakeside, ready to conquer the eight laps ahead of me. I removed my rugby coat, as if I was to enter the Aviva stadium, ready to engage in battle. I searched for Simon to tell him that I would lead the first two laps, but he was nowhere to be found. As I walked down the slope towards the lake, I encountered Jim Page. Jim was usu-

ally a very positive individual, but this morning, he appeared visibly upset. In that instant, I knew the reason behind his sorrow. 'Is Simon on his way?' I inquired with concern. Jim didn't respond with words; he simply shook his head. Poor Jim was clearly hurting, having provided so much support to Simon throughout the week. It felt as though Simon's departure from the race was a personal blow to him. Curiosity got the better of me, so I asked, 'What happened?' Jim explained that Simon had only finished his day eight triathlon at 6am, and the organisers decided he wouldn't be able to continue.

I didn't even have a moment to fully grasp the news, as I found myself wading through the lake, immersed in conversation with Jim Page as he stood on the lakeside. Suddenly, the horn sounded, marking the start of day nine and I began my first lap. As I swam, concentrating on my stroke and navigating between buoys throughout the eight laps, I couldn't help but think about Simon. I pondered on how he must have been feeling after being forced to withdraw from the race so near to the finish line. Among all the other competitors who had a Did Not Finish (DNF) designation, Simon undoubtedly had the strongest grounds for feeling aggrieved.

I continued with my usual swim pace and completed it in 1 hour and 16 minutes, which was a solid average time. Surprisingly, losing Simon didn't seem to affect my swim time, although it definitely had an effect on my morale. I was relieved to be done with that day's effort in the lake, but I still remained curious about what had happened with Simon.

Following a smooth transition, I hopped on my bike, trailing just behind Rob Duddington as per usual. There was no pressure on me, given the considerable lead we had attained. I simply wanted to enjoy the sunshine and bask in the atmosphere of day nine. The end felt so near and the rest of the guys were also in high spirits. We all recognised that we were approaching the finish line with a good chance of completion.

Every morning on the bike course when Simon and I would see each other for the first time after the swim, Simon would initiate a high five while we were on our bikes coming towards each other. It was more of a low, side five as a high five would be a bit too risky. It became a daily ritual where we would connect our hands with a loud slap as our bikes passed each other. It was a small gesture, but it brought us closer. Simon's absence was profoundly felt by all.

During the bike leg of day nine, I spotted Simon sitting in a chair, his injured leg propped up on another chair. Despite his disappointment at being unable to continue, he remained in good spirits, donning sunglasses and clapping for every lap completed by the final five competitors.

At the end of the bike leg Simon was strolling around, preparing to depart, but he had a desire to bid farewell and offer good luck to the remaining racers. Jim informed me, "Simon is over there and wants to say goodbye." I understood that this would be difficult. Despite hardly knowing him, I felt a strong connection with him. It felt as though we would be forever linked due to our shared experiences in the Deca and the daily swims. He embraced me tightly, expressing his emotions openly. "You have been incredible all week; now go out there and claim your prize," he said to me.

Moved and at a loss for words, I knew I would miss having him in the race and was disheartened that he wouldn't be able to finish. He also acknowledged his own mistakes and the lessons he had learned. Instead of blaming equipment, injuries, or any external factors, he took responsibility for his errors. I understood that he would be physically and emotionally hurting for a few days, but I also knew he would gain multiple valuable lessons from the way his event concluded.

The arrival of Miriam and the boys infused me with a surge of energy. My Mam, Coach Bjorn, and his family also came, bringing with them a wave of excitement that lifted my spirits as they cheered me on. We were all blessed with a gorgeous, sun-filled day. The swim felt noticeably warmer compared to previous days and went smoothly.

When Miriam had arrived the day before, she had brought a gift from my dad: one of the swim caps he had worn during the Transplant Olympic Games. These games, akin to the Olympics, are exclusively for transplant recipients and are held annually in various locations worldwide.

The cap was white, with a large green shamrock on the front and within that shamrock, in white, the name of our beloved country, Ireland. With immense pride, I wore it on the morning of my ninth swim. I wasn't sure if Dad had sent it as a symbol of patriotism for me to don or because he couldn't be there in person, so he sent a small piece of himself with the swim cap. Dad, being a traditional man, often struggles to express his emotions through words, as do many men of his generation. I've inherited this trait to some extent, though my generation is generally more inclined to express their feelings.

The bike leg on the ninth day of the race was incredibly enjoyable. I started off at a comfortable pace and maintained it throughout. I made sure not to rush my food intake, either. After a few hours, I was joined by Martin Curran and we began chatting. Martin had been struggling with foot issues since the first day. He had finished second to last ahead of me on day one. Approaching the finish chute that evening, I closed the gap on Martin, but instead of passing him as he walked towards the finish line, I resisted the temptation. However, when he looked back and saw me approaching, he burst into a sprint while laughing. He made it a point to remind me throughout the rest of the event that he had beaten me on day one and he continues to do so to this day.

We were engaged in a lively conversation, discussing various aspects of the event, the pleasant weather, our favourite food and the ups and downs of life. Of course, I couldn't help but complain about my sore undercarriage, while Martin couldn't stop laughing about it.

Though I tried to maintain a sense of humour, the pain was undeniably intense. My saddle sore had been growing increasingly painful with each passing day and by day ten, it had reached a ten on the pain scale.
The day seemed to fly by in a blur and I was connecting with the competitors I had shared the road with for the past nine days. I informed Martin that I needed to make a stop to address my saddle sore problem, while he decided to take a break to refuel. Martin had been accompanied by one crew member from the beginning: his brother Derek. Occasionally, as I cycled past, poor Derek would be caught napping, exhausted from the constant demands of the race.
Martin's marathon times allowed him only two to three hours of sleep each night, leaving even less time for his dedicated brother Derek. Despite this, Derek would go the extra mile by joining Martin for some laps on the run course. As Martin mostly walked during these laps, Derek decided to keep him company, especially during moments when Martin wasn't listening to his music. Their camaraderie was truly admirable.

On the ninth day, as I was nearing the end of my bike section, Derek surprised us all by ordering pizza from a local Domino's Pizza place. He made a special effort to ensure that I had a vegan pizza. It was truly appreciated. I took time out from my ride to stop and enjoy the pizza delivered to my camper and at the same time get medical attention for my saddle sore.

After finishing my visit with Nurse Miriam, I climbed back onto my bike and prepared to continue the race. Martin was doing the same, providing us with an opportunity to chat further.

I was shocked when Martin caught up with me later and began filling me in on some rumours circulating at the headquarters area. Somebody had approached the organisers with allegations of drafting. I couldn't help but wonder who might be guilty of this offence, as I hadn't witnessed anyone drafting. Shockingly, the accusations were directed at both Martin and me. To say I was furious would be an immense understatement.

At the time I was trying to push through the pain and to battle demons within my body and mind. Dealing with these allegations on the ninth day of the race was upsetting. I could vividly imagine myself dismounting my bike and confronting the person or people who had made the accusations against me. After a few laps, the initial rage subsided and a new worry took its place. What if I ended up being disqualified over this bullshit?

Martin, on the other hand, wasn't bothered by the situation and reminded me that I had let my imagination run wild. He cheekily remarked, "They're just concerned that the Celts are teaming up now." His light-hearted comment offered some perspective. To me, drafting was a serious violation of the rules. Using another competitor as a wind-shield to make the cycling portion easier was not something I would ever consider doing. However, it seemed that the accusations were based on Martin and me simply cycling side by side and talking.

Day nine marked the first time that I had the chance to relax and engage in a longer conversation with someone. The accusations left me wondering, "Why would they say such things? Did I upset someone and if so, how? Or, was it because someone didn't want me to win the overall title?

Could it be a case of sour grapes? That's what my crew speculated. Determined not to give anyone a reason to disqualify me, I informed Martin that I would finish the rest of the bike leg and speak with him later. "I don't want to let this distract me". Martin, understanding my frustration, took the initiative to discuss the matter with the organisers on my behalf.

Later, one of the organisers ran alongside me after I had made a turnaround at the HQ end. They reassured me, saying, "Hey, if you want to talk to anyone, go ahead and talk. You've been working your ass off with the rest of the guys for the past nine days and you have every right to engage in conversation." I felt a sense of relief and gratitude.

It was important to remember that the organisers were closely monitoring the athletes, ready to take action if any rule violations were observed. Ultimately, the accusations stemmed from frustration and were not given any serious consideration.

Mentally and emotionally, I felt good on the bike, but the pain I was experiencing made me anxious about the upcoming marathon. Despite this, I knew the finish line was within my reach. Starting the run then elevated my spirits and mood, especially since my legs felt a bit better than the previous nights.

To add to my motivation, my two youngest boys, Ben and Reece, joined me for a few laps before their bedtime. Riding their yellow fold-up bikes, they kept my mind occupied and distracted me from the leg pain, brightening my mood. After about an hour in the dark, Linda drove the two boys back to their hotel in her car.

While running alongside Dave Kershaw, he asked me an unexpected question: "Gerard, what would you say is your greatest accomplishment?" As we reflected on our past races and celebrated Dave's impressive athletic background, I was filled with deep admiration for him. However, without a moment's hesitation, I responded, "Persuading my wife to marry me and raising extraordinary children."

We both chuckled, acknowledging the touch of cheesiness in my answer. Yet, in the midst of the intense exhaustion that accompanies ultra-endurance events, our heightened emotional states sometimes lead us to express things that we may not ordinarily verbalise. But perhaps, amidst the fatigue and strain, there was an undeniable truth in my reply.

Day nine was a remarkable day and I was filled with elation after completing the race in a time of 16:21.31 and still top of the leader-board. Dave Kershaw was second in 16:34.29. As always, we parked our camper near the picturesque lake. Without wasting any time, I seized the opportunity for cryotherapy and submerged myself in the rejuvenating cold water. Once I had invigorated my body, I promptly hopped into the shower, which happened to be an electric one housed within a Portaloo. Feeling refreshed, I made my way back into the cosy confines of our camper.

Paula, ever attentive and prepared, had arranged my large coat, hot water bottles and a soft duvet on the front seat, ensuring that I would stay warm and comfortable after the long race. Her care and consideration made these post-race moments a little more enjoyable and comforting.

Once I had finished the race, I changed into my thermal gear and made my way into the front seat of the camper. However, to my surprise, there was no heating turned on. In a playful tone, I sarcastically exclaimed, "No heating? This simply won't do! Unacceptable! You're fired!" Paula, playing along, cheekily replied, "Go and ask me bollocks." We shared a laugh, but little did I know, there was a surprise waiting for me.

From the back of the camper, I instantly recognised two familiar voices. One of them said, "He never shuts up," and the other chimed in with, "Ah, just hire someone else." I turned around in my seat and to my surprise, it was my friends Jonner Mangan and Noel Dempsey. There was an eruption of applause and cheering all around. The lads had decided to catch a last-minute flight to join me and help me complete the Deca. It was a truly heart-warming surprise and a perfect way to end the day.

Day 9				
Name	Total	Swim	Bike	Run
Gerard Prendergast	16:21:31	1:16:03	8:58:02	6:07:27
Dave Kershaw	16:34:29	1:33:32	9:03:36	5:57:22
Rob Duddington	17:46:07	1:08:54	9:54:43	6:42:32
Graham Smedley	19:49:01	1:18:33	9:59:30	8:30:59
Martin Curran	20:37:06	1:36:28	9:19:18	9:42:21

Race Commentary

After completing eight full iron-distance triathlons in eight days, Simon Jacob's tremendous effort came to an end as he was pulled from the event. While Jacob was determined to continue, the organisers made the difficult but necessary decision to prioritise his well-being. At the top of the leaderboard, Ger Prendergast claimed another victory, closely followed by Dave Kershaw, in a fiercely contested battle for the overall title. Kershaw finished just 13 minutes behind Prendergast, leaving him with an uphill battle on day ten if he hopes to surpass the Irishman. Their riveting race at the forefront has captivated spectators.

Meanwhile, Martin Curran and Graham Smedley are pushing through adversity. Curran, finishing day four in a taxing twenty hours, has had less than four hours to eat and rest before plunging back into the lake for the final day. Similarly, Smedley, initially a frontrunner until an injury on day five, is persevering day after day to complete the event. Their determination in the face of injuries and sleep deprivation is awe-inspiring. These two athletes are showcasing unwavering resilience and fortitude. The question remains: can Prendergast maintain his momentum, or will Kershaw stage an unlikely comeback to overtake the leader? Can Curran and Smedley overcome their obstacles just one more time to continue their remarkable journey? The stage is set for an exhilarating conclusion to the event, where the competitors' physical and mental strength will be put to the ultimate test.

Friday 13th, October, 2017 - Day 10: Live and Die on this Day...

Strategy

Initially, I had planned to approach day ten of the race with a relaxed mindset, simply enjoying the day as I had on day nine. My intention was to take it easy, methodically completing each lap at a steady pace. I convinced myself that winning day ten was not a priority and my main goal was to reach the finish line that night without pushing myself too hard. After all, I was in first place, three and a half hours ahead of my closest rival, Dave Kershaw.

Diary

In my tenth vlog entry, I summed up my experience at Eton Dorney's lake on the final day of DecaUK.
The water was pleasantly not too cold, my laps were consistently smooth and the support I received was exceptional. By now, my time in the lake had simply

become a routine part of my day. Over the ten days, the swim portion of the competition hadn't presented many physical consequences, as is often the case with this discipline. Swimming is made easier because the water provides natural buoyancy and support for our bodies. In contrast, when running, our bones and joints systems have to bear the weight of our bodies, which is multiplied by four with each foot strike on the ground. Additionally, the coldness of the water acted as a therapy, helping with recovery. So, most days, despite feeling stiff and sore initially, I would emerge from the lake feeling rejuvenated.

As I moved from the swim to the bike stage that morning, I couldn't help but notice how impeccably clean and shiny my bike looked. Coach Bjorn informed me that he had given it a tune-up while I was changing and fuelling up. I was pleased to have a freshened up bike for the occasion and as I set off on my first lap, I could immediately feel the difference. In my Vlog for the day, I exclaimed, "I swear Coach Bjorn must have installed an engine in my bike!" The service had made it noticeably smoother and faster, allowing me to breeze through the course. The crew supporting me struggled to keep up with me during the food laps, because they hadn't expected me to return so quickly after each lap.

Although I was still dealing with the discomfort of a saddle sore, my excitement overshadowed the pain, at least initially. As the bike leg progressed, the saddle sore became more prominent, demanding my attention. I managed to complete the first twenty laps with incredible speed, but eventually, the pain became overwhelming and I had to address it.

Because saddle sores had never troubled me before, I blamed this new problem on my recently acquired custom cycling kit. While it felt comfortable and looked stylish, it was the only new element in my gear that could potentially be causing this issue. Despite diligently applying generous amounts of Sudocrem to the affected area in an attempt to alleviate the pain, the pressure on the saddle remained excruciatingly uncomfortable.

I had never experienced this issue before, I was unsure of the best course of action. There were moments when I could mentally block out the pain for extended periods of time, but there were also times when the discomfort became unbearable, forcing me to take breaks. I made an effort to complete at least ten laps before stopping, seizing those moments to grab some food or a bottle of water from the support crew.

One of the crew members had an idea that involved using sanitary towels and more Sudocrem to address the saddle sore issue. At that point, I was open to trying anything. We generously applied Sudocrem to a sanitary pad and positioned it where I felt the most friction. Initially, it seemed to work, but unfortunately, after an hour, the pain returned and I was once again in considerable discomfort. We added more pads to alleviate the discomfort, but they ended up being even more bothersome as they would shift around and create additional hindrances rather than providing any real help. After a few laps, I decided to remove the pads and surprisingly, it brought some relief. I carried on with the cycle and thankfully, the discomfort seemed to subside slightly for the remainder of the ride.

It didn't take long after this for my plans to take a complete U-turn. The overwhelming exhilaration of nearing the end of such an extraordinary event overpowered me. I couldn't believe the privilege of being in this position. It seemed like just a short time ago, I was struggling to complete a humble five-kilometre road run in Dublin's Phoenix Park. And now here I was, on the brink of not only accomplishing but potentially winning the ultimate test of endurance triathlon races, the Deca.

A wide smile stretched across my face and I was overcome with excitement. At that moment, I made a bold decision to throw caution to the wind and go all in. I knew that nothing could stand in my way now.

Throughout the past nine days, I had faced countless challenges, yet not a single one had broken my spirit. On day ten, I was determined to keep that unwavering resolve intact. As I continued to accumulate laps, I couldn't help but notice that the other competitors were taking more frequent and longer breaks. The physical and mental toll of the event was clearly weighing heavily on them. However, instead of feeling sympathy, I found that my determination and motivation only grew stronger. It was as if I had become a parasite, drawing strength from their struggles. Like Superman basking in the rejuvenating power of the sun, I felt a wave of renewed energy, propelling me forward. Nothing could deter me now.

As I observed the other competitors taking longer breaks, I decided to maximise my laps completed before they returned from their food and rest stops and managed to complete three full laps while one of the guys took his food break. While they started to slow down, I found myself gaining momentum. We were all grappling with fatigue, but I concealed mine and drew motivation from their visible struggles.

My total biking time for the day was 8 hours and 14 minutes, surpassing Dave Kershaw's bike split by 41 minutes, the second-fastest time of the day. It was also my fastest bike split throughout the entire ten-day competition. Several factors contributed to this achievement:

1. The service Coach Bjorn performed on my bike automatically enhanced its speed.
2. The excitement of the day infused adrenaline into my body, driving me to excel.
3. I desired to finish earlier on that particular day so that I could spend quality time with my family and fully enjoy the significance of the occasion.
4. Knowing that I wouldn't have an early start the next morning allowed me to push myself a little harder on day ten.
5. The accusations from the previous day had agitated me and I wanted to respond with a stellar performance, proving my commitment and abilities.

Approaching the turnaround point for the final lap, I had requested that Matt Brown, one of the crew organisers, have the last lap sign ready for me. Each day, it was an uplifting sight to see him proudly waving a bright yellow sign, bearing a beaming smile. I was thrilled to find him prepared and as I neared the turnaround, he rang a cattle bell that he had attached to the sign. It was an incredibly special moment as I embarked on my very last lap, reaching out to touch the sign.

The support I received from everyone present; my family, crew, organisers and onlookers, was overwhelming. Despite the presence of only about fifty people, the cheers were so loud that it felt as if there were five hundred voices cheering me on. The encouragement and energy generated by the crowd created an unforgettable atmosphere, one that I hoped to experience again later that night when I completed my final marathon run.

When I dismounted from the bike, I was surrounded by my jubilant family and crew. Cheering and applause filled the air as we commemorated the moment with photographs and shared in the incredible atmosphere.

On my way to the run course, a wave of cheers, loud howls and enthusiastic applause greeted me. It was an overwhelming display of support and encouragement. Ben and Reece joined me on their bikes, while Miriam accompanied me on foot as we set off. The first two laps seemed to fly by in no time at all.

For the following two laps, Jonner and Noel, who now wanted to be known as DecaNoel, joined me. They were filming a DecaNoel video and in their playful skit, DecaNoel 'took over' as the race leader. He couldn't resist teasing me about my plant-based nutrition. "Look at this guy, eating nuts and seeds," he exclaimed, humorously showcasing his own unconventional 'hydration plan' by running with a can of Fosters lager in one hand. With a mischievous grin, he proclaimed, "You can eat my dust," while simultaneously opening the can of Fosters lager and taking large swigs from it.

Approaching the finish line, each step seemed to intensify the pain in my quads. Yet, mentally, I felt invigorated. I mustered all my strength to keep pushing forward. The focus on nutrition during this marathon slipped from my mind. I couldn't recall eating anything at all. When I reached the turnaround at the finish line, I would gulp down water mixed with cordial from a 1-litre bottle as a means of hydration.

To my surprise and delight, Coach Bjorn hopped on his bike and accompanied me for a couple of laps. Our conversation deviated from the usual training-related topics and veered into more personal territory. It provided a welcome distraction from the physical exertion.

Coach Bjorn had a habit of starting sentences with "As my Dad would say" and then concluding them with some classic old-school saying. Despite his South African background, the sayings he shared were remarkably similar to the ones my Irish father used to tell me. Almost every time Coach Bjorn shared one of these sayings, I found myself responding with a hearty laugh and exclaiming, "Jaysis, my dad used to say the exact same thing!"

As the darkness enveloped us, Ben and Reece, my sons, stood by the finish line, eagerly awaiting my arrival. Miriam was determined to join me in running once again, while Reece then insisted on accompanying us on his bicycle. He had brought along his older brother Jake's Bluetooth speaker, using it to amplify motivational tunes. It was a powerful moment when he played the song that served as the inspiration for our Deca motto, "Gotta keep it movin'." The music stirred deep emotions within me and I couldn't help but sense Mick's presence throughout the duration of the track. For this final marathon, I had purposefully worn a pair of socks that he had borrowed and returned to me before his untimely passing, hoping that somehow they would channel his energy to guide me across the finish line.

As the familiar notes of 'Moving' by Bugzy Malone blared into the darkness, a wave of emotions washed over me. I felt sadness, anger, happiness, pride and excitement. My mind wandered back to day seven, when I had been on my knees and I couldn't help but imagine that he - Mick - was there, extending a hand to pull me up from the grass, propelling me forward. As the song played, I could almost feel his presence.

When the song came to an end, we continued on, propelled forward by Reece's choice of the next track - the same song from Rocky, 'Gonna Fly Now,' with a twist—it was a 20 minute version that raised a few eyebrows but brought us all good-natured amusement. With each step, I drew closer to my last lap.

I instructed the guys to prepare my tricolour. Coach Bjorn joined me for the final lap. As we reached the far end of the course, at the turnaround point, I bade a heartfelt farewell to the blinking cone at the far end of the run course, a constant companion throughout the past ten days. With renewed determination, I ran on towards the finish line. Crossing the final bridge, only 200 metres stood between me and the end of this incredible adventure.

The guys met me at the bridge, armed with a refreshing drink, my phone and my beloved Irish flag. Visions of Linda's reminder to have it displayed correctly flashed through my mind, but truth be told, I hadn't managed to get it right. Fortunately, with the magic of Photoshop, we could fix it later. Feeling prepared and eager, I set off.

Approaching the turn to the finish line, a warm welcome awaited me. Crew members from other teams and enthusiastic supporters had gathered. With my phone live-streaming, I realised the dim lighting made visibility challenging. Trying to exchange high-fives while clutching my phone and holding my flag proved to be quite a juggling act.

The supporters gathered there at the finish line and embraced me with pats on the back and words of congratulations. I took a moment to shake hands with strangers who had come to show their support. I then pressed on towards the finish line. With immense pride, I hoisted my flag high into the night sky. The crowd erupted with cheers, with my wife and children leading the charge with colourful banners and joyful noise.

As I finally crossed the finish line, the air was filled with a celebratory shower of champagne, drenching me. The flashes from countless cameras illuminated the scene, momentarily blinding me. It was indescribable, the culmination of hard work, resilience and the support of a united community.

Amidst it all, my mam handed me her phone and uttered one of the most quintessentially Irish things a mother could say: "Talk to your Da there, will ya?". In that whirlwind of noise and excitement, my mam was determined to connect me with my Dad, something I'm now truly grateful for. It was a truly Irish moment, filled with a unique blend of chaotic joy and heartfelt connection.

In the midst of this, we broke into a collective chorus of 'Everywhere we Go-oh,' a song beloved by Ballymunners, a way to proudly announce our origins no matter where we find ourselves. These few moments allowed me to bask in the pride of representing my hometown, knowing that I had been fully supported by the entire community from the very beginning. The knowledge of their unwavering support filled me with immense pride.

Jim Page, a member of the crew, expressed that he had never witnessed a more extraordinary race finish. Words fail to capture the multitude of emotions I experienced in that moment, but I can confidently say that it was one of the highlights of my life.

Despite all the excitement, I still had to look after my tired legs and I plunged into the cool, refreshing lake. The guys insisted that I indulge in the champagne and although I don't drink alcohol, I obliged with a small sip. The taste rattled my palate, causing me to shudder. Swiftly passing it back, I made my way to the shower, relishing in the warmth as the hot water cascaded over me for a blissful 20 minutes.

Once refreshed, I bundled up in my trusty fleece jumper and comfortable tracksuit bottoms and adorned my reliable full-length rugby bench coat and accepted a steaming cup of tea.

A camping chair at the finish line, eager to watch the arrival of other competitors, I allowed myself a moment of reprieve, taking in the sight and significance of their remarkable achievements.

Dave Kershaw, didn't keep me waiting for long after my refreshing lake swim and shower. We seized the opportunity to capture a photo together, proudly displaying our hard-earned medals.

Finishing this monumental ten-day race marked the greatest accomplishment of my life. Now that it was over, it was time to celebrate. Amidst a flurry of phone calls, live streams and expressions of gratitude towards the supporters both present and far away, my crew had stocked up on champagne and other drinks for the post-race festivities. They leapt around, cheering and dancing and when they turned to include me in their celebration... they found me peacefully asleep in my camping chair.

They put me to bed in the camper. Afterwards, I made them promise to wake me up when the next finisher was about to arrive. As it happened my exhausted crew fell asleep themselves and I didn't wake up in time to greet the remaining finishers - Rob Duddington, Martin Curran and Graham Smedley. I had completed the Deca in 158 hours and 9 minutes. Behind me came Dave Kershaw in 162:36.51, Rob Duddington in 166:56.18, Graham Smedley in 178:48.43 and Martin Curran in 193:44.53.

The following morning, I awoke at 8am, feeling surprisingly energetic. It seemed as though I could embark on another race. I grabbed a cup of tea from the HQ tent and meandered around, chatting to those who were awake. I ended up chatting with Kathy, the photographer who had spent the entire night capturing precious moments on camera and had slept on the cold ground in the HQ marquee. Jim Page emerged into the tent, accompanied by Claire Smith and Paul Smethurst. They appeared as if they had just completed their own Deca, having accumulated more hours on their feet than I had over the entire event.

After one last dip in the lake to soothe my aching muscles and bid farewell to the serene waters, I felt completely relaxed.

During breakfast, I enjoyed chatting with the other guys who had completed the race. Physically, I felt amazing and was on cloud nine. Coach Bjorn and I had a conversation about recovery and then he headed off to Legoland with his partner, Orlaith and their son, Jonah. As they departed, Coach Bjorn playfully beeped his bus horn to the tune of La Cucaracha, which brought on a chorus of cheers from everyone present.

Shortly after, Jonner and Noel followed suit, leaving for the airport in their rental car. As they drove off, they rolled down the windows and, at the top of their lungs, joined in the rendition of La Cucaracha that Coach Bjorn had just played. It was a hilarious moment that exemplified the fun and positive energy the guys had brought to the crew, uplifting me whenever I needed it.

Though I bid my fellow competitors a final farewell, I knew that our paths would cross again in the future at another major event.

Day 10				
Name	Total	Swim	Bike	Run
Gerard Prendergast	15:35:11	1:13:40	8:14:58	6:06:34
Dave Kershaw	16:44:26	1:32:23	8:55:17	6:16:47
Rob Duddington	17:20:10	1:08:35	9:45:13	6:26:23
Graham Smedley	20:30:00	1:20:11	10:12:35	8:57:15
Martin Curran	21:26:02	1:32:20	9:37:55	10:15:48

Race Commentary

In what Triathlon 220 magazine has hailed as one of the most gruelling triathlons in history, Irish athlete Ger Prendergast emerged triumphant in the inaugural DecaUK ultra endurance triathlon. Going head-to-head against competitors from all corners of the world, Prendergast not only conquered the challenge but also claimed victory in the race.

Prendergast left no stone unturned on the bike section, delivering his best performance of the ten days on two wheels. The podium was a familiar sight, with the usual suspects securing second and third places. Dave Kershaw claimed the overall runner-up position, closely followed by Rob Duddington in third.

However, it's noteworthy to highlight the remarkable feats accomplished by Martin Curran and Graham Smedley. Against all odds, they demonstrated extraordinary resilience, grit and determination by crossing the finish line on day ten and earning the prestigious title of Deca finishers. Their accomplishments showcase their indomitable spirit.

Overall Standings	
Name	Total
Gerard Prendergast	158:09:00
Dave Kershaw	162:36:51
Rob Duddington	166:56:18
Graham Smedley	178:48:43
Martin Curran	193:44:53

The final overall standings after day 10 show the five finishers of DecaUK 2017. Ger Prendergast is named the DecaUK 2017 winner with an overall time of 158 hours and 9 minutes. He finished four and a half hours ahead of a very deserving Dave Kershaw, who pushed Prendergast hard in the final few days. Rob Duddington took third place overall with an impressive display of resilience himself; he was three and a half hours behind second placed Kershaw. Martin Curran and Graham Smedley realised their goals and both got their finishers medal.

2XU
DECAUK
FINISHER

FINIS
JR BOOTCAMP
NO EXCUSES

DECA DAILY SCHEDULE

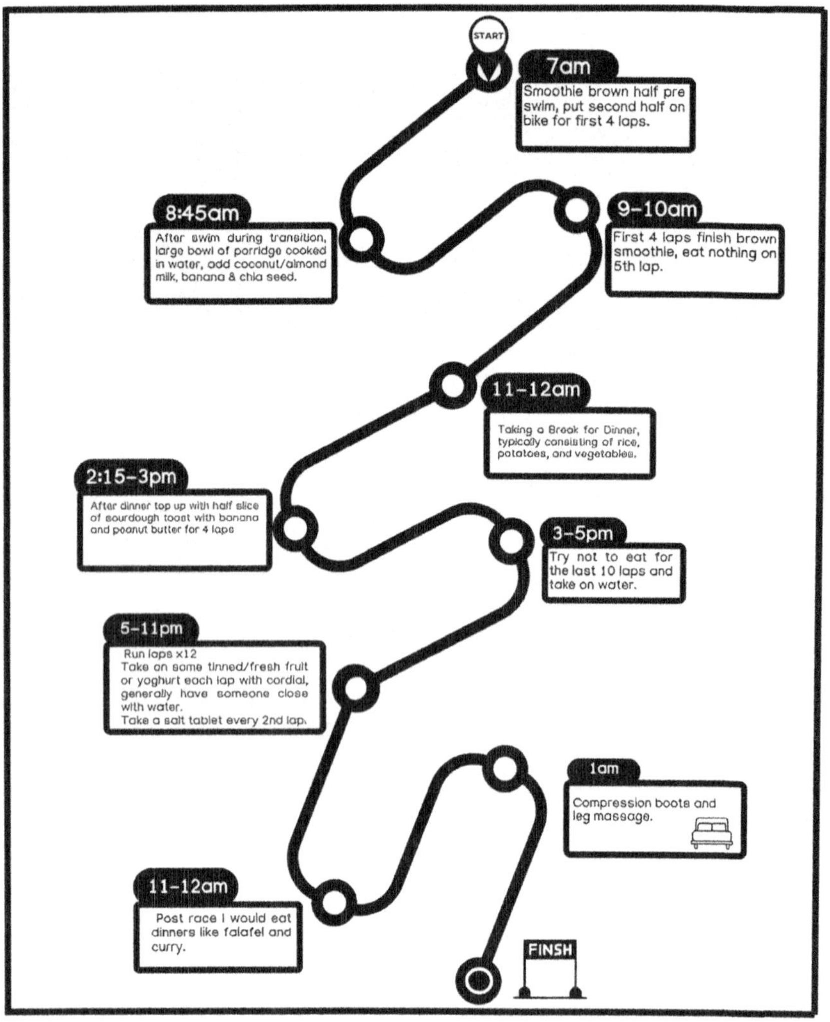

Stats for Deca

Fastest Swim Time 1:12:22 Day 7

Slowest Swim 1:19:59 Day 2

Fastest Bike 08:14:58 Day 10

Slowest Bike 9:14:45 Day 2

Slowest Run 7:09:28 Day 7

Fastest Run 4:58:03 Day 4

Total 1st Place Finishes 6 (days 3, 5, 6, 8, 9 & 10)

Other Stats:

Last Place after Day 1
First after Day 10
Fastest Finish Time 14:46:35 Day 5
Slowest Finish Time 17:10:42 Day 7

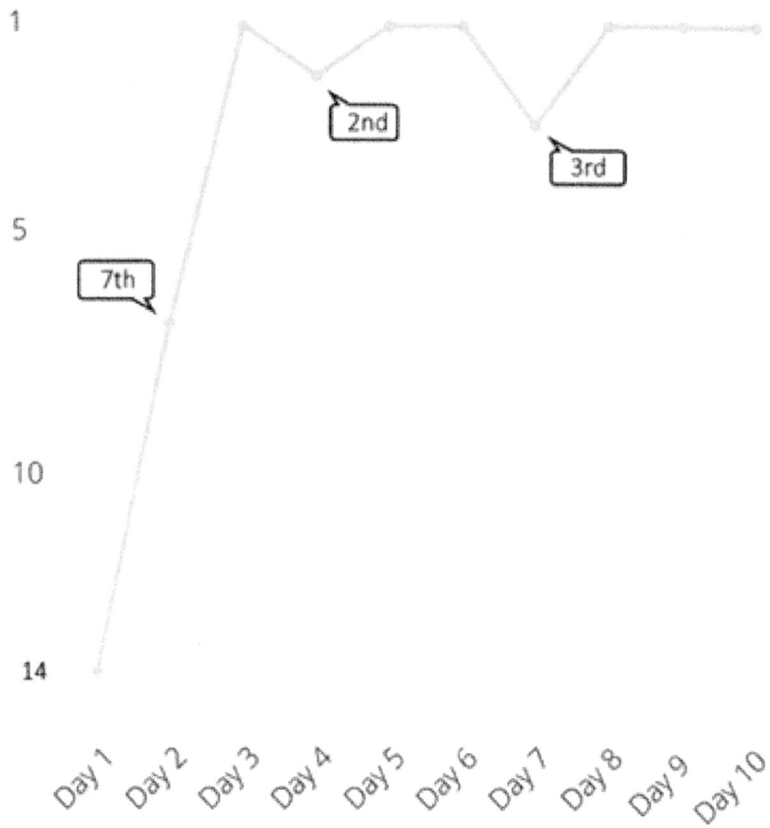

Ger positions through the days

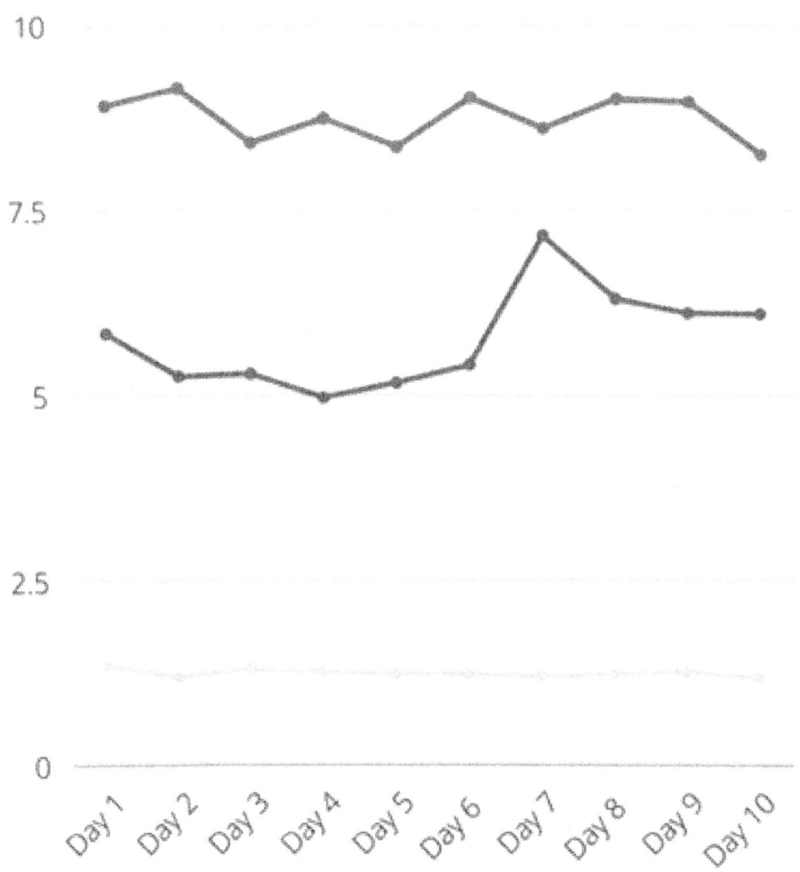

The impact of each discipline on the final result

Part 4

The Finish Line and Beyond

Chapter 7: The Aftermath

When Miriam and I initially organised our travel arrangements for DecaUK, our plan was to allow for a day of recovery after the race, which concluded on a Saturday. The following day, Sunday, we had planned to take the children to nearby Legoland, close to Lake Dorney. We would return to Ireland on Monday morning, driving from Windsor to Holyhead and catching the evening ferry. However, due to my physical condition, we made the decision to modify our plan and forgo our visit to Legoland. Instead, we opted to take an earlier ferry and head straight home.

During this time, I was facing challenges with my hands and feet. Both hands lacked strength and I experienced numbness in my fingers. These sensations extended to my feet as well.

My feet continued to feel numb, reinforcing the notion that it would be irresponsible for me to take on the long drive. Thankfully, Paula offered to accompany us and handle the driving. With her help, we started on our journey. To ensure we were on the right path, we relied on the GPS on my phone for accurate directions.

Initially, everything seemed to be going well. However, as I entered Holyhead into Google Maps, I was pleasantly surprised to see an estimated arrival time of four and a half hours. Given our previous trek that took us six hours, I thought this was great news.

Unfortunately, as the drive progressed, it became clear that the GPS was leading us on a different route out of Windsor. After some time had passed and I noticed the lack of motorways on our route, I began to suspect that something was amiss. It was becoming increasingly clear that we were spending the majority of our drive on national roads, with minimal usage of motorways. Consequently, the estimated arrival time continued to extend, contrary to our initial expectations. As Paula grew increasingly tired after several hours of driving, it became clear that I would have to take over behind the wheel. Miriam did not drive at the time, leaving me as the only available option. Despite the late hour, the roads were relatively empty, which provided some relief. However, my focus was constantly challenged by trucks and other large vehicles ahead of us, with red tail lights almost hypnotising me.

Although we were steadily approaching Holyhead, a new concern arose: our dwindling fuel supply. The camper included a digital screen that displayed the number of miles remaining before running out of fuel. When I took the wheel, we had enough fuel for a 40-mile (approximately 64 km) range, with 30 miles (about 48 km) of road still to drive. However, as we neared Holyhead, the discrepancy between the miles shown on the dashboard and the distances indicated on the road signs towards the ferry began to close. This heightened the risk of running out of fuel before reaching our destination.

As I searched for a petrol station, I noticed none in sight along the roadside. Realising the need to find fuel, we started taking the motorway exits into nearby towns. Unfortunately, this approach only wasted more fuel. Eventually, we stumbled upon some stations, but it was already past 11pm and they had closed for the night. With no other options, we continued towards the ferry, hoping and praying that we wouldn't run out of petrol along the way. The situation grew increasingly dire as the dashboard screen displayed fewer miles than indicated on the road signs, causing immense stress. Finally, with just one mile left on the dash, we arrived in Holyhead. However, there was still no petrol station available, so I could only pray that Dublin Port would have one upon our arrival.

While aboard the boat, I began to feel an uncomfortable sensation in my feet. It was so overwhelming that I had to remove my shoes. Finding no relief, I took off my socks as well, allowing my feet to breathe. To my surprise, when I looked at my feet, they had swollen up like balloons. Normally, my feet appear quite vascular and bony, with prominent tendons. But now, they looked as if they had been inflated, with no visible veins, tendons, or even my ankle bone. I quickly put my feet and legs inside my sleeping bag and laid down on an empty sofa we found on the ferry. Within moments, I fell into a deep sleep, only waking up when it was time to disembark. As soon as I was awake, my mind was consumed with the worry that we had only one mile of fuel left. I turned to Google Maps and searched for the nearest petrol station. It showed a petrol station a mere six hundred metres away and it was open. We inched along in the traffic leaving the ferry and, after what felt like an eternity, we reached the petrol station without running out of fuel. Relieved, we filled up, entered the port tunnel and were home within 30 minutes.

On the day we returned home, I felt a sense of accomplishment. Despite experiencing various physical issues, the adrenaline from the event had kept me on a high. However, in the following days, my body began to rebel. The most noticeable problems were still in my hands and feet. During the later days of the Deca, I started experiencing numbness in my fingers and I also lost strength and dexterity in my hands. This was particularly evident in my left hand. This condition persisted for several months and while there was gradual improvement, the progress felt agonisingly slow. Simple tasks like opening jars or packets became challenging and I often had to rely on my children or Miriam to assist me. It was ironic for me, since in the past, Miriam would come to me for help with opening jars. Now I needed her assistance. Handing me back the opened jars, she would playfully tease me with a cheeky grin and a comment like, "There you go, precious." My toes also experienced numbness, but they were gradually getting better.

The night terrors became the most distressing consequence. After returning home on a Sunday morning, I managed to get a few hours of sleep before waking up feeling refreshed. We spent the day enjoying meals and visiting family and later on, I was taken to my workplace for a surprise celebration. By 11pm, we called it a night and I fell asleep almost instantly. However, my respite was short-lived as I abruptly woke up, drenched in sweat and overwhelmed by confusion. In that disoriented moment, I found myself wondering which lap of the bike race I was on and how many more laps remained. I realised that my arms were instinctively outstretched in the same cycling position I had while on the bike during the Deca. It was a deeply unsettling experience. On one hand, I was aware that I was drenched in sweat and back in my own bed at home. But in the confusing realm of my dream, I still felt trapped in the intensity of the race. The sensation was so vivid yet so surreal. Initially, due to the dampness, I even wondered if I had regressed to childhood and wet the bed.

I felt a mix of embarrassment and fear as I struggled to comprehend why these night terrors were occurring. However, inspecting the wetness beneath me, I soon realised it was only from the overwhelming amount of sweat I had produced, unlike anything I had experienced before.

Despite feeling unsettled, I tried to go back to the damp and cold sensation from the soaked bed sheets made it difficult to drift off again. I desperately wanted to fall asleep as quickly as possible and the freezing temperatures made me reluctant to get out of bed to change the sheets. So, I lay back down, pulled the blanket over me and managed to sleep once more.

This cycle repeated itself three more times throughout that night. Each time, when I awoke, an unpleasant wave of panic washed over me, but it was short-lived as I quickly realised it was just a dream.

This continued for the next three nights. Most of the time, I believed I was on the bike, but sometimes I thought I was on the run course. The sweats and panic remained a constant feature. On Thursday night of that week, I only woke up once and this time there was no sweating, only the panic of not knowing how many laps remained in the race I was dreaming of. By Friday, the terror had completely passed. I only woke up to use the toilet that night. After that, my sleep pattern became normal.

In the days that followed, I attended some physiotherapy sessions at my brother Kevin's house. He skillfully worked on cracking the bones in my feet and wrists, aiming to improve blood flow to those areas. Remarkably, after just one session, the swelling in my feet had subsided. Kevin also provided effective treatment for my thigh problem, greatly alleviating the discomfort.

Additionally, I sought the expertise of Damien Harold, my trusted masseuse.

Over the years, Damien had worked wonders on my body, leaving me feeling rejuvenated after each visit to his clinic.

After completing the Deca, I experienced discomfort in my right thigh, specifically the inner side known as Vastus Medialis. This was the first challenge that needed to be addressed. To expedite my recovery, I made regular visits to Kevin's house for physiotherapy sessions on the weekends. Fortunately, this treatment quickly alleviated the pain. However, I still remained unsure if my thigh would fully recover until I resumed running.

Another issue I faced was persistent tiredness and weakness. I recognised that this was a natural response that would gradually fade over time. However, I was determined to ensure it wouldn't become a persistent problem. To promote healthy blood circulation and active recovery, I incorporated swimming sessions into my routine for the following week. My intention was to stay active while avoiding the risk of over-exertion or injuries that could arise from abruptly returning to full training. By gradually reintroducing training sessions, I aimed to establish a steady momentum and limit the chances of setbacks or injuries.

It wasn't until I returned home to Dublin from the race that I noticed an issue that is challenging for me to discuss. I believe it's important to address it openly. Although it threatens my sense of masculinity, as a father of three boys and considering that everything has always worked down there, I feel comfortable talking about it without feeling my manhood is compromised. This topic is rarely spoken about by men, making it difficult to put into words. Essentially, I was suffering with Wangxiety.

The prolonged hours in the saddle during the race placed immense pressure on the perineum, the area between the anus and penis. It's where the nerves and blood vessels responsible for supplying blood to the penis are located. The constant pressure hindered blood flow and caused the issue. Before conducting any research, I was genuinely concerned that this problem might be permanent. Experiencing erectile dysfunction created significant psychological stress for me. It became a constant worry and preoccupied my thoughts throughout the day. Seeking answers, I conducted online research and discovered that cycling-induced erectile dysfunction is typically temporary and reversible. This finding offered some hope for my eventual recovery. As time passed without any improvement, there was a lingering fear that I might be among the small percentage mentioned in these studies who suffered permanent effects.

Realising the importance of seeking professional guidance, I decided to visit a doctor, and I regret that I didn't do so earlier. In early January, I finally shared my concerns with the doctor. He clarified matters I had previously found during my own research. If I had sought medical assistance earlier, it could have eased my fears.

Cyclists who spend hours on their bikes often encounter this common issue. In my experience, I raised my saddle height during DecaUK, thinking it would improve my posture while riding. Unfortunately, this adjustment resulted in increased pressure on my perineum, causing blockage in the blood flow to the area. Just like when a beaver uses logs to obstruct a river, the continuous pressure for eight hours a day, over ten days, had a similar effect.

Thankfully there are methods to aid the healing process. Firstly, reducing cycling activity while the issue persists is recommended. Additionally, studies indicate that using a no-nose saddle can alleviate perineum pressure, thereby reducing interference with blood flow. Lastly, seeking a professional bike fit from an expert who employs pressure maps to determine the ideal saddle position for optimal performance and comfort can also be beneficial.

In hindsight, if someone were to ask me whether participating in DecaUK was worth the time, financial investment, and knowing all the physical issues, my answer would be a resounding "Yes." The expense turned out to be money well spent, not just because of the significant effect my success had on me but also because it seemed like the correct goal for me to pursue at that time in my life. Completing the event dramatically improved my self-confidence, not just in sport but in all aspects of my life. The experience pushed me to stretch my limits and ultimately inspired me to embark on new ventures. Following DecaUK, I took the leap and wrote this book. Additionally, I launched my own podcast called the Ger Prendergast podcast and started my own triathlon coaching business called GP Tri-Coaching. All of these ventures stemmed from the incredible experience I had at DecaUK.

At the time of the race, I was fortunate to be in a position where attending the event was feasible. I didn't have a full-time job or a business that I couldn't take time away from, allowing me to dedicate the necessary time for training while the children were in school and, Miriam, was at work. This minimised any impact on my family. I felt a strong drive to undertake something significant, not only for myself but also for my loved ones, especially after the loss we had all experienced.

Chapter 8: The Role of Sport in My Life

Looking Back: Reflections on My Life and Competitive Journey

- Sport has played a fundamental role in shaping the person I have become today. When I lost the vision in my left eye, it was through sports that I found equilibrium and was able to seamlessly blend in with my peers. Sports helped me overcome fear, insecurity and the constant concern of how others saw me, enabling me to embrace my true self. During those years, football/ soccer became my passion. Although I no longer actively participate in the sport in my forties, I remain immensely grateful for how it aided in my personal healing process.
- Following that, I faced a battle with alcohol and came to the realisation that abstaining from drinking was crucial to becoming the person I aspired to be. During this period, my ambition was to excel in futsal and proudly represent my nation. Once again, it was my passion for sports that provided the catalyst for my personal healing and growth.
- Later, in 2017, sports came to my rescue once more after the devastating loss of Mick. My family and I were engulfed in grief, facing an incredibly challenging time. However, within me, there was an innate understanding that my body craved the healing power of sports, not only for my physical well-being but, crucially, for my mental health. I channelled my energy into training and relied on DecaUK to provide me with a sense of purpose and aid in overcoming the deep void that grief had left in our lives. Once again, sport became the medicine through which I healed myself.

Boundaries and Blessings in One Park Run

In recent years, I challenged myself to complete a marathon every Saturday for an entire month. However, at the time, the world was grappling with the Cov-id-19 pandemic and strict restrictions were in place, confining individuals to a two-kilometre radius around their homes
With that in mind, I would run the marathons around my local park, which is

500 metres from my house and also has a one-mile perimeter around the outside of the park. During one of these marathon runs, I came across a lady with a young boy, approximately four years old. They were out for a morning walk in the park. The park gates were not opened for access into the park yet, as it was only 8am at this point. The park rangers opened the gates at 9:30am, a fact myself, the lady, or the people who were in the park already, did not know. As I ran by, I heard her asking a man who was already in the park, "What time did the gates open?" The man who had jumped over the park fence, which is approximately 4 feet in height and made up of 5 horizontal bars, almost like steps, which made it quite easy to get over and into the park, replied, "I'm not sure." The park was quite full of other runners and walkers at this point, too.

The lady faced difficulties entering the park, as she found it difficult to get through the fence due to her poor physical fitness.

Each time I completed a 1-mile lap, I came across the lady and her little boy, who could not access the park until 9:30am and was standing at the gate impatiently while gazing at the other people inside.

I felt concern for the lady and after several laps and time passing, I considered offering her assistance to get over the fence. However, I hesitated, recognising it might be inappropriate or unwelcome. Almost ashamed to run past her while she couldn't access the park due to closed gates, I felt empathy for her struggles, especially given her current physical condition. During that time, a range of emotions swept over me—empathy, compassion and even shame for not helping.

I want to clarify that my intention isn't to pass judgement on others but to reflect on my own journey and the profound impact of sports on my life.

After experiencing a wave of emotions, gratitude overwhelmed me. This episode suddenly prompted me to reflect on what my life could have been if, as a slightly overweight child, I hadn't had the chance to engage in any sports. If my father hadn't provided me with all those inputs, if I didn't have my brothers around, or if I had lived in a central urban area, my life might have taken a radically different path.

Instead, because of my childhood experiences, I now have the ability to jump a fence to get into the park, to spontaneously start running, or to sprint and catch a frisbee thrown by one of my sons. I am immensely grateful for the opportunity to have grown up practising sports.

Growing up immersed in various sports profoundly impacted my life. Playing numerous sports as a child not only made me fit and healthy but also ignited a passion for diverse athletic experiences. This passion endures into adulthood, keeping me in good health.

Witnessing others not enjoying such opportunities makes me realise how fortunate I am. I owe my gratitude to the childhood chance to express my sports passion, an opportunity I truly cherish.

Winning DecaUK and reflecting on my journey underscored the immense value of my sports-filled upbringing. The physical fitness I gained from my childhood passions now serve as pillars for my well-being and success. Beyond the physical benefits, sports provided mental resilience, confidence, and powerful tools for combating stress and anxiety.

In expressing gratitude, I thank my family and appreciate the meaningful connections forged through sports. This journey highlights the profound impact of sports on shaping my identity and fostering mental well-being beyond the field. Sport, a conduit for connection, confidence and resilience, stands as a beacon against life's challenges and this book is a celebration of the profound and multifaceted gifts that sports bestow upon us—a legacy of gratitude and triumphs that transcend the finish lines of any race.

The End

Part 5
Further Exploration

Multidisciplinarity

Reflecting on my childhood, I realise how crucial it was for me to engage in a variety of sports. Back in the day, alongside my friends, I enthusiastically dabbled in golf, rugby, hockey, basketball, tennis and even explored numerous other athletic pursuits. The sheer range of sports I participated in kept me invigorated and constantly eager to stay active.

This is precisely why triathlon has such a magnetic appeal for me. With triathlon, I have the opportunity to train for and compete in three distinct sports as one collective event. Alternatively, I can choose to compete in each sport individually, such as road running, road cycling, or swimming. Moreover, the comprehensive fitness and skills cultivated in triathlon can also be used in related sports like sea swimming, mountain biking, trail running and others that integrate elements of swimming, biking or running.

During my childhood, soccer was my main sport, but I found it refreshing to explore other games like basketball. Playing basketball provided a welcome respite for my legs from the repetitive impact of kicking a soccer ball with force. Additionally, it offered a chance to engage my arms more intensely through shooting the basketball.

In a similar manner, when I had the chance to play hurling, I discovered that it placed a greater emphasis on my back, shoulders, arms and core rather than solely focusing on my legs. This variety in sports allowed me to target different muscle groups and experience a well-rounded physical workout.

Upon reflection, I can identify numerous advantages to playing multiple sports:

1. Development of Different Muscle Groups and Movement Patterns: Each sport targets various muscle groups and requires different movement patterns. By participating in multiple sports, we can develop a well-rounded physique and improve our coordination and agility.
2. Motivation, Interest and Challenge: Incorporating variety into our training sessions helps maintain motivation, interest and a sense of challenge. This, in turn, increases our likelihood of consistently showing up for training sessions and ensures more consistent progress.
3. Cross-Training Benefits: Engaging in different sports provides the opportunity for cross-training. Working different muscles helps strengthen areas that support the primary muscles used in our primary sport. This not only enhances performance but also allows overworked muscles to rest and recover.
4. Prevention of Burnout and Overuse Injuries: Specialising in just one sport

can lead to physical burnout and overuse injuries. Playing multiple sports promotes a more balanced physical activity routine, reducing the risk of strain and supporting overall physical well-being.

5. Enhanced Interest in Physical Activity: Playing multiple sports offers a broader range of activities and keeps individuals engaged and interested in physical activity. This is particularly beneficial for youths, as it helps maintain their interest and enthusiasm for being active.
6. Cognitive and Emotional Benefits: Research suggests that participating in multiple sports promotes neuroplasticity, which is the brain's ability to form new neurons and connections and reorganise neural networks. This can improve cognitive function, attention and mood. Engaging in a variety of sports can help stimulate the brain and foster overall mental well-being.

I encourage everyone to embrace the challenge of engaging in a new sport each year. This is a practice I personally follow and also recommend to my clients. It involves exploring various activities that push our limits and expand our horizons. For instance, I have participated in obstacle course races, ventured into indoor wall climbing and even braved the exhilarating experience of winter sea swimming, among other endeavours. As part of my future goals, I aspire to learn Brazilian Jiu-Jitsu, diving into the world of martial arts. Embarking on these new sporting ventures not only keeps us active and engaged but also allows us to continually grow and discover hidden talents and passions within ourselves.

In the United States, numerous athletes who have reached the pinnacle of professional sports, such as MLB, NFL and NBA, have a background of interchanging between different sports. One notable example is Tom Brady, widely regarded as one of the greatest American football quarterbacks of all time. Prior to his football career, Brady excelled in baseball at a high level. This showcases the potential benefits of exploring various sports before ultimately choosing a specific path.

In a similar vein, here in Ireland, many top rugby and Gaelic Athletic Association (GAA) players have a history of practising multiple sports before focusing their efforts on one for their professional careers. Rob Kearney, a highly esteemed rugby player who proudly represented the Irish national rugby team for more than a decade and earned 95 caps, is a prime example. Additionally, he had the honour of representing the British and Irish Lions on two tours, which is the pinnacle of professional rugby. Kearney's journey to success began with a foundation in Gaelic football. Even after retiring from professional rugby, Kearney returned to the sport that initially shaped him into such a high-level athlete. These examples exemplify the advantages of engaging in multiple sports, as it allows athletes to develop a diverse skill set, gain different perspectives and potentially discover a passion and aptitude for a particular sport. The experience of participating in multiple sports can complement and enhance an athlete's overall athletic abilities, contributing to their success in their chosen field. It underscores the versatility, adaptability and transferable skills that arise from engaging in a variety of sports.

Goal Setting and Motivation

In order to accomplish anything in life, it is essential to create a plan outlining how we will achieve our goals. However, before establishing these goals, we must take a moment to reflect on why we desire them. Why do we want to finish an Ironman? Why are we willing to endure potentially seventeen hours of relentless struggle? Similarly, it is important to ask ourselves, "Why do we want to earn seventy thousand euros per year?" if that is our financial goal.

Regardless of the nature of our goals, it is crucial to understand the underlying motivation behind them. If our aspirations to complete a marathon or Ironman are simply based on the fact that our neighbour accomplished the feat, our 'why' may not possess enough power to rouse us from our bed at 4 a.m. on a cold, dark and rainy Monday morning for a run. However, if our 'why' is strong and deeply rooted, it can serve as the fuel that propels us forward when faced with challenging circumstances. We require a compelling 'why' to navigate through the obstacles that inevitably appear along our journey.

Upon winning the Deca event, I experienced a profound sense of elation. This victory was particularly significant for me, as I had been struggling to come to terms with the loss of my brother-in-law to suicide. Returning home, I felt an overwhelming wave of positivity that my success at DecaUK had generated within the community where I grew up and have deep roots. Additionally, I recognised the positive impact it had on my wife and her siblings. It provided them with something to focus on and raised their spirits. Reflecting on how proud my late brother-in-law, Mick, would have been, I shifted the prevailing negativity to a more positive outlook. The satisfaction of bringing that sense of pride and accomplishment to my loved ones amplified the gratification I felt about my own achievements. While my story may be unique in its circumstances, I pose a question to you:

Can you identify a genuine and impactful 'why' for yourself?

Once you have formulated your answer, take time to reflect on it and assess its resonance within you. Is this 'why' truly representative of your motivations for competing and setting goals?

When approaching DecaUK, I did not have expectations of winning. However, I did arrive well-prepared and trained, which instilled in me the confidence to take on such a formidable challenge. I also possessed the awareness to differentiate between allowing myself some rest and slacking off. Whenever I felt the inclination to slack off, I reminded myself of my goal and questioned whether indulging in complacency would serve me in reaching that objective. This self-accountability and focus played a crucial role in my success.

When my motivation starts to dwindle, I find it helpful to remind myself of my goal and the reasons why I want to achieve it. Take, for instance, my current goal of completing 30 Iron distance triathlons in 30 days. Why do I want to achieve this feat? My aim is to become Ireland's most renowned Ultra Endurance Triathlete, so that when people think of Ultra Triathlon, they associate it with my name. But why is this ambition meaningful to me?

1. Firstly, I envision leaving a lasting legacy. It would be gratifying to know that I will be remembered for accomplishing something significant long after I have passed.
2. Furthermore, I aspire to elevate my profile as an athlete to establish a platform from which I can offer advice and guidance on training and nutrition for overall fitness. By growing my influence, I hope to make a positive impact and help others achieve their fitness goals.
3. Lastly, I am driven by the desire to build a thriving business that can serve as an asset for my family, ensuring their future security. The thought of this should be enough to ignite a fire within me and compel me to embark on a rigorous run or dedicate an hour to training at the gym.

If these compelling reasons fail to ignite my passion, it's important for me to reflect and identify if there's something missing or if I need to reassess my goals. Having a strong and meaningful 'why' is crucial in fuelling my motivation and drive to push through challenges and stay committed to achieving my objectives.

Once we have identified our goal, such as completing a marathon or Ironman, the next step is to refine and focus on that goal.

- Is your goal Specific?
- Is your goal Measurable?
- Is your goal Achievable?
- Is your goal Realistic?
- Is your goal Time Bound?

This enables you to monitor progress and increase the attainability of the goal. Then, we must determine the steps necessary to reach the goal. If it involves a physical challenge like a marathon or an Ironman, creating a training plan is essential. We should incorporate our training into our daily routine and use visualisation as a powerful positive psychological technique to aid in accomplishing our goals. Personally, I am a great admirer of Brian Tracey, who suggests envisioning ourselves as already having achieved our goal. Imagine the satisfaction of completing each training session and the exhilaration of crossing the finish line. Brian Tracey also advocates for daily goal writing, using the present tense as if we have already reached them. This exercise rewires our brain to believe we have accomplished our aspirations and prompts us to act accordingly.

According to Dr. Gail Matthews, a psychology professor at Dominican University in California, writing down your goals daily increases your chances of achieving them by 42%. In a study involving 267 participants, Dr. Matthews discovered the significant impact of simply putting your goals on paper. It's truly amazing, isn't it?
As a triathlon coach, I strongly emphasise the importance of accountability. This is why many people choose to hire a coach. While it would be great if following a generic online training programme could guarantee effortless goal attainment, the reality is that most individuals face challenges along the way. They require a structured system of accountability to ensure success and this is precisely what a coach can provide.
Having a coach serves as a valuable support system, allowing individuals to express their thoughts, emotions and uncertainties. Being accountable to someone helps to maintain focus and motivation. Additionally, a coach plays a crucial role in tracking progress, which can be extremely valuable. The feeling of accomplishment and encouragement that comes from witnessing positive advancements can be very motivating and uplifting.

G.P. Formula to Success

Success is the attainment of the specific goal or objective that you have set for yourself. What success looks like can vary greatly from person to person. For one, crossing the finish line of a 5k road race may be a significant achievement, while for another, completing an Ironman may be the ultimate goal.
Over the years, drawing from personal experiences, extensive reading, and guidance from coaches, I have developed a framework that breaks down success into its constituent parts. I've chosen to articulate these elements in a formula, illustrating their interrelationships and offering my perspective on success. While applying this formula may pose challenges, I believe it can significantly assist you in clarifying your thoughts, defining your vision, and focusing efficiently on the next steps. This, in turn, enhances the likelihood of a more seamless integration of all the puzzle pieces on your journey toward success.
"Success consists of going from failure to failure without loss of enthusiasm." - Winston Churchill

1. Motivation (Mn)

After setting a goal and finding your reason for pursuing it, your motivation will initially be high. However, it is important to be aware that motivation is a powerful emotion that tends to diminish over time. This phenomenon is evident every January when gyms are filled to the brim with enthusiastic individuals, but by February, the once bustling gyms become noticeably quieter.

2. Consistency (Cy)

Consistency involves the repetition of actions or behaviours. Whether we are swimmers, cyclists, runners, gym enthusiasts, yoga practitioners, or engaged in any chosen activity, consistent practice is vital in order to improve and achieve our goals. The more we engage in a particular activity, the more familiar it becomes to us. Our bodies absorb the information and integrate it into our nervous systems, transforming it into a natural movement pattern over time. You may have heard the expression "consistency is key." While I don't believe it is the sole key to success, it is certainly an essential ingredient in the formula for achieving success.

3. Self-Discipline (SD)

The distinguishing factor that sets apart the top athletes in any sport is their unrelenting commitment to completing their training and preparation, even when they have no desire to do so.

If it's raining, they will put on a coat and brave the weather to get their session done.

If it's snowing, they will bundle up in hats and gloves to venture outside and complete their session.

If there's a heatwave, they will apply sunblock, stay hydrated and still push through their session.

Even when it's 5am and they yearn to stay in bed, they will rise, don their prepared workout gear and head outside to get their session done.

This dedication is what contributes to their success. They understand that starting a session can be challenging, but once they warm up and get into it, it becomes easier. Eventually, they wonder why they made such a fuss about it in the first place.

Is it motivation that drives them? No, it's self-discipline.

Like most people, I struggle with breaking the habit of procrastination. It's a constant battle that requires conscious effort. Breaking poor habits is not easy, but just like starting a training session, once you initiate the habit, it becomes easier and you find that it wasn't as daunting as you initially thought. Breaking habits may be challenging at first, then there's a period of adjustment and eventually it becomes the new normal.

Every day, I remind myself to resist the temptation to procrastinate. Even if I would rather relax and watch TV, I know that once I start and get into the task, it won't feel as difficult. The key is to procrastinate less and focus on building positive habits.

4. Momentum (M)

Momentum is a state that we can attain through the development of positive habits. Take regular exercise, for example. Initially, it may be challenging to go to the gym, unsure of what we're doing and experiencing discomfort afterwards. However, if we persist, we will eventually find pleasure and ease in our routine. We establish familiarity with the gym and the pain we once felt becomes a distant memory.

Once these habits are ingrained, we experience momentum, or flow. It's like having a tailwind propelling us forward. We have already put in the hard work of battling against the headwind to get from point A to point B. Upon turning around to return to point A, we suddenly feel a surge of ease, as if someone is gently pushing us along. While striving to achieve our goals in any aspect of our lives, we encounter resistance and significant challenges. However, as time passes, the struggle diminishes until what was once a challenging task has become automated in our behaviours. This is the power of momentum and once we attain it, we become reluctant to lose it.

So, when you find yourself tempted to take a day off or take it easy for no legitimate reason, remember that preserving momentum is crucial. Once it dissipates, regaining it can be difficult. Losing momentum can set back months of progress. This is a lesson I've truly come to understand during the process of writing this book.

5. Self-Confidence (SC)

Maintaining the confidence to persevere towards our goals, despite the challenges we may encounter, is crucial. The journey to success is seldom linear or effortless. It is a path filled with obstacles, setbacks, highs and lows. However, if we remain determined and stay on track, we will eventually reach our desired destination. We can be confident in the knowledge that our goals will be achieved.

Once we make the decision to pursue our aspirations, it is important not to overthink or allow the fear of failure to hold us back from becoming who we aspire to be. The fear of how others may perceive us has often prevented us from pursuing our good ideas or attempting new ventures. Even in my own experience of writing this book, there have been times when I have taken extended breaks due to bouts of fear.

What if people view me as a fraud?
What if they see me as arrogant?
Who would even read or care about this book?
However, I have come to find that reading a motivational book can often eliminate these doubts and remind me of the worthiness of completing my own book. The same can apply to each and every one of us, whether it's writing, recording podcasts, or any other form of creative expression. We should not underestimate the value we can bring to others through our work.

6. Dedication (D)

Maintaining focus and a strong commitment to our goals is of utmost importance. In a world filled with countless distractions, it is crucial that we cultivate awareness of these external factors and remain dedicated to our objectives. Effective time management is an invaluable tool for staying committed to our training. Setting aside specific and non-negotiable slots for activities, such as swimming sessions on Monday, Wednesday and Friday evenings at 7pm, is essential for staying on track.

7. Courage (Ce)

Courage and self-confidence go hand in hand, but it is particularly important to tap into our courage when we find ourselves in a negative headspace or caught up in overthinking. Despite our fears, we must summon the courage to reconnect with our self-confidence and push forward. When faced with adversity and the overwhelming knowledge of what lies ahead and the tasks that must be accomplished, it is crucial to display courage. We must confront these challenges head-on, demonstrating resilience and determination. This requires finding the inner strength to persevere and push through, even when faced with uncertainty or fear.

Step-by-Step Process

After contemplating our desires, we proceeded to jot down our S.M.A.R.T. goals. These goals possess specific attributes, such as my intention to complete Ironman Cork next year. Furthermore, they are measurable, allowing us to track our progress and make necessary adjustments. With the right approach, attaining these goals is feasible, as evidenced by countless individuals who cross the finish line of an Ironman with a mere hour remaining before the cut-off time.

However, it is crucial for our goals to remain realistic. For instance, it would be impractical to expect that one could finish an Ironman without any prior experience in swimming or cycling, particularly if the event is only a week away. Ultimately, to ensure a sense of urgency, we establish a time-bound element to our goals. In the case of the Ironman, the race day serves as the designated deadline.

After deciding to take the plunge, we can follow these steps:

- Step 1: Ignite Motivation - The initial surge of motivation that arises from setting our goal is the first vital component of the equation.
- Step 2: Embrace Consistency - Motivation can only carry us so far; now it's time to incorporate consistency. Even when we lack the desire, we must commit to showing up daily.
- Step 3: Develop Self-Discipline - Through the multiplication of consistency, self-discipline emerges, making the process gradually more effortless and automatic.
- Step 4: Harness Momentum - By combining motivation, consistency and self-discipline, we unlock a state of flow known as momentum. Everything becomes smoother, the struggle fades and our performance sees a remarkable boost.
- Motivation + (Self Discipline x Consistency) → Momentum
- Step 5: Embrace Self-Confidence - The blend of motivation and doubt becomes a thing of the past. After enduring uphill battles, we have reached the peak. The self-belief that has been growing within us surfaces, instilling a newfound sense of confidence in our daily pursuit of our goals.
- Step 6: Unyielding Dedication - Multiply the newly acquired self-confidence with a deep-rooted, unconscious, unwavering willpower that surpasses any level of commitment. Let this dedication anchor us in the face of challenges.
- Step 7: Embrace Courage - Courage becomes crucial, particularly when circumstances deviate from our expectations. At any point in the equation, courage can be applied, for setbacks and obstacles are inevitable at any stage of the journey.

{[Motivation + (Self-Discipline x Consistency)]Momentum} + [(Self-Confidence x Dedication) + Courage] = Success
{[Mn + (SD x Cy)]Mo} + [(SC x D) + Ce] = Success

Success - If you find yourself falling short of your goal, it is essential to engage in an open and honest dialogue with yourself regarding the execution of each step in the formula. Evaluate your progress using the following scoring system, providing an honest rating on a scale of 1 to 10, with 1 representing the lowest level and 10 indicating the highest level of implementation for each step.

Were you motivated to start?

1 2 3 4 5 6 7 8 9 10

○ ○ ○ ○ ○ ○ ○ ○ ○ ○

Were you doing it for the right reason?

1 2 3 4 5 6 7 8 9 10

○ ○ ○ ○ ○ ○ ○ ○ ○ ○

Were you consistent enough with the tasks that needed to be done?

1 2 3 4 5 6 7 8 9 10

○ ○ ○ ○ ○ ○ ○ ○ ○ ○

Was your self-discipline strong?

1 2 3 4 5 6 7 8 9 10

○ ○ ○ ○ ○ ○ ○ ○ ○ ○

Did you make excuses to skip training sessions?

1 2 3 4 5 6 7 8 9 10

○ ○ ○ ○ ○ ○ ○ ○ ○ ○

Did you feel things get easier as time passed and momentum grew?

1 2 3 4 5 6 7 8 9 10

○ ○ ○ ○ ○ ○ ○ ○ ○ ○

Were you confident in the process and gave it your all?

1 2 3 4 5 6 7 8 9 10

○ ○ ○ ○ ○ ○ ○ ○ ○ ○

Were you seriously dedicated to the plan you set out?

1	2	3	4	5	6	7	8	9	10
○	○	○	○	○	○	○	○	○	○

Did you allow outside influences to affect you? i.e., comparing to others.

1	2	3	4	5	6	7	8	9	10
○	○	○	○	○	○	○	○	○	○

Were you courageous when things started to get difficult?

1	2	3	4	5	6	7	8	9	10
○	○	○	○	○	○	○	○	○	○

Total score _______

Determining whether your score is high enough to classify your efforts as successful is subjective, as success is unique to each individual and depends on the specific goals being pursued. However, answering these questions provides you a way to measure different parameters of your activities and figure out what is lacking.

It is important to recognise that reaching our goals according to our intended timeline is not always possible.

We may encounter failures along the way, but it is crucial to view these setbacks as valuable feedback and opportunities for growth. When we have diligently applied the seven steps of the formula in our pursuit but fall short of achieving our goal, we can find reassurance in the knowledge that we have no regrets.

Feeling successful comes from knowing we have given our all, grown personally and developed as individuals, athletes, or in any other endeavour we have strived for.

We can take this experience, learn from it and try again, using the lessons learned to move forward towards future accomplishments.

Part 6

Resources

Part 6

The following section provides a collection of valuable tools, information, and references to support your journey in endurance sports, nutrition, and personal development. These resources have been carefully curated based on my experiences and the knowledge I've gained throughout my athletic career, particularly during my preparation for and participation in DecaUK.

Here you'll find detailed nutritional guides, including meal plans and recipes that fueled my performance. There are also training tips, equipment recommendations, and a list of suggested readings that have influenced my approach to ultra-endurance events and overall wellness. Whether you're an aspiring athlete, a seasoned competitor, or simply interested in adopting a healthier lifestyle, these resources offer practical advice and inspiration to help you on your path. Use them as a starting point to customise your own approach to training, nutrition, and personal growth.

Equipment and Costs

It is important to shed light on the financial aspects of participating in events like DecaUK, as it can be valuable information for individuals contemplating similar challenges. Given the magnitude of the event, a substantial investment

in equipment was necessary. I found myself allocating a significant amount of money towards new cycling clothing, cycling accessories, food, travel and accommodation, even before factoring in the entry fee. The expenses quickly added up, reaching an overwhelming figure.

The entry fee for DecaUK came to €2000, which was covered by a generous contribution made by Rob Murphy, the esteemed owner of Supervalu Ballymun. Rob, being an active member of the triathlon community himself, understood the financial burdens and hurdles that come with participating in such an event. After I approached him for support and explained my goal, he readily extended his support. There were additional expenses to consider, such as food while travelling, goggles, hats, gloves, contact lenses and other necessary items, which pushed the total cost close to the €8,000 mark. Listed below are the necessary items required for entry into the event and to ensure I had everything I needed to complete it.

Healthy Nutrition

Game-Changer: Unlocking the Protein Potential of Plants

Funny thing – meat eaters often worry vegans lack essential nutrients. But the truth is, it may be the meat eaters who are missing the bounty of vitamins and minerals packed into plants. Meat gets all the glory because it naturally contains all nine essential amino acids. However, you can obtain these essential amino acids from a variety of plant sources as well. It might take some planning and possibly supplementation to ensure there are no nutrient deficiencies, but it's definitely doable. In fact, by understanding protein complementarity–such as combining beans and rice–you can create a complete amino acid profile solely from plant sources. Moreover, some plant-based foods naturally contain all nine essential amino acids, although this fact may not be widely known.

Additionally, while plant-based diets can be rich in many vitamins and minerals, it is crucial to be aware that nutrients like Vitamin B12, iron, zinc, and omega-3 fatty acids are generally more absorbable from animal sources. Vegans need to plan their diet carefully or consider supplements for these nutrients to maintain optimal health.

It's crucial to understand that simply adopting a vegan label doesn't automatically make one's diet healthier; the key lies in well-planned nutritional choices that ensure a balance of all essential nutrients. The idea that meat is the only protein game in town is a myth. Since I had some difficulty myself in finding this crucial and useful information, I decided to break down the science of plant-based protein into five easy steps, making it accessible and straightforward to ensure a nutritious, plant-based diet:

1. Identifying the nine essential amino acids and where to find them.
2. Table of Recommended Dietary Allowances (RDA) for amino acids.
3. Calculating your own daily RDA quantity.
4. Table of amino acids in plant-based foods.
5. Suggestions on how to set up your personal diet plan.

This guide will equip you with the knowledge to create and customise your own delicious, protein-packed plant-based diet.

1. What Are the Nine Essential Amino Acids and Where Can You Find Them?

Have you ever wondered how to ensure you're getting all the essential amino acids on a plant-based diet? It can be overwhelming trying to figure it all out. I've personally encountered challenges in sourcing this information, which is why I've compiled it to simplify your life.

Disclaimer: It's important to recognise that individual needs may vary due to our unique medical profiles. With this in mind, I'm providing fundamental, evidence-based insights to equip you with the knowledge necessary to tailor this information to your specific circumstances and confidently progress towards your health goals.

So, let's dive in! Below you can find the list of the 9 essential amino acids and which foods, including processed foods, contains them:

Where you can find the 9 essential Amino Acids

Essential Amino Acid	Plant-Based Food Sources	Non-Plant-Based Food Sources
Histidine	Soy Products (tofu & tempeh), brown rice, chickpeas, lentils, quinoa, hemp, black beans, sesame seeds, chia seeds, buckwheat, soy beans, spirulina and nutritional yeast	Meat, poultry, fish, dairy products
Isoleucine	Soy products, lentils, chickpeas, quinoa, pumpkin seeds, hemp, black beans, sesame seeds, oats, chia seeds, buckwheat, soy beans, spirulina and nutritional yeast	Meat, fish, poultry, eggs, dairy products
Leucine	Soy products, lentils, chickpeas, quinoa, peanuts, hemp, black beans, sesame seeds, oats, brown rice, chia seeds, buckwheat, soy beans, spirulina and nutritional yeast	Meat, poultry, fish, eggs, dairy products
Lysine	Soy products, lentils, chickpeas, quinoa, pumpkin seeds, hemp, black beans, peas, sesame seeds, chia seeds, buckwheat, soy beans, spirulina and nutritional yeast	Meat, poultry, fish, dairy products
Methionine	Lentils, chickpeas, quinoa, sunflower seeds, sesame seeds, hemp, black beans, sesame seeds, chia seeds, buckwheat, nuts, soy beans, spirulina and nutritional yeast	Meat, fish, poultry, eggs, dairy products
Phenylalanine	Soy products, lentils, peanuts, quinoa, almonds, pumpkin seeds, hemp, black beans, sesame seeds, nuts, chia seeds, buckwheat, soy beans, spirulina and nutritional yeast	Meat, poultry, fish, dairy products

Threonine	Soy Products, lentils, chickpeas, quinoa, spinach, hemp, black beans, sesame seeds, chia seeds, buckwheat, soy beans, spirulina and nutritional yeast	Meat, poultry, fish, dairy products
Tryptophan	Soy Products, lentils, quinoa, pumpkin seeds, oats, hemp, oats, black beans, sesame seeds, chia seeds, buckwheat, soy beans, spirulina and nutritional yeast	Meat, poultry, fish, dairy products
Valine	Soy products, lentils, chickpeas, quinoa, peanuts, almonds, hemp, black beans, nuts, sesame seeds, chia seeds, oats, brown rice, buckwheat, soy beans, spirulina and nutritional yeast	Meat, fish, poultry, eggs, dairy products

2. Recommended Daily Allowances (RDAs) for Each Amino Acid

In the table below you can find the recommended milligrams of each amino acid per day, per kg.
Estimates of Amino Acid Requirements (from WHO 1985)

Requirements, mg/kg per day, by age group	
Amino Acid	**Adults (3)**
Histidine	8–12 mg
Isoleucine	10 mg
Leucine	14 mg
Lysine	12 mg
Methionine plus cystine	13 mg
Phenylalanine plus tyrosine	14 mg
Threonine	7 mg
Tryptophan	3.5 mg
Valine	10 mg
Total without histidine	84 mg

Based on the highest estimate of requirement to achieve nitrogen balance. Data from several investigators (reviewed in FAO/WHO, 1973).
Source: https://www.ncbi.nlm.nih.gov/books/NBK234922/table/ttt00008/?report=objectonly

3. RDA Personal Calculation

To calculate the daily quantity of amino acids you should consume as an athlete weighing 80 kg, we'll use the provided values per kilogram of body weight from the table above 'Estimates of Amino Acid Requirements (from WHO 1985)'.
Here's the calculation:
Let's multiply each of these values by the weight (80 kg):

- Histidine: 8-12 mg/kg/day * 80 kg = 640-960 mg/day
- Isoleucine: 10 mg/kg/day * 80 kg = 800 mg/day
- Leucine: 14 mg/kg/day * 80 kg = 1120 mg/day
- Lysine: 12 mg/kg/day * 80 kg = 960 mg/day
- Methionine plus cystine: 13 mg/kg/day * 80 kg = 1040 mg/day
- Phenylalanine plus tyrosine: 14 mg/kg/day * 80 kg = 1120 mg/day
- Threonine: 7 mg/kg/day * 80 kg = 560 mg/day
- Tryptophan: 3.5 mg/kg/day * 80 kg = 280 mg/day
- Valine: 10 mg/kg/day * 80 kg = 800 mg/day

These values give you an idea of the approximate quantities of each amino acid you should aim to consume daily. As you can see, the quantities are very manageable because most of the time they are less than a gram per day.

4. Table of Amino Acids in Plant-Based Food

The great news is that there are plant-based foods that encompass all nine essential amino acids; these are often termed 'complete proteins'. While we do provide an extensive list of such plant-based foods at the start of the following table, I recommend diversifying your diet by incorporating a variety of plant-based foods into your daily meals.
I've gathered the specifics of the amount of each necessary amino acid in each plant-based food from many sources to assist you in organising your meals based on your tastes. This way, you'll be able to design your own diet.
In the table below you can find the approximate amounts of each essential amino acid per 100 grams of the listed foods.
Disclaimer: Keep in mind that these values can vary slightly depending on factors such as variety, processing, and preparation methods.

PLANT PROTEIN

1 gram edible protein per **100g (3,5 oz)** in weight

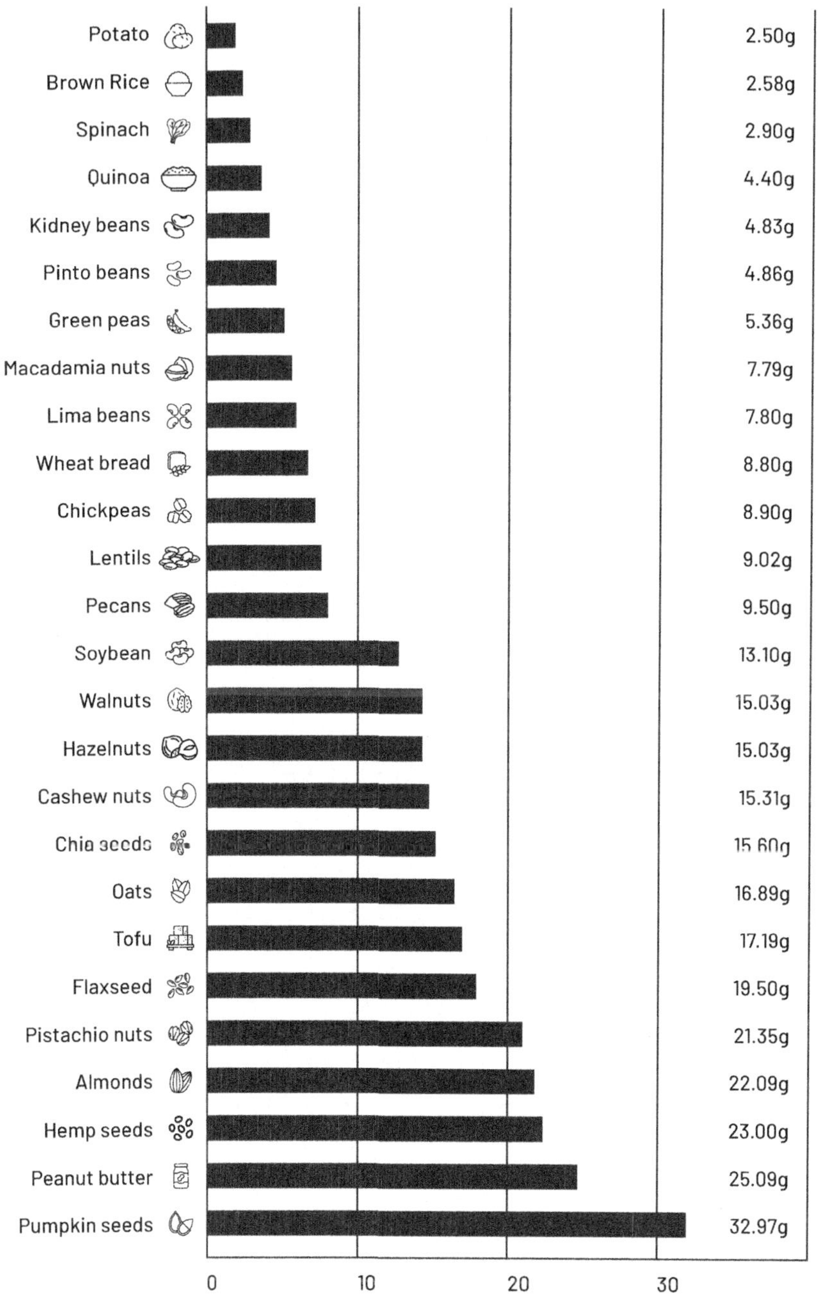

Food category	Food type	Methionine	Threonine	Tryptophan	Histidine	Leucine	Isoleucine	Lysine	Phenylalanine	Valine
Nuts and Seeds	Hemp Seeds	Methionine + Cysteine 5.88g	3.79g	0.26g	3.20g	Isoleucine + Leucine 5.21g	Isoleucine + Leucine 5.21g	2.88g	Phenylalanine + Tyrosine 9.63g	4.53g
Beans and Legumes	Black beans	0.133g	0.373g	0.105g	0.247g	0.708g	0.391g	0.608g	0.479g	0.464g
Yeast	Nutritional Yeast	1.5g	3.5g	1.0g	2.0g	8.0g	5.0g	6.5g	5.0g	4.5g
Nuts and Seeds	Sesame Seeds	0.739g	0.916g	0.309g	0.618g	1.65g	0.859g	0.672g	1.12g	1.1g
Nuts and Seeds	Chia Seeds	0.588g	0.709g	0.436g	0.63g	1.37g	0.801g	0.97g	1.02g	0.95g
Pseudocereal	Quinoa	0.33g	0.45g	0.12g	0.29g	1.09g	0.63g	0.74g	0.69g	0.78g
Pseudocereal	Buckwheat	0.21g	0.46g	0.14g	0.43g	0.87g	0.45g	0.43g	0.64g	0.57g
Legumes	Soybeans	0.29g	0.58g	0.15g	0.52g	1.37g	0.76g	0.99g	0.92g	0.82g
Alge	Spirulina	0.118g	0.306g	0.096g	0.112g	0.509g	0.331g	0.312g	0.286g	0.362g
Nuts and Seeds	Pumpkin Seeds			0.12g	0.41g	1.49g	0.78g	0.63g	0.06g	0.20g
Beans and Legumes	Chickpeas (garbanzo beans)	0.04g	0.13g	0.03g						
Beans and Legumes	Lentils	0.06g	0.15g	0.04g						
Beans and Legumes	Kidney beans	0.13g	0.13g	0.13g						
Beans and Legumes	Peas	0.02g	0.02g	0.03g						
Nuts and Seeds	Almonds			0.04g					0.14g	0.15g
Nuts and Seeds	Walnuts			0.02g					0.10g	0.12g
Nuts and Seeds	Cashews			0.02g					0.10g	0.14g

Nuts and Seeds	Sunflower Seeds			0.05g					0.14g	0.18g
Nuts and Seeds	Flaxseeds	0.17g		0.14g					0.19g	
Whole Grains	Brown rice	0.03g	0.09g	0.02g						
Whole Grains	Oats	0.07g	0.15g	0.03g						
Whole Grains	Barley	0.04g	0.11g	0.02g						
Whole Grains	Millet	0.05g	0.15g	0.04g						
Whole Grains	Amaranth	0.05g	0.15g	0.05g						
Gluten	Seitan	0.12g	0.17g	0.05g						
Vegetables	Spinach	0.06g	0.14g	0.02g						
Vegetables	Broccoli	0.04g	0.12g	0.03g						
Vegetables	Brussel Sprouts	0.05g	0.14g	0.04g						
Vegetables	Asparagus	0.02g	0.08g	0.02g						
Vegetables	Cauliflower	0.02g	0.05g	0.01g						
Fruits	Avocado	0.02g	0.01g	0.02g						
Fruits	Banana		0.03g	0.01g					0.05g	
Fruits	Oranges		0.01g						0.02g	
Fruits	Apples		0.01g						0.01g	
Fruits	Berries (strawberries,-blueberries,raspberries)		0.02g	0.01g					0.04g	
Legume-based Pastas	Chickpea Pasta	0.05g	0.10g	0.02g						
Legume-based Pastas	Lentil Pasta	0.06g	0.10g	0.04g						

Data source for Hemp Seeds: This is the only data source available for Hemp Seeds but it contains aggregated data for some of the amino acids. However Hemp has one of the highest quantities of amino acids: https://www.researchgate.net/figure/Amino-acids-composition-of-hemp-protein-isolate-HPI_tbl2_364710359
Data for Black beans: https://fitaudit.com/food/135594/amino
Data for Spirulina: https://fitaudit.com/food/121447/amino
Data for all the other foods comes from: United States Department of Agriculture (USDA). National Nutrient Database for Standard Reference, FoodData Central. Accessed 11/04/2024 from https://fdc.nal.usda.gov/

5. Suggestions on How to Set Up Your Personal Diet Plan

It's very simple to add some of these plant-based ingredients into meals you may eat already, for example if I'm having a salad I'll always sprinkle on some chia seeds or if I'm having pasta, I'll serve with a nice pinch of nutritional yeast over the top.

The possibilities are endless, here are some examples to get you started:

- Sprinkle Hemp Seeds on Salad: Add a tablespoon of hemp seeds to your salad for extra protein and essential amino acids.
- Top Porridge/Oats with Almond Butter: Stir in a spoonful of almond butter into your oats for added protein and essential amino acids.
- Stir Chickpeas into Curry: Add chickpeas to your vegetable curry for a boost of protein and essential amino acids.
- Top Avocado Toast with Pumpkin Seeds: Spread mashed avocado on whole-grain toast and sprinkle with pumpkin seeds for extra protein and essential amino acids.
- Add Nutritional Yeast to Pasta Sauce: Sprinkle nutritional yeast over pasta dishes or mix it into the sauce for a cheesy flavour and added essential amino acids.
- Sprinkle Hemp Seeds on Salad: Add a tablespoon of hemp seeds to your salad for extra protein and essential amino acids.
- Top Porridge/Oats with Almond Butter: Stir in a spoonful of almond butter into your oats for added protein and essential amino acids.
- Stir Chickpeas into Curry: Add chickpeas to your vegetable curry for a boost of protein and essential amino acids.
- Top Avocado Toast with Pumpkin Seeds: Spread mashed avocado on whole-grain toast and sprinkle with pumpkin seeds for extra protein and essential amino acids.
- Add Nutritional Yeast to Pasta Sauce: Sprinkle nutritional yeast over pasta dishes or mix it into the sauce for a cheesy flavour and added essential amino acids.

- Mix Quinoa into Stir-Fry: Use quinoa as a base for your vegetable stir-fry instead of rice for a complete protein source.
- Blend Tofu into Smoothies: Add silken tofu to your fruit smoothie to increase the protein content and essential amino acids, if it's not your thing just go with cashews.
- Make Lentil Soup: Cook lentils into a hearty soup with vegetables for a nutritious meal packed with essential amino acids.
- Spread Hummus on Sandwiches: Use hummus as a spread on sandwiches instead of mayonnaise for a protein-rich option.
- Snack on Edamame: Enjoy edamame as a snack or add it to salads for a protein boost and essential amino acids.
- Make a Chia Seed Pudding: Mix chia seeds with plant-based milk and sweetener of choice to make a delicious pudding packed with essential amino acids.
- Blend Spinach into Smoothies: Add a handful of fresh spinach to your fruit smoothie for added nutrients, including essential amino acids. I find frozen spinach great for staying fresh and also keeping my smoothie cool.
- Mix Tofu Scramble with Veggies: Make a tofu scramble with sautéed vegetables like bell peppers, onions, and spinach for a protein-packed breakfast option.
- Use Black Beans in Tacos: Fill your tacos with seasoned black beans, lettuce, tomato, and avocado for a plant-based meal rich in essential amino acids.
- Snack on Almonds and Dried Fruit: Create your own trail mix by combining almonds with dried fruits like raisins or apricots for a convenient and nutritious snack.
- Add Lentils to Salads: Toss cooked lentils into your salads for added protein, fibre, and essential amino acids.
- Spread Cashew Cheese on Crackers: Enjoy cashew cheese spread on wholegrain crackers as a satisfying snack or appetiser.
- Stir-Fry Tempeh with Vegetables: Cook tempeh with your favourite vegetables in a stir-fry sauce for a flavorful and protein-rich dish.
- Make Peanut Butter Banana Sandwiches: Spread peanut butter on wholegrain bread and add sliced bananas for a delicious and protein-packed snack or meal.
- Sprinkle Sunflower Seeds on Soups: Top your soups or stews with roasted sunflower seeds for added crunch and essential amino acids.

Welcome to Your Week-Long Plant-Based Food Plan!

This meal plan offers a variety of delicious recipes to inspire your plant-based culinary journey while emphasising different goals each day, such as recovery, increased energy, and a focus on fat burning. Whether you're seeking nourishment for an active lifestyle or aiming to shed some extra pounds, this plan has you covered.

Preparing plant-based meals at home is not only satisfying but also promotes overall health and well-being. By following this meal plan, my hope is that you'll realise how easy it is to thrive on a plant-based diet when armed with knowledge and preparedness. Having the right ingredients on hand and knowing what to eat ensures consistency and success on your journey towards a healthier lifestyle.

Let's dive in and discover the abundance of flavours and nutrients that plant-based eating has to offer!

Optimal Protein Intake: Maximising Utilisation and Minimising Excess

Concluding our exploration of protein's role, a study in the 'American Journal of Clinical Nutrition' by Katsanos et al. (2008) revealed that a moderate serving of protein (around 20-25 grams) maximally stimulates muscle protein synthesis in both young and elderly individuals. If you consume more protein in one meal than your body can use immediately for muscle protein synthesis, several outcomes may occur with the excess protein:

1. Fat storage: Excess amino acids are converted into fatty acids and stored as fat in adipose tissue.
2. Glucose production: Some amino acids can be converted into glucose in the liver through gluconeogenesis.
3. Increased urea production: Breaking down excess amino acids leads to higher urea production, excreted by the kidneys in urine. This is generally not a concern for healthy individuals.
4. Potential nutrient imbalance: Excessive protein intake may disrupt the balance of macronutrient intake, overshadowing the consumption of other essential nutrients.

Occasional consumption of higher protein amounts in a single meal is generally safe for healthy individuals. However, consistently exceeding your protein needs can lead to weight gain and strain on the kidneys. Spreading protein intake evenly throughout the day optimises muscle protein synthesis and nutrient utilisation.

MIND AND BODY FITNESS	Breakfast	Lunch	Snack	Dinner
Day 1 Energy Boost	Quinoa Breakfast Bowl with Almond Milk, topped with Mixed Berries and Chia Seeds	Chickpea Salad with Mixed Greens, Cherry Tomatoes, Cucumber, and Avocado. Dress with Olive Oil and Lemon Juice.	Apple slices with Almond Butter.	Tofu and Vegetable Stir-Fry (including bell peppers, broccoli, snap peas) served over Brown Rice.
Day 2 Strength and Recovery	Green Smoothie with Spinach, Banana, Protein Powder (plant-based), and Almond Milk.	Lentil Soup with Whole Grain Bread.	Coconut Yoghurt with Mixed Nuts and a drizzle of maple syrup.	Baked Sweet Potato topped with Black Bean and Salsa, Guacamole, and a side of Steamed Broccoli.
Day 3 Fat Burning Focus	Overnight Oats made with Oats, Almond Milk, Chia Seeds, and a sprinkle of Cinnamon. Topped with Sliced Almonds and Fresh Berries.	Quinoa Salad with Mixed Greens, Grilled Tofu, Roasted Vegetables (such as courgette, bell peppers, and cherry tomatoes), and a Lemon-Tahini Dressing.	Celery and Carrot Sticks with Hummus.	Courgette Noodles with Pasta Sauce and a side of Steamed Green Beans.
Day 4 Muscle Recovery	Protein-Packed Smoothie Bowl topped with Granola, Banana Slices, and Hemp Seeds.	Tempeh/Tofu Wrap with Whole Wheat Tortilla, Lettuce, Tomato, Cucumber, and Mustard. Served with a side of Carrot Sticks.	Trail Mix made with Almonds, Walnuts, Pumpkin Seeds, and Dried Cranberries.	Stuffed Bell Peppers with Quinoa, Black Beans, Sweet Corn, and Salsa, topped with Avocado.
Day 5 Energy Boost	Acai Bowl topped with Fresh Fruit, Coconut Flakes, and a drizzle of Peanut Butter.	Chickpea and Vegetable Curry served over Brown Rice.	Sliced Apples with Cashew Butter.	Spaghetti and Roasted Sweet Potato with Pasta Sauce and a side of Steamed Broccoli.
Day 6 Strength and Recovery	Tofu Scramble with Spinach, Mushrooms, and Tomatoes, served with Whole Grain Toast.	Lentil and Vegetable Stir-Fry with Quinoa.	Coconut Yoghurt with Mixed Berries and a sprinkle of Granola.	Baked Portobello Mushrooms stuffed with Quinoa, Spinach, and Vegan Cheese, served with a side of Roasted Brussels Sprouts.
Day 7 Fat Burning Focus	Chia Seed Pudding made with Almond Milk and topped with Sliced Almonds and Fresh Berries.	Black Bean and Sweet Corn Salad with Avocado, Tomato, Red Onion, and Coriander, dressed with Lime Vinaigrette.	Carrot Sticks with Hummus.	Stir-Fried Tofu with Mixed Vegetables (such as bell peppers, snap peas, and broccoli) over Cauliflower Rice.

Note: Remember to adjust portion sizes based on individual energy needs and goals. Additionally, it's so important to stay hydrated throughout the day, and consider consulting with a registered dietitian for personalised advice.

Individual protein requirements vary based on factors like age, sex, body composition, and activity level. Consulting with a registered dietitian or nutritionist for personalised recommendations is advisable.
The body excretes excess protein beyond its needs. Despite marketing suggesting otherwise, a balanced diet with diverse plant-based protein sources is typically sufficient for health and fitness. Quality protein sources and adequate caloric intake support muscle repair and growth, challenging the misconception that more protein is always better.

Considerations on Excessive Protein Intake

Research explores potential adverse effects of high protein intake on bone health, renal function, cancer risk, liver function, and heart disease. Individual responses vary due to factors like age, sex, diet, activity level, and health conditions. While research suggests risks, it's essential to consider individual protein tolerance. Consult healthcare professionals or dietitians for personalised guidance on protein intake and dietary choices.
References:

1. Bone disorders and calcium homeostasis:

- Darling et al. (2009). Dietary Protein and Bone Health: A Systematic Review and Meta-Analysis. The American Journal of Clinical Nutrition, 90(6), 1674–1692.
- Mangano et al. (2017). Protein Intake and Bone Health. Current Osteoporosis Reports, 15(3), 214–222.

2. Disorders of renal function:

- Moe et al. (2011). Effects of Dietary Protein Intake on Outcomes in Hemodialysis Patients. Clinical Journal of the American Society of Nephrology, 6(4), 829–836.
- Knight et al. (2015). Impact of Protein Intake on Renal Function Decline in Women with Normal Renal Function or Mild Renal Insufficiency. Annals of Nutrition & Metabolism, 66 (Suppl. 4), 39–41.

3. Increased cancer risk:

- Song et al. (2016). A Meta-Analysis of the Association between Dietary Protein Intake and the Risk of Cancer. Oncotarget, 7(27), 42422-42436.
- Ekmekcioglu et al. (2017). Dietary Protein: Its Role in Satiety, Energetics, Weight Loss and Health. British Journal of Nutrition, 108(S2), S105–S112.

4. Disorders of liver function:

- Nguyen et al. (2006). A Low Protein Diet Alters the Balance of Renal Nitric

Oxide and Endothelin-1 Regulatory Factors in Chronic Kidney Disease. Kidney International, 69(9), 1502-1510.
- Figurelli et al. (2012). Renal Protein Handling and NH3 Metabolism in Liver Cirrhosis. Current Opinion in Nephrology and Hypertension, 21(6), 649–654.

5. Progression of coronary artery disease:

- Chiang et al. (2014). The Impact of High Dietary Protein Intake on the Progression of Coronary Artery Calcification: A Longitudinal Study. Clinical Nutrition, 33(6), 996–1002.

A Testament to Strength and Performance

The athletic world is witnessing a surge of world-class athletes embracing plant-based diets, challenging the notion that strength and fitness hinge solely on animal products. Here are some notable examples:
Lewis Hamilton - F1 World champion
Four-time Formula 1 world champion Lewis Hamilton won his fourth title this week after adopting a vegan diet earlier in 2017.

Venus Williams - Tennis
The tennis star adopted a raw vegan diet after she was diagnosed with Sjögren's syndrome in 2011 and doctors advised it would relieve some of her symptoms, such as extreme fatigue and joint pain.

Scott Jurek - Ultrarunner
Scott Jurek is an American ultramarathon runner, winner of 16 prestigious ultramarathon titles and holds a personal record of running 165.7 miles over a 24-hour period – averaging 8:42 per mile.

Jermain Defoe - Football
Defoe is the seventh-best goalscorer in Premier League history, scoring over 150 goals in the league to date. He plays for Bournemouth FC and the England national team – both as a striker.

David Haye - Boxer
'Apes are 20 times stronger than humans and they don't rely on a meat-based diet. They eat plants all day long. It's a myth that you need meat for strength.' David Haye[4].

4 Source: businessinsider.com Former World Champion explains how heavyweight boxer David Haye can thrive on a plant-based diet - Alan Dawson Feb 24, 2017.

Barny Du Plessis - Bodybuilder
Du Plessis went vegan after retiring from bodybuilding in 2013 due to an ever-growing list of health concerns, which included hernias and acid reflux. After adopting a vegan lifestyle, the bodybuilder saw his fitness radically improve and he returned to the stage, winning the prestigious Mr. Universe title in 2014.

Kendrick James Farris – Weightlifter
Kendrick Farris is an American Olympic weightlifter who finished 11th in his weight class at the 2016 Olympic Games in Rio de Janeiro.

Tia Blanco - Surfing
Tia Blanco is a professional surfer and winner of the Open Women's World Surfing Championship in 2015 and 2016.
Blanco grew up vegetarian and decided to adopt a vegan diet in 2013 based on her love for the environment, the sea and animals brought about by her passion for surfing.

Nate Diaz - MMA
Nate Diaz is a mixed martial artist currently competing in the UFC, the world's biggest mixed martial arts organisation.
Diaz first became vegan at age 18, inspired by his older brother and former welterweight champion in Strikeforce and WEC, Nick Diaz.

Timothy Shieff – Free runner
Timothy Shieff is a professional free runner.
Shieff went vegan after suffering from mild tendonitis – a common condition where tendons become inflamed from overuse.

Jack Lindquist – Track cyclist
Jack Lindquist is an American sprint cyclist and keen blogger. The cyclist adopted a vegan diet in 2005 after some close vegan friends explained the benefits of the regime to him.

Griff Whalen – American Football
The Oakland Raider wide receiver Griff Whalen went vegan just a few years ago and credits his success in the NFL to his plant-based diet. In 2016, he told ESPN that ‹nutrition plays a huge part in how quickly you can recover and how hard you can push yourself the next day.›

Kyrie Irving - Basketball
"Playing a great game isn't just luck," according to Celtic's player Kyrie Irving. In fact, the NBA star says adopting a vegan diet helped significantly improve his game.

Patrik Baboumian - Strongman

Baboumian has been a vegetarian since 2005 and became a vegan in 2011. In November 2011, he became the new face of a campaign by the animal rights organisation PETA, advocating a vegan diet.

Patrik stands out as he eradicates the notion or common misconception that all vegans are weak and scrawny. As a vegan, Patrik Baboumian has performed at the highest standards of strongman competition and even broken some records in the process.

- 2011 Germany's Strongest Man
- 2012 European Champion in Powerlifting Class –140 kg division (GPA)
- 2012 World Record beer keg lifting 150.2 kg (331 Pounds)
- 2012 World Record: Front Hold 20 kg (1:26,14 minutes)
- 2013 Veg Fest yoke-walk, 550.2 kg (1,213 pounds) over 10 m (33 feet) in Toronto
- 2015 Veg Fest yoke-walk, 560 kg (1,230 pounds) in 28 seconds

These athletes shatter stereotypes and showcase the potential of plant-based diets. Achievements across a variety of sports show that nourishing the body without relying on animal products is not only feasible but can lead to peak performance.

DecaUK Nutritional Daily Schedule

Intro

As a plant-based athlete, careful planning of my daily nutrition at DecaUK was essential to sustain me through the long days of intense activity. This nutritional strategy was crucial to completing such a demanding event. Before entering DecaUK 2017, I heard many claims that a plant-based diet would make finishing an event like this impossible. However, I knew that not only would a plant-based diet help me complete the event, but it would also allow me to finish stronger than if I had consumed a meat-based diet.

I choose not to consume meat or dairy products, so I opt for almond milk in my smoothies. Almond milk is a great alternative, as it is free of cholesterol and saturated fat. While it may have a lower protein content compared to cow's milk, I don't prioritise protein as the most essential nutrient. While protein is significant, fats and carbohydrates are equally important.

In my smoothies, I include nuts and seeds, which are excellent sources of protein, so I don't worry about a protein deficiency. For a healthier option with no added sugar, I use half-unsweetened almond milk. While 400ml of unsweetened milk alone doesn't taste as appealing, I prefer adding 200ml of coconut milk or a blend of coconut and almond milk to enhance the flavour.

Bananas are my absolute favourite fruit. I don't follow the commonly suggested

limit of 1–2 bananas per day. Instead, I enjoy them freely, whether it's just one or even five or more on certain days. Bananas are rich in potassium and vitamin C. They are often consumed by individuals post-workout to replenish muscles with essential nutrients like sodium, magnesium and potassium.
Such a plan is specific only to optimise performance in a multi day endurance race such as DecaUK.

- 7am - Smoothie brown half pre swim, put second half on bike for first 4 laps
- 8:45am - After swim during transition, large bowl of porridge cooked in water, add coconut/almond milk, banana & chia seed
- 9am to 10am - First 4 laps finish brown smoothie, eat nothing on 5th lap
- 10am to 11am - Next 4 laps have a half slice of sourdough toast with ¼ an avocado each lap for four laps, nothing 5th lap
- 11am to 12pm - Next 4 laps eat soup with spinach blended in
- 2pm stop for dinner which was generally rice, potatoes, veg
- 2:15pm to 3pm - After dinner top up with half slice of sourdough toast with banana and peanut butter for four laps
- 3pm to 5pm - Try not to eat for the last 10 bike laps and take on water.
- 5pm to 11pm - 12 run laps
- Take on some tinned/fresh fruit or yoghurt each lap with cordial, generally have someone close with water.
- Take a salt tablet every 2nd lap of the run, approximately every 1.5hrs
- 11pm to 12am - Post race I would eat dinners like falafel and curry
- 1am - Bed

The Secret Recipes from DecaUK

Deca Delight

Ingredients:

- 200ml Unsweetened Almond Milk
- 200ml Coconut Milk
- 1 Banana
- 3-4 Dates
- Small Handful of Goji Berries
- Large Handful of Mixed Nuts
- 1 tablespoon Milled Chia Seeds
- 1 tablespoon Pumpkin Seeds
- 1 tablespoon Milled Flax Seeds
- ½ tablespoon Cacao Powder

Instructions:

1. Prepare Ingredients: Gather all your ingredients.
2. Blend: In a blender, combine unsweetened almond milk, coconut milk, banana, dates, goji berries, mixed nuts, milled chia seeds, pumpkin seeds, milled flax seeds and cacao powder.
3. Blend Until Smooth: Blend until all ingredients are well combined and the smoothie reaches your desired consistency.
4. Serve: Pour into a glass and enjoy your nutrient-packed Deca Delight !

Gers Green Ginger Zinger

Ingredients:

- 2 Handfuls of Spinach
- 1 Celery Stick
- ¼ - 1/3 Cucumber
- 1 Banana
- 1 tablespoon Milled Chia Seeds
- 1 tablespoon Milled Flax Seeds
- Water or Coconut Water (as needed for desired consistency)

Instructions:

1. Prepare Ingredients: Gather spinach, celery, cucumber, banana, milled chia seeds and milled flax seeds.
2. Combine in Blender: In a blender, add spinach, celery, cucumber, banana, milled chia seeds and milled flax seeds.
3. Add Liquid: Pour water or coconut water into the blender to reach your desired consistency.
4. Blend Until Smooth: Blend until the mixture reaches a smooth and creamy texture.
5. Serve: Pour into a glass and enjoy your St. Patrick's Smoothie packed with green goodness!

Feel free to adjust the ingredient quantities based on your taste preferences. Cheers to a healthy and delicious smoothie!

Overnight Porridge

Ingredients:

- 2 tablespoons Oats
- 2 tablespoons Milled Chia Seeds
- Almond/Coconut Milk (to immerse)

- 1 teaspoon Maple Syrup

Toppings (next morning):

- Banana
- Blueberries
- Pumpkin Seeds
- Walnuts

Instructions:

1. Prepare in a Mason Jar: In a mason jar, combine oats and milled chia seeds.
2. Immerse in Milk: Pour almond or coconut milk into the jar until the oats and chia seeds are fully immersed.
3. Add Maple Syrup: Stir in 1 teaspoon of maple syrup.
4. Overnight: Seal the jar and refrigerate overnight.

Next Morning:

1. Add Toppings: In the morning, top your overnight porridge with sliced banana, blueberries, pumpkin seeds and walnuts.
2. Enjoy: Stir everything together and savour your delicious and nutritious Overnight Porridge!

Feel free to adjust the ingredient quantities based on your preferences. Enjoy your convenient and healthy breakfast!

Mick's Favourite Curry

Ingredients:

- 2 Red Onions
- 4 Cloves of Garlic
- 1 Thumb-sized Piece of Ginger
- 2 Red Chillies
- 200g Red Lentils
- 1 400g Tin of Chickpeas, rinsed
- 1 400g Tin of Chopped Tomatoes
- 1 400g Tin of Coconut Milk
- 1 tsp Coriander
- 1 tsp Turmeric
- 1 tsp Smoked Paprika
- 1 tsp Fenugreek
- 1 tsp Cumin
- 2 tsp Garam Masala
- 2 tbsp Tamari Sauce
- 1 tsp Salt
- 1 tsp Black Pepper

- 2 litres Vegetable Stock
- 1 tbsp Nutritional Yeast
- 1 tsp Maple Syrup
- Juice of 1/2 Lime
- 1 Head of Cauliflower, cut into florets
- 1 kg Organic Potatoes, diced
- 4 Carrots, chopped
- Fresh Coriander
- 1 Red Pepper, sliced

Instructions:

1. Prepare Vegetables: Cut all vegetables into uniform pieces and wash thoroughly. Keep them separate.
2. Rinse Chickpeas: Rinse chickpeas in a sieve until no froth is left.
3. Sauté Aromatics: In a large pot with hot olive oil or coconut oil, sauté diced onion, garlic, ginger and chilli until fragrant.
4. Add Red Lentils: Add red lentils to the pot and coat them in oil for a minute.
5. Combine Ingredients: Stir in chopped tomatoes and coconut milk. Add coriander, turmeric, smoked paprika, fenugreek, cumin, garam masala, Tamari sauce, salt and black pepper. Cook for five minutes.
6. Prepare Vegetables: Leave skins on organic potatoes and carrots. Cut them into pieces that retain their shape. Add them to the pot, coating in the curry mixture.
7. Add Stock: Pour in 2 litres of vegetable stock, preferably using organic vegetable stock cubes.
8. Simmer and Add Cauliflower: Bring to a simmer and add cauliflower florets. Stir to prevent lentils from sticking.
9. Cook Potatoes: Once potatoes are cooked, reduce heat. Add chickpeas, lime juice, red pepper and torn fresh coriander.
10. Infuse Flavours: Allow the curry to infuse for at least 30 minutes.
11. Serve: Serve with your choice of accompaniment, such as brown rice, quinoa, couscous, or bulgur wheat. Enjoy!

Plant-Based Recipes

Irish stew:

For a vegan version of Irish stew, you can substitute the traditional meat and animal-derived ingredients with plant-based alternatives. Here's a recipe for vegan Irish stew:

Ingredients:

- 2 tablespoons olive oil
- 1 large onion, chopped
- 3 cloves garlic, minced
- 3 medium potatoes, peeled and diced
- 2 carrots, peeled and sliced
- 2 stalks celery, sliced
- 1 cup pearl barley (optional, for added texture)
- 4 cups vegetable broth
- 1 teaspoon dried thyme
- Salt and pepper to taste
- Fresh parsley for garnish (optional)
-

Instructions:

1. Heat the olive oil in a large pot over medium heat. Add the chopped onion and minced garlic, and sauté until softened, about 5 minutes.
2. Add the diced potatoes, sliced carrots, and sliced celery to the pot. Stir to combine.
3. If using pearl barley, add it to the pot at this stage.
4. Pour in the vegetable broth and add the dried thyme. Bring the mixture to a simmer.
5. Reduce the heat to low, cover the pot, and let the stew simmer for about 25-30 minutes, or until the vegetables are tender and the barley is cooked through (if using).
6. Season the stew with salt and pepper to taste.
7. Serve the vegan Irish stew hot, garnished with fresh parsley if desired.

Shepherd's pie:

Ingredients:

For the filling:

- 1 tablespoon olive oil
- 1 onion, finely chopped
- 2 carrots, diced
- 2 cloves garlic, minced
- 8 ounces (225g) mushrooms, chopped
- 1 can (15 ounces) lentils, drained and rinsed
- 1 tablespoon tomato paste
- 1 cup (240ml) vegetable broth
- 1 tablespoon soy sauce or tamari
- 1 teaspoon dried thyme

- Salt and pepper to taste
- 1 cup (150g) frozen peas (optional)

For the mashed potato topping:

- 2 pounds (900g) potatoes, peeled and chopped
- 1/4 cup (60ml) unsweetened plant-based milk (such as almond, soy, or oat milk)
- 2 tablespoons vegan butter or olive oil
- Salt and pepper to taste

Instructions:

1. Preheat your oven to 400°F (200°C).
2. In a large skillet, heat the olive oil over medium heat. Add the chopped onion and diced carrots, and sauté until softened, about 5 minutes.
3. Add the minced garlic and chopped mushrooms to the skillet and cook for another 5 minutes, until the mushrooms have released their moisture.
4. Stir in the drained lentils, tomato paste, vegetable broth, soy sauce or tamari, dried thyme, salt, and pepper. Simmer the mixture for 10-15 minutes, or until thickened. If using peas, add them during the last few minutes of cooking.
5. While the filling is simmering, prepare the mashed potatoes. Place the peeled and chopped potatoes in a large pot of salted water. Bring to a boil, then reduce the heat and simmer until the potatoes are fork-tender, about 15 minutes. Drain the potatoes and return them to the pot.
6. Mash the potatoes with a potato masher or fork until smooth. Stir in the plant-based milk, vegan butter (or olive oil), salt, and pepper, until well combined.
7. Transfer the lentil and vegetable filling to a baking dish and spread it out evenly.
8. Spoon the mashed potatoes over the filling, spreading them out with a spatula to cover the entire surface.
9. Use a fork to create a decorative pattern on the surface of the mashed potatoes.
10. Place the baking dish in the preheated oven and bake for 20-25 minutes, or until the mashed potatoes are golden and crispy on top.
11. Serve the vegan shepherd's pie hot, straight from the oven.

This vegan version of shepherd's pie is packed with flavour and hearty enough to satisfy even the biggest appetites. Enjoy!

Part 7
Appendices

The following appendices provide supplementary information and materials to complement the main content of this book. They offer additional context, details, and insights that may be of interest to readers looking to delve deeper into certain topics or gain a more comprehensive understanding of the DecaUK experience and related subjects.

In these appendices, you'll find testimonials from team members and fellow participants, offering unique perspectives on the DecaUK challenge. Additionally, I've included information about my current services and recent achievements since completing DecaUK.

Appendix A: Introducing the DecaUK 2017 Team Members

Paula

Paula Cumisky is my elder sister, with a three-year age gap between us. She is an active participant in my fitness classes at the gym in Ballymun and was the first person to extend her support to DecaUK. Out of the entire team, Paula was the only member who stayed for the entire event, taking on the responsibility of driving the campervan all the way from Dublin to Windsor and back again. As the head crew member, Paula took charge of overseeing all aspects, including clothing, equipment, food, water and sleeping arrangements—she had it all covered! Despite having no prior experience in triathlons, Paula eagerly contributed her skills and dedication to our team.

Paddy

Paddy Cumisky is Paula's husband and he accompanied us on the trip to Windsor two days before the start of DecaUK. Paddy was able to stay with us for the initial three days of the event but had to return to Dublin for work commitments. During those initial days, Paddy played a crucial role as Paula's right-hand man. Whenever any issues arose, Paddy was quick to address and resolve them. Similar to Paula, Paddy lacked experience in triathlons; nonetheless, he displayed great dedication and willingness to assist.

Kevin

Kevin Prendergast is my younger brother, just one year apart. He pursued his studies abroad for several years, a feat I believe I would have struggled with, but Kevin managed it successfully with the support of his now wife and fellow Deca crew member, Linda. Not only did he excel academically, finishing at the top of his class, but he also returned home as a highly qualified osteopath. Whenever I have any injuries, Kevin is my go-to therapist and I willingly drive an hour each way every week for body maintenance because of his exceptional skills—not just because it's free for me. Kevin took on the role of team medic during the event and his expertise was even sought after by other athletes, which he happily provided. Despite having no previous experience in triathlons, Kevin's dedication to helping others and his exceptional abilities made him an invaluable member of the team.

Linda

Linda Prendergast, my sports enthusiast sister-in-law and wife to Kevin, holds a special place in my heart. Having dedicated her entire life to playing Gaelic Football and actively participating in my fitness classes at the gym in Ballymun, Linda was among the first individuals to join the Deca Crew. During her time with us, Linda took on the vital roles of strategist and coach, showcasing her exceptional skills and contribution, particularly on day five of the event. Despite not having any prior triathlon experience, Linda's passion for sports and her ability to strategise made her an invaluable member of the team.

Chris

Chris Fitzpatrick is one of my oldest friends. He is not just a close friend but also the godfather to my firstborn son, Jake and even took on the role of best man at my wedding. Given the depth of our friendship and the high regard I hold for his opinions, I was thrilled when Chris agreed to join the Deca crew. As an IT manager, I knew that his work commitments would limit his presence during the entire event. However, the days he was able to make the trip over were filled with top-class input and a no-nonsense approach. Despite not having prior experience in triathlons, Chris's friendship, expertise and efficient nature made him an invaluable part of the team.

Ciaran

Ciaran Mangan, another lifelong friend of mine, is a highly accomplished professional. He arrived on the same day as Chris, who happened to be his childhood friend and neighbour. It was a joy to have both of them as part of the crew for a few days. Ciaran played a crucial role, utilising his exceptional motivational skills, which he jokingly referred to as "saving day 7 and saving the Deca." His presence brought a vibrant and enjoyable atmosphere to the team. Despite not having any prior triathlon experience, Ciaran's expertise, combined with his ability to uplift and motivate, made him an invaluable addition to our crew.

Jonathan

Jonathan Mangan, fondly known as 'Jonner,' and I have been best friends since our teenage years. We even had the opportunity to work together for a significant amount of time, allowing us to develop great chemistry and familiarity. When Jonner joined the Deca crew alongside Noel Dempsey, they formed an entertaining double act that brought joy and lifted the spirits of all the athletes and crew members. Their presence was particularly valuable during the final few days of the event, when everyone was truly feeling the physical and emotional toll of DecaUK. Despite not having prior experience in triathlons, Jonner's friendship and ability to lighten the atmosphere made him an invaluable asset to our team.

Noel

Noel Dempsey joined us on the journey alongside Jonner as they travelled together. Much like Jonner, Noel had a tremendous impact on me, the crew and everyone present at DecaUK. While he may not have had an official title, Noel could be aptly described as the chief cheerleader and the influence of this role should not be underestimated. His positive energy and uplifting spirit resonated with all of us, bringing a sense of joy and motivation to the entire team. Despite not having any prior experience in triathlons, Noel's enthusiasm and ability to inspire made him an invaluable force in our collective experience.

Bjorn

Bjorn Ludick was an athlete I held in high regard ever since I delved into the world of triathlon in 2012. Whether I was searching for triathlon races and events in Ireland, Bjorn's name would consistently appear, often having secured a top-three finish. In 2011, Bjorn even emerged as the champion of the triathlon national championships. My initial encounter with Bjorn took place at a Triathlon Ireland camp for kids, where I enrolled my son, Reece. I was thoroughly impressed by Bjorn's coaching skills, observing his exceptional guidance and mentorship towards the young participants. I had the opportunity to attend some swim and bike sessions coached by Bjorn and his advice greatly contributed to my progress. So, when I sought a coach to assist me in my journey of completing DecaUK, Bjorn was undoubtedly the right choice. Accompanying Bjorn on the trip were his amazing wife, Orlaith and their delightful little boy, Jonah. They travelled in their self-converted camper van and exuded a cool, adventurous vibe. Bjorn's extensive triathlon experience, which includes being the 2011 Irish

National Champion and having raced as a semi-professional for both Ireland and South Africa, combined with his background as a full-time triathlon coach, made him the perfect coach to support me on my DecaUK journey.

Miriam

Miriam Lematy is my amazing wife, my inspiration and my closest confidante. Her unwavering support has been the backbone of my journey. While every member of the crew played a vital role, Mirz had been by my side long before the event even began. She attended swim, bike and run sessions, ensuring that I had everything I needed for training. Mirz always had a nutritious meal ready for me after long training sessions, prepared recovery baths, provided massages, emotional support and truly everything one could ever wish for in a partner. On the eighth day of the event, she arrived with our kids and immediately took charge of nourishing me and supporting my post-race recovery. Miriam's love and dedication have played a pivotal role in my success. Mirz is not only a budding triathlete herself, having completed sprint, Olympic and half Ironman triathlons, but she is also an unwavering pillar of support throughout my journey at DecaUK.

Appendix B: DecaUK Testimonials

Team Testimonials

Testimonial by Paula Cumiskey

Myself, Paddy and Ger made the initial trip over to the Deca Ironman UK. To be honest, I really didn't know what to expect from this, but I was there to do a job and help him complete the event. As soon as we reached London and settled into our campsite, I was down to business, strategies and what needed to be done. Ger is plant-based, so all of his food was freshly made daily.

Our mornings started at 5.30am and could go on until anytime after 12pm. Once Ger had finished, we got him back into the lake for leg recovery, into the shower, food and then into bed. I had placed 2-3 hot water bottles to heat up his bed and we then tucked him in. I then drove the camper back to the site and got ready for the following day. The first few days were slow, but soon we got our rhythm, changing up things like eating on the go and not sitting down, which saved us precious time. Day five is a day I'm sure both Ger and I will never forget.

That was the day where it was just the two of us and like any other day previous to it, we did our after race recovery in the shower and the past few days Ger was getting a leg rubdown from Kevin, which helps recovery, who had shown me what to do after he had left. Ger was in the shower, I had the bed set up in the locker room back at the campsite, waiting for him to finish. I had left his orange juice there, which got knocked over. Ger, tired and grumpy, just wanted to go to bed but after some persuasion, I got him onto the bed and began his rubdown.

As I was messaging his calf area, I could feel myself bending down when suddenly crash, bang and all of a sudden Ger was on the floor, probably in shock. We can laugh about it now, obviously, he won the bloody Deca. I have so many fun stories I could share, but then it would be me writing the book!

That has to be one of my most memorable experiences and one I will cherish for life. Not only was it the most intense, gruelling 10 days, but I saw how the mind is truly powerful and can achieve anything once there is the will to 'keep moving forward' and the strength to keep going. I saw my brother at his lowest and all I wanted to do was to finish it for him, but his determination and the memory of Mick pushed him on. I am so very grateful that he asked me to be part of his crew, but most of all, I am unbelievably proud of the most amazing man I have the pleasure of calling my brother. It was one hell of a journey.

Testimonial by Kevin Prendergast - Osteopath

Before the DecaUK event, Ger faced challenges that added complexity to an already demanding challenge. A calf strain, initially estimated to clear in 4-6 weeks, forced a shift to low-impact training, emphasising swimming and cycling. A bout of cold/flu struck just weeks before, demanding a few days for recovery.

By the time I arrived, Ger had already completed several iron distance triathlons. Nutrition became a focal point as indigestion and stomach cramps hindered Ger's run. Struggling with a lack of bowel movements, his performance suffered until a strategic remedy involving chewable Rennies and orange juice provided relief.

Running alongside Ger for segments on Friday and Saturday nights, I experienced firsthand the toll on his body. The weather added another layer of difficulty—calm but cold mornings and nights.

Expecting a somewhat leisurely experience, I quickly realised Ger had understated the intensity of the event. His laid-back demeanour didn't reflect the full-on nature of the challenge.

Arriving on Friday, I found myself on a whirlwind of activities. From renting the smallest car available to navigating through breakfast cafes and shopping runs, the day was a frenzy of preparations for the long days ahead.

A brief session of osteopathic treatment and mobilisations prepared him for the swim. Ger's biking routine was complex, involving laps, nutritional strategies and dealing with saddle soreness. Challenges like a punctured back wheel were expertly handled by the crew and makeshift solutions like Sudocrem in cycling shorts provided relief. The transition from bike to run required strategic stretching and more mobilisations, considering Ger's fatigue. Prolonged hours on the bike were contributing to numerous issues, including left painful levator scapula muscle which caused significant shoulder and upper back pain on the left side.

Post-run recoveries in the lake, despite the cold temperatures, were essential for Ger's overall well-being.

As the days progressed, Ger faced physical and mental hurdles. Ciaran's concern about Ger's condition on day 7 prompted quick action. Despite the challenges, Ger's resilience shone through, culminating in an emotional swim on day 8.

Testimonial by Chris Fitzpatrick

The best way to describe being part of a Deca crew is to compare it to a start-up business – you go into being part of the crew with a strategy based on the capabilities of the athlete, but the key to success depends on the crew and the strategy being agile enough to adapt to 'external factors' that are beyond your control—weather, competition, mechanical failure. Like a start-up, the crew experiments with different tactics; they quickly need to figure out what works for the athlete and what doesn't. The crew needs to be mobile, vocal and motivated. Communication with the athlete is key. There is no 'downtime'. As with any successful business, having a team or crew that has a differentiated skill set is essential. Individual crew members need to be focused on various aspects of the strategy simultaneously: cooking, hydration, supplements, monitoring weather forecasts, competition and recovery. The crew is heavily invested in the event, even though they are not 'in' the race. The real hard work is done by the athlete on the course, but the crew is a small yet essential part of any Deca attempt.

Testimonial by Coach Bjorn Ludick

The first time I heard about the event was when Ger sent me an email saying that he wanted to do a Deca Triathlon. At the time, I didn't really know what it was, but after looking into it for a few days, I realised that this was not going to be a run around the park. "You know this is ten Iron distance triathlons in ten days, one after the other?" I asked him on a phone call after researching the event. I was sure he had believed it was going to be something completely different.

Once we started talking about the reason why Ger wanted to attempt such an enormous challenge, I knew he was serious and I would have to do everything in my power to be the best coach and friend that I could be. I needed to make sure that all the boxes were ticked to get Ger in the best possible shape that I could for him to have any chance of even attempting this challenge.

In doing my research into ultra-endurance triathlon, I quickly realised that this was going to be more of a mental test than a physical one. I could coach Ger to be in the best possible shape that he can be, BUT if his head is not in the right place, he will fail.

Ger did an amazing job with the training; it was flawless. Early morning and late evening training sessions were done with no complaints. The week-long preparation camps worked great; we completed two separate camp weeks. I think they opened Ger's eyes to what he had signed up for.

I came to the conclusion that it would be best for myself and Ger's family to arrive later into the event. This gave him something to look forward to and kept

him motivated. We learned a lot from the first few days to make sure we would be able to make it to the end. I was talking to Ger every day to give him some tips and nuggets of information to get him through the day.
We put a structure in place so that we would have to do all the little things right to give his body the best possible chance to recover with the time that we had available.
I went over to Dorney Lake with my family in our campervan. To see Ger for the first time in the Deca was great. He was so full of energy and smiling the whole time.
I was trying to talk to Ger on a regular basis while also giving him space. Getting closer to the latter part of the event, I could see that Ger was feeling the effects of the days that had passed. He had been through a lot, but there was one night I could see that he needed someone with him. I cycled with him for long periods of the marathon, talking about all things non triathlon related. I learnt a lot from him as a person during that run. His brother-in-law meant a lot to him and Ger really missed him. Ger is a very passionate and proud man and will do anything in his power to achieve his goals. He loves his family and friends very much and I'm very lucky to be his friend and coach.
One thing I have to say. Ger's Team/Family was amazing!! I don't think there could have been a better crew. Well done team DECA GER!!

Participant Testimonial

Graham Smedley

I was aware Ger was off to a good start in the swim on day one. The next time I saw him was he was walking back towards HQ with a flat tyre.
I, myself, had a great start on 'Day One.' I tried to go at a steady pace and was noticing people flying by me on the bike all morning. Not getting off the bike at any stage of the cycle meant I was in the top three to finish the bike and soon after I was running in second place. I did not want to win 'Day One' as I could imagine everyone talking about how I must have gone out too fast! I ran very conservatively, but in the end, I did get past the leader. I overtook him in the dark without realising it. Happily, I was able to back that up with a second placed finish on day two, again taking it easy but enjoying the fact that my easy run was keeping me in pace with TC, who won the second day. Day three for me was an off day as I slowed a little on the run and I didn't take that into account with my nutrition and ended up bonking towards the end. I did notice that Ger had a storming 'Day Three' and also noticed how smooth his running stride looked. Ger won 'Day Three' and after seeing that, I told TC on the morning of 'Day Four'

that it was Ger he needed to keep a watch-out for rather than me. 'Day Four' ended with me finishing first again, just ahead of Ger, but during the run I noticed Ger was gaining a little each lap, until half way. After that, I saw he was taking big chunks out of my half-lap lead each time we passed, so smooth. Then disaster struck for me. With three laps to go, I felt my Achilles start to tighten, so I was pleased to stand in the lake to recover a little after the run. I'd done this for the first two days, but a later finish on day three led to me skipping my cryotherapy dip in the lake. The night of day four, Ger and I were chatting in the dark, cold lake whilst we watched the head torches of the other athletes go back and forward.

That was the end of the 'race' for me. I had trained with the aim of being competitive, but walking to the toilet block on the morning of 'Day Five' I knew just finishing would be a tall order. My Achilles had fully tightened up and although the cold swim did it some good, the pressure of the pedals on the bike caused further pain. I went out really slowly on the run, I knew the two and a half hour lead I had held after 'Day Four' would disappear, so I resigned myself to shuffling along and just finishing. Towards the back end of the marathon, even that idea disappeared as I felt a burning pain slice through my Achilles and I could no longer put any weight on it. As I made the return lap, my head was down and I was hardly moving. One of the other athletes, Ziv from Israel, came back as he passed me to check to see if I was okay. Even though he was struggling with late finishes himself and would ultimately have to call it a day himself, he had the mindset to reach out. I will never forget that. And that would have been me done. Mentally, I was in a bad place, but thankfully, Jim Page of the Brutal Team, came out to see me and try to help me with some words of encouragement. Jim had got me going again, bringing me around from thinking it was all over to then really wanting to finish the whole event. I was totally reliant on Claire, my wife, getting me to the start each morning after we'd both had just an hour or so of sleep. I shared some cold, sad and lonely nights out on the run course with Martin Curran as we battled to finish in time to get any sleep at all. Had Martin not been a day ahead of me in terms of minimal sleep, I would not have believed it possible, but he kept going - so I did.

I had one good day on the bike when I was able to win back a little extra sleep, but I was getting very tired and very emotional. I tried to hold back the tears whilst swimming on day nine because Simon Jacob had not been able to start the penultimate day. On the last day, it was a celebration for most, but I really had a bad time and it was very difficult to deal with. People were happy that we would all soon be finished, but I knew I had hours upon hours of misery ahead before I could finally stop. But the time eventually came for me to stop and I'd finished the Deca. It did not go how I wanted it to go and for a long time after the event, I struggled to see it as a positive, but thanks to those around me during the event, I have a Deca medal and very few people in the world can say that!

Appendix C: Book Suggestions

The Three Self-Development Key Books:

- 'Eat the Frog' by Brian Tracy (2014):
  - » Wake-up call to address chronic procrastination.
  - » Initial impact on self-development journey.
  - » Authored by Brian Tracy, known for "No Excuses, the Power of Self-Discipline."
- 'No Excuses, the Power of Self-Discipline' by Brian Tracy:
  - » Ignited a powerful desire for personal growth.
  - » Played a significant role in instilling discipline.
  - » Fueled determination to transform positive changes into lasting habits.
- 'The 5 AM Club' by Robin Sharma:
  - » It offers valuable suggestions on daily approach and morning routines.
  - » Unique storytelling approach with captivating narrative.
  - » Resonated personally, engaging throughout the journey.
  - » Focuses on achieving success through unconventional means shared by an eccentric billionaire.

Considering the impact that these books had on me, I would like to recommend a few other titles that I believe could be incredibly beneficial to you:

- 'Atomic Habits' by James Clear - This book provides practical strategies for making small changes that lead to significant personal and professional growth.
- 'The Power of Now' by Eckhart Tolle - A transformative read that explores the importance of living in the present moment and finding inner peace.
- 'Mindset' by Carol S. Dweck - Dweck delves into the concept of mindset and how the way we perceive our abilities and failures can affect our personal and professional achievements.
- 'Man's Search for Meaning' by Viktor E. Frankl - This poignant memoir explores the author's experiences as a Holocaust survivor and the powerful lessons he learned about finding meaning in life.
- 'Eat and Run' by Scott Jurek - Jurek's memoir intertwines his incredible achievements as an ultramarathon runner with valuable insights on nutrition and mindset.

- 'Peak Performance' by Steve Magness & Brad Stulberg - This book delves into the science behind achieving optimal performance and offers practical strategies for reaching your full potential.
- 'Ego is the Enemy' by Ryan Holiday - A thought-provoking read on the dangers of ego and how it can hinder personal growth and success.
- 'Start with Why' by Simon Sinek - Sinek explores the concept of finding your purpose and understanding the 'why' behind your actions to inspire others and drive meaningful change.
- 'The Subtle Art of Not Giving a F*ck' by Mark Manson - Manson's refreshing and unfiltered book challenges conventional wisdom and offers practical advice on finding happiness and living a fulfilling life.
- 'Running Man' by Charlie Engle - Engle's memoir reflects on his own journey as an ultramarathon runner, overcoming addiction and finding strength and purpose in the face of challenges.
- 'Primal Endurance' by Mark Sisson and Brad Kearns - This book challenges traditional endurance training methods and provides a comprehensive guide to optimising performance through a primal approach.
- 'Can't Hurt Me' by David Goggins - Goggins' inspiring memoir details his journey from a painful past to becoming a Navy SEAL and renowned endurance athlete. He offers valuable tools for pushing past mental and physical limitations.
- 'Who Moved My Cheese' by Dr. Spencer Johnson - This insightful parable explores the importance of adapting to change in life and work and offers practical strategies for embracing change and finding new opportunities.
- 'Goal Setting' by Jim Rohn - Rohn's book highlights the power of setting clear and meaningful goals, providing guidance on how to create effective goal-setting strategies and achieve success in all areas of life.
- 'The War of Art' by Steven Pressfield - This book delves into the creative process and the internal battles we face when pursuing our passions. Pressfield offers insights and strategies to overcome resistance and unleash our true creative potential.
- 'The Compound Effect' by Darren Hardy - This book explores the power of small actions and compounding results to achieve long-term success and personal growth.

I hope these recommendations may prove valuable on your own self-development journey.

Appendix D: Recent Achievements and Milestones After DecaUK

- 29/12/2018 Podcast Launch: Initiated 'The Ger Prendergast Podcast' to share experiences, reaching a wider audience and contributing to the Irish triathlon community.

- 01/01/2018 - 31/01/2018 Fundraising for Mental Health Ireland: Raised €12,000 in 2018 by completing 52 triathlons in 52 weeks, showcasing commitment to both personal challenges and charitable causes.

- 2020 & 2019 Adaptation Amidst COVID: Seized the opportunity during the pandemic to become a well-rounded athlete, completing yoga courses, triathlon coaching, and adopting positive psychology techniques.

- 17/07/2022 Continuous Deca at DecaUK 2022: Undertook an extraordinary challenge, completing a 38 km swim, 1800 km bike ride, and 420 km run, emerging as the champion with a total time of 227 hours.

- 07/2022 Historic Milestones: Became the first Irish individual to achieve a Continuous Deca, solidifying the position as a trailblazer. Achieved the unprecedented feat of completing both Deca formats, breaking records for the longest triathlon ever undertaken by an Irish individual.

- 07/2022 Global Recognition: Stood as the fifth person in the world to emerge victorious in both Deca formats, leaving an indelible mark on the history of endurance sports.

Appendix E: Candid Chronicles

Father Son Tri Training - Ger Prendergast

In this photo, I'm standing proudly beside my eldest son, Jake, both of us dressed in matching cycling suits as we prepare to start the cycle leg of a half Iron distance triathlon. I had organised this event for a group of my triathlon coaching clients at Lilliput Adventure Centre, and it turned out to be an amazing day filled with training, fun, and memorable moments shared with everyone involved.

The Lord Mayors Award 2023 - Ger Prendergast

At the Mansion House in Dublin City Centre, I had the incredible honour of receiving the Lord Mayor's Award 2023, presented by the Lord Mayor of Dublin, Caroline Conroy. This prestigious award recognised my sporting achievements and contributions to my community. Sitting in the same chair where some of the most famous and influential figures have been before me, I felt deeply humbled and proud. This moment represents not just a personal achievement but a tribute to the journey and dedication that led me here.

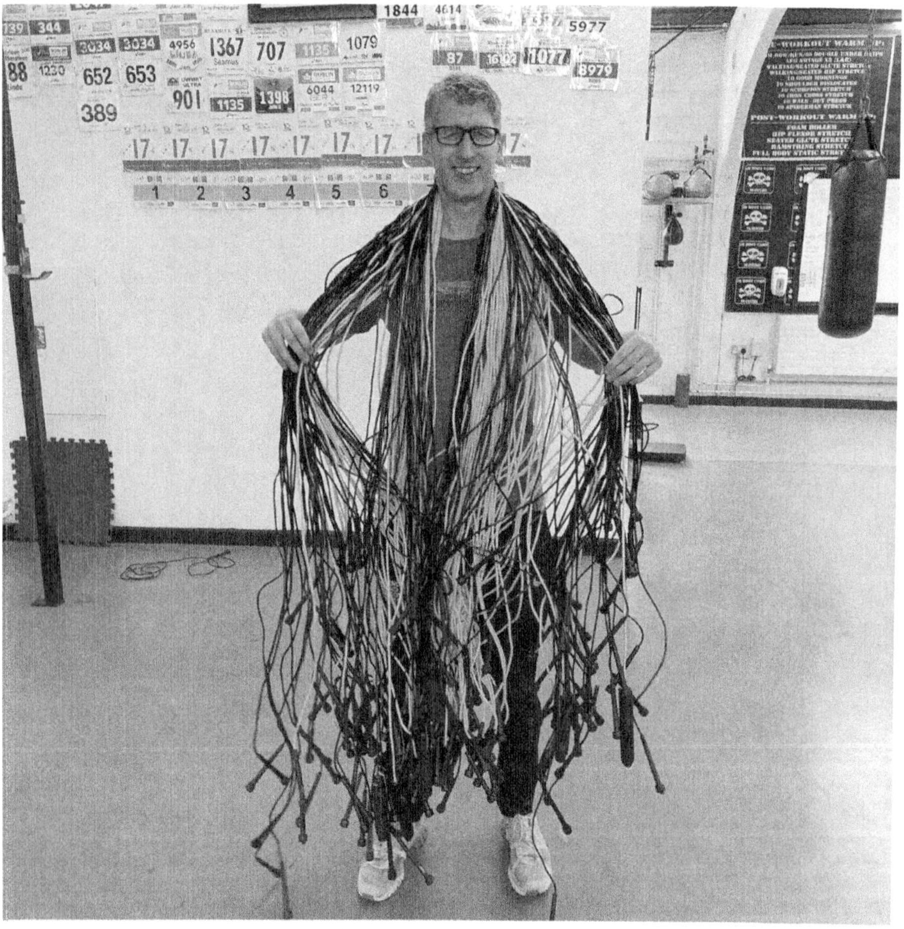

Skipping World Record - Ger Prendergast

In this photo, I'm wearing 100 skipping ropes around my neck, gearing up for a special event we organised in Ballymun as part of the Ballymun Running Festival. This mini-event was an ambitious attempt to break the world record for the most people skipping simultaneously online. We handed out ropes to everyone at the festival, encouraging them to join in—and they did! Together, we successfully set a new world record, making the day even more memorable.

The Lord Mayor at the Ballymun Scouts - Ger Prendergast

In this photo, I'm standing beside Lord Mayor of Dublin, Caroline Conroy, wearing my Scout uniform at a celebration for my Scout group, Ballymun 200th Dublin. It was a special night for me as the Scout leader watching on as some of our new members were officially invested and became Scouts. Having the Lord Mayor there to speak to our young Scouts made the event even more memorable and an incredible honour for everyone involved.

4 Peaks Challenge - Ger Prendergast.
Davy Hill and I are geared up and ready to tackle the final leg of the Four Peaks Challenge at Slieve Donard. The challenge involved climbing the highest peaks in each of Ireland's four provinces, and our goal was to break the fastest known time for the event. With determination in our eyes and poles in hand, we set out to conquer the last summit—and successfully set a new record, completing all four peaks in just 21 hours.

Mizen to Mailin challenge - Ger Prendergast

Triathlon clients, Paul, Davy and I straddling our bikes just before we embarked on an epic challenge: cycling nearly 600 kilometres from Mizen Head, the most southerly point in Ireland, to Malin Head, the most northerly. Our goal was ambitious—to complete the journey in under 24 hours—and I'm proud to say we succeeded. This moment captures the excitement and determination that fueled us throughout this unforgettable adventure.

On our wedding day, Miriam and I took a moment to pose on a Mark II Raleigh chopper, capturing the playful spirit of our celebration. Surrounded by old-school bikes—Raleigh choppers, a tandem, and other quirky bikes, we invited our guests to join in the fun and kick off the reception with a bit of nostalgia and laughter. This photo perfectly reflects the joy and love that filled one of the best days of my life, making it truly unforgettable.

Dublin City Marathon - Ger Prendergast

In this photo, I'm celebrating with my triathlon client David Hill and good friend Ken Coakley, all of us proudly showing off our medals after finishing the Dublin City Marathon. I love this picture because it captures a special moment shared with two guys who truly inspire me. Ken and I have a tradition of somehow finding each other during the race and finishing together, which has now happened at least three times. Additionally, I'm thrilled to have helped Davey achieve a remarkable personal best, finishing in 3 hours and 30 minutes—an incredible improvement of one hour and one minute on his PB he set at the previous edition of the Dublin City Marathon.

Soft launch of Gotta Keep It Movin' - Ger Prendergast

On stage at the soft launch of Gotta Keep It Movin' at the Access Centre in my hometown of Ballymun, I sat alongside Coach Bjorn, who had been with me every step of the way from start to finish. The room was packed with familiar faces, making it a truly special day. This photo captures a moment of pride and reflection, shared with the person who helped guide me through the entire journey.

Ballymun Summit, Elite Athlete Talk hosted by Ger Prendergast - Ger Prendergast
At the Ballymun Summit during the Elite Athlete Talk, I had the privilege of hosting a distinguished panel of speakers, including John Kelly of Irish Taekwondo, Roddy Collins, Joey Malone, Noel King, Sean Boyland, Oisín Fagan, Davey Byrne, and Kelly Harrington. This photo captures a moment of inspiration and shared expertise, with each speaker contributing their unique experiences and insights to a memorable event.

Kerry Way Ultra 2020 - Ger Prendergast

Running through the breathtaking Black Valley in the Kerry Mountains during the Kerry Way Ultra in 2020, this race became a deeply personal journey for me. After DNF'ing in 2020 and 2021, and missing the 2022 race due to my father's passing, I returned in 2023 with a mission: to finish all 200 km in his honour. After years of perseverance, I crossed the finish line in 32 hours, carrying my father's memory every step of the way.

Before the swim on day 1 of DecaUK 2017 - Ger Prendergast

Day 1 of DecaUK 2017 at Eton Dorney, and I'm suited up in my wetsuit, sliders, and holding my swim cap, ready for the challenge ahead. But as I'm walking toward the lake, I'm looking back the other way, giving the impression that I have no idea where I'm supposed to go! A moment of pre-race confusion perfectly captured, reminding me that even on day one, the journey to the start line wasn't exactly straightforward.

Charity Triathlon - Ger Prendergast

I'm being directed and advised by a Water Safety Specialist just before starting the swim section of an Iron Distance Triathlon in Cork in December 2022. The conditions were extreme, with freezing temperatures and crazy currents in the harbour. Alongside my clients, Seany Kinsella and David Hill, we alone, took on the 3.8km swim, 180km cycle on dangerous roads, and a 42km run through Cork City—all to raise money and awareness for Penny Dinners, a homeless charity in Cork. Despite the challenges, we completed the event and were treated like heroes by everyone involved with the charity, who took great care of us after the event.

Before the start of day 10 at DecaUK 2017 - thatcameraman.com
Just minutes before the final swim of 10 Iron Distance Triathlons in 10 days at DECA UK 2017, the reality hit me hard in the pre-race tent: one last 3.8k swim, a 180k cycle, and a 42k run to go. Surrounded by my fellow competitors and our crews, I put my face in my hands and asked my sister-in-law Linda, 'Whose fucking poxy idea was this?' Her smiling reply, captured perfectly in this photo: 'It was yours. Now go and get it done.' A moment of doubt turned into motivation, thanks to a well-timed dose of honesty!

Meeting David Goggins - Ger Prendergast
Standing beside David Goggins at one of his talks in 2024, I had the chance to briefly chat with him about various events and challenges. It was a memorable moment, made even more special when Goggins signed my book for my son, Jake. This photo captures the excitement of meeting an inspirational figure and sharing that experience with my family.

After completing 10 Iron distance triathlons in 10 days at DecaUK 2017, I thought I could muster the strength to stay awake and congratulate every fellow competitor. I managed to greet Dave Kershaw, but after that, my body had other plans. Exhaustion took over, and I was out cold in a camping chair, fast asleep while the finish line celebrations continued without me.

DecaUK 2017 Finish line day 10 - Kathi Harman

Crossing the finish line on day 10 of DECA UK 2017, I was on top of the world, hoisting the Irish tricolour above my head and screaming with joy. The only catch? In my exhaustion-fueled excitement, I managed to raise the flag backward—orange, white, and green instead of the other way around. Despite my sister-in-law Linda's best efforts to guide me, my tired brain took a 50-50 shot...and missed. But hey, even in triumph, there's room for a little comedy!

DecaUK 2017 - Kathi Harman. Crossing the finish line at DecaUK 2017, I had barely caught my breath before being handed the winners trophy and medal. Just as I was savouring the victory, my Ma made sure I didn't get too carried away by shoving the phone to my ear and shouting 'talk to your Da there, will you?'

Appendix F: Beyond DecaUK

Ironman Cork 2022
Tackling St. Patricks Hill AKA Heartbreak Hill at Ironman Cork 2022.

Day 10 of my Indoor Deca I completed in 2018 at Ballymun Leisure centre. 3.8k pool swim followed by a 180k indoor bike ride on my turbo trainer that I brought to the centre and finished off with a 42k treadmill run, everyday for ten consecutive days.

A hike up the Dublin mountains in a beautiful spot called Fairy Castle.

Ironman Cork 2022

Passing beneath the famous Youghal Clock gate tower at Ironman Cork 2022

Ironman Cork 2023
Holding my power at 190 watts during Ironman Cork in 2023 which helped me knock 32 minutes off my bike time from the previous year on the same course.

Ironman Cork 2023

Passing beneath the famous Youghal Clock gate tower at Ironman Cork 2023

Ironman Cork 2023

Pounding the streets of Youghal at Ironman Cork 2023

Ironman Barcelona 2023

Exiting the water in Calella at Ironman Barcelona 2023. It was a difficult swim against a strong current for the longest stretch of the swim.

Ironman Cork 2023

Crossing the finish line at Ironman Cork 2023 with the Tri-colour

Acknowledgements

During my training for DecaUK in both 2017 and 2022, I drew inspiration from a variety of sources, but the most significant were the uplifting musical scores from some of my favourite movies. Foremost among these were the Batman trilogy by Christopher Nolan, featuring the remarkable music composed by Hans Zimmer, as well as the soul-stirring melodies from 'The Last of the Mohicans'' and 'The Grey.'

A conscious choice I made during my training was to forgo using music while running, allowing me to focus solely on my thoughts and the rhythm of my footsteps. However, during my indoor bike training sessions, I embraced a different approach. I found motivation in a treasure trove of motivational videos on YouTube, many of which incorporated the music from these movies.

One particular source of inspiration came from a poem featured in the movie 'The Grey,' 2011, directed by Joe Carnahan and starring Liam Neeson. This poem, recited by Neeson in the film, resonated with me on a deep emotional level. It became a guiding force in my journey, occupying my thoughts as I ventured into the cold waters on the first day of DecaUK and again on the tenth day. Its impact was so profound that I felt compelled to include it in this memoir, marking the beginning of my challenge with the poem's first line as the subheading for day one, 'Once More into the Fray...,' and concluding with the poem's final line on day ten, when I knew victory was within reach, 'Live and Die on this Day....'

"Gotta Keep It Movin'" is a phrase borrowed from the lyrics of the song 'Moving' by Bugzy Malone. It was a song that my brother-in-law, Mick, used to sing passionately, adopting it as his personal mantra when facing immense challenges in his life. Following his passing, I embraced this mantra as my own, finding inspiration in it as I confronted my own monumental challenge, DecaUK 2017.

The Services from MIND AND BODY FITNESS

Discover My Services

Thank you for being a part of this journey. I want to share the range of services I offer to help you on your wellness and fitness journey.
Ready to transform your fitness journey? Join Ger today and experience the unparalleled benefits of our personalised training sessions. Whether you're aiming for a high-energy cardio blast, strength training mastery, a mindful yoga fusion, or triathlon performance enhancement, Ger can guide you every step of the way.

High-Energy Cardio Blast:
Join our dynamic fitness classes designed to elevate your heart rate, burn calories, and boost your overall cardiovascular health. With a perfect blend of energising music and expertly crafted routines, our classes make working out feel like a party. Whether you're a fitness enthusiast or a beginner, our instructors will guide you through an invigorating and fun workout experience.

Strength Training Mastery:
Unleash your inner strength in our power-packed strength training classes. Led by certified trainers, these sessions focus on building lean muscle, improving endurance, and enhancing overall strength. We provide a supportive and motivating environment to help you reach your fitness goals, whether you're looking to tone up, build muscle, or increase your functional strength.

Mindful Yoga Fusion:
Immerse yourself in the transformative world of my yoga fitness classes. Blending traditional yoga practices with modern fitness elements, these classes offer a holistic approach to wellness. From stress reduction to improved flexibility, I will guide you through each session, promoting mindfulness, balance, and a deep connection between mind and body.

Personalised Personal Training:
Elevate your fitness journey with our personalised training sessions. Experi-

ence the benefits of one-on-one attention as I tailor workouts to your individual needs. Whether your goal is weight loss, strength building, or overall fitness improvement, our personal training sessions offer focused guidance and motivation for your specific objectives.

Triathlon Prep and Performance:
Dive into the world of triathlon with our specialised coaching sessions. Whether you're a seasoned triathlete or a beginner looking to conquer your first race, I provide comprehensive personal training plans. From swim technique refinement to cycling efficiency and running endurance, our triathlon coaching covers it all. Join us and take your triathlon performance to new heights.

Contact Ger now to schedule your first session and embark on a path to a healthier, stronger, and more vibrant you. Let's achieve your fitness goals together because you deserve the best version of yourself. Take action now and make every workout count!

Ready to take the next step? Contact Ger today!
Email: gerard.prendergast@gmail.com
Phone: (+353) 085 2721770
Website: http://gpmindbodyfitness.com

Address:
Trinity Comprehensive School Gym
Ballymun Road
Dublin 11
Rep. of Ireland

Social:

Instagram
https://bit.ly/insger

Facebook
https://bit.ly/fbger

Join Our Newsletter to receive updates and exclusive content, send an email to gerard.prendergast@gmail.com with the subject "Subscribe to Newsletter".

Printed in Great Britain
by Amazon

46946972R00165